Anna G. Ross

Nov '68

Hors d'œuvre and
Cold Table

A Selection of Hors-d'œuvre

HORS D'ŒUVRE AND COLD TABLE

A Book of Tried and Trusted

Recipes and Methods

WILLIAM HEPTINSTALL

FABER AND FABER LTD

24 Russell Square

London

First published in 1959
by Faber and Faber Limited
24 Russell Square London W.C.1
Second impression 1960
Third impression 1968
Printed in Great Britain by
Latimer Trend & Co Ltd Whitstable

SBN 571 03602 3

À

PIERRE AUBIN

QUI, LE PREMIER,

M'A RÉVÉLÉ LES GRANDEURS

DE LA

CUISINE FRANÇAISE

HOMMAGE DE RESPECTUEUSE ADMIRATION

W. H.

Foreword

In Gastronomy, just as in sport, a good start may win the race: it is important. Hors-d'œuvre come first and they are important: they may make or mar the meal. Yet, strictly speaking, hors-d'œuvre are forefare and they are not part of the meal any more than the foreword is part of the story in a book: they are outside—*hors*—the meal—*œuvre*, which is why, whether there be only one derelict sardine or a galaxy of canapés, bouchées, barquettes and the rest, there is still but one meal to follow, and *œuvre* should never be in the plural: *Les hors-d'œuvres* is quite common, of course, but it is just one of those errors as common as common sense is uncommon.

Hors-d'œuvre are intended to stimulate but not to satisfy our appetite: they must be attractive in shape and colour to appeal to the eye; they must be tasty to stimulate the flow of our salivary glands and gladden our little taste buds; there must be a number of them, as different as possible both in looks and in taste, so that each one of us may have a chance to choose those which he or she fancies most at the time, and to enjoy the contrast of different flavours and savours; they should be small, light, dainty, so that they do not dull the appetite.

Food is fuel for us all, just as it is for the birds of the air, the fish in the sea, and four-footed beasts. But for some of us food is fun as well as fuel, and of all our foods none lends itself more readily to being fun than *hors-d'œuvre*. The soggy beetroot, tomato and potato salads which so often masquerade as hors-d'œuvre may be food but they are certainly not fun. If you want to know how different and how excellent hors-d'œuvre can be, ask the master, the man who has the imagination of a poet, the fairy touch of the artist, the consummate skill of the practitioner, and a rare gift of expression, William Heptinstall: his book is the answer.

ANDRÉ L. SIMON

Introduction

Another cookery book? Why not? This one will appeal to you: it deals with one branch only of the art, and is unique. Of course there are books on the same subject, but none of them that I know deals exhaustively with it. Had there been one, it would have saved me many years of being tied to this chariot.

The whole of the civilized world has contributed. Friends, not alone those *du métier*, from many lands have supplied mixtures and salads, given help and advice. The careful nursing of an editor of this publishing house at a time when I came near to making a bonfire of the manuscript, I acknowledge with thanks. I also record my indebtedness to the lady who prepares twenty varieties of hors-d'œuvre every Sunday morning before breakfast.

You will find recipes for hors-d'œuvre which may also be used as savouries—gastronomically incorrect though this may be—and some satisfying ones which will give a single *plat*, perhaps a supper dish. You may have a television or bridge party in view; here are the dishes you may prepare well in advance, so that you may spend all your time with your friends and still offer them interesting and sustaining food.

This book began quite simply as a few notes to help the trainee cooks in my kitchen, and to relieve myself of that ever-present question, 'What shall I do next, please?' This was at a time when I was initiating the hors-d'œuvre display at Sunday luncheon and the mass of notes accumulated. Then my old and valued friend André Simon came to stay with me, and to him I submitted the pile of scraps of paper, old envelopes and menu cards. He it was who brought order out of chaos, and more, gave me a plan to follow if ever I thought of writing a book on hors-d'œuvre.

WILLIAM HEPTINSTALL

Fortingall Hotel, Perthshire,
April 1959

Contents

Contents

Contents

Contents

2. Flesh and Fat

Contents

Contents

3. Herbs, Condiments and Spices

4. Sauces, Dressings and Seasonings

5. Flavoured Butters, Pastes and Spreads: Beurres Composés et Fromages

Contents

6. Pickled Fruits, Fungi and Vegetables

7. Aspics, Moulded Creams, Royales

B   17

Contents

8. Vegetables

Contents

19

Contents

Contents

Chicken, peas, pimentos, rice — Potato, red cabbage,
julienne of white of egg and Victoria plum — Prunes,
sausage and potato — Prunes, tomato, ham, gherkins

12. Zakouska, Canapés, Toasts and Derivatives

21

Contents

13. Hot Hors-d'œuvre

Contents

23

Contents

Contents

Contents

26

Contents

Contents

HOT HORS-D'ŒUVRE—RUSSIAN SPECIALITIES

1. Fish

FISH ROE

This is the name given to the seed or spawn of fishes, that of the male being known as soft roe or milt and that of the female as hard roe or spawn. The varieties which interest us most are (*a*) the family of acipenser which gives the different kinds of caviar; (*b*) cod roe, a hard roe; (*c*) herring roes, both hard and soft; (*d*) salmon roe, the hard roe furnishes the so-called red caviar and the soft may be used poached; (*e*) tunny, a hard roe, and (*f*) grey mullet, a hard roe.

CAVIAR

There are four foremost hors-d'œuvre: caviar, oysters, raw smoked fish or ham and melon in that order of importance. The most renowned caviar comes from the delta of the Volga on the Caspian Sea, the area known as Astrakhan, and is yielded by five members of the Acipenser family. First the Beluga or Huse, a fish measuring more than twelve feet in length and bearing upwards of three hundred and fifty pounds of supreme quality caviar. Next, the Sturgeon, whose length is roughly six feet, the Sevruga slightly less, with the Waxdick still less, and finally the Sterlet averaging two feet in length. Beluga Malossol caviar (mildly salted) has, as one would expect from the largest fish, the largest grain and of course the highest price, but is followed closely by Ocietrova (sturgeon) Malossol, not quite so large in grain and slightly less in price. Next comes Sevruga Malossol at about two-thirds of the price of the Beluga caviar. We do not meet Waxdick caviar under its own name and rarely with that of the genuine Russian Sterlet. This last used to be reserved exclusively for the Russian Court on account of its quality and small grain, and has reappeared from French and Portuguese sources since Russian and Persian supplies became scarce. The flesh of the Sterlet is the prime of the Acipenseres—the fish being about the size of a salmon. That of the huge Beluga or Sturgeon after either salting and drying or freezing is rarely found out of Russia.

Many people think that the light-grey coloured varieties of caviar are the best and most delicious. It is, however, a scientific truth that the colouring of the roe is adapted to the colour of the river bottom where the fishes spawn. Further, it is quite erroneous to assume that pressed caviar is prepared from inferior roe, it is in fact more nutritious than the globular variety. There are varieties of Astrakhan caviar which carry more salt and are cheaper than those mentioned above. They are useful, as also is the pressed, for sandwiches, canapés, barquettes and the like. Great skill has to be shown in the making, i.e. the salting of caviar, and the art has remained in certain families for generations and been handed from father to son. Of every hundred who wish to become caviar makers about twenty make the grade but only five become experts. The rest give it up in despair. During the salting process the outer film of the globule seems to crack in every direction; one must know when to stop mixing the roe, it is a gift—and only five in a hundred ever acquire it.

1.

To serve caviar see first that it is in a perfectly fresh condition, for ageing caviar loses all its qualities. Encrust it in ice, do not let metal touch it—use a bone or ivory spoon for service—and please, please keep away from it chopped onion, even chopped parsley or chopped hard-boiled egg. Endeavour to serve this, the finest hors-d'œuvre of all, in its natural state. To accompany the dish put a halved lemon at hand together with a few slices of rye bread, in default toast or, better still, Bliny. These are little pancakes made from a fermented batter of buckwheat with sometimes an admixture of plain flour or even from plain flour alone.

2.

Bliny (plural of blin). Weigh ¾ lb. flour either buckwheat or mixed and make a small ferment of ½ pint of warm milk, ¾ oz. yeast and a little of your weighed flour, say 2 oz. Cover this in a warm place and allow it to 'drop', then make it into a batter with the remainder of the flour, 1 pint of warm milk and 4 yolks. Allow this to stand until required (about half an hour), add the well-beaten whites carefully and make your Bliny in very small pancake pans. This quantity of batter will make roughly seventy to eighty.

Note. Caviar may be rolled in bliny and served with sour cream (smetane) on top.

Herring Roes

Cod Roe

3.

To prepare and serve. This must first be cooked, and to do this successfully it is advisable to roll the roe in a cloth tightly—like a galantine—for it disintegrates very easily. If you will wrap it up as I suggest and poach it slowly in water to which has been added salt and vinegar, then allow it to cool in its own liquor before unwrapping, you are more likely to make a success of it than otherwise. Having unwrapped the cold cooked cod roe, you may slice it but not too thinly and arrange it on a service dish with a sauce over it made from the cooking liquor and vinaigrette dressing in equal parts. The débris may be made into a spread or butter and will be of use when we consider canapés, etc.

Herring Roes

4.

For hard roes make a 'cuisson' as follows: Take sufficient water, season it with salt, peppercorns, thyme, bay leaf, a small pinch of coriander seed, parsley stalks, carrots and onion sliced very thinly on the 'mandoline', and vinegar. Bring this mixture to the boil and allow the vegetables to cook thoroughly. Having arranged your herring roes in an earthenware dish, pour the above pickle on them and place the dish in a cool oven with a greased paper over it to prevent any drying of exposed roes. After an hour, remove the dish from the oven and put away to cool until the following day. Before serving sprinkle chopped parsley over.

5.

Soft roes are best poached in white wine with the juice of a lemon added. It is not necessary to make an elaborate marinade which would only mask the delicate flavour of the roes.

6.

Mayonnaise of soft roes. This dish is prepared in exactly the same way as any other mayonnaise of fish. Shred some lettuce and, having seasoned it, place it at the bottom of a glass dish. Upon this dress some drained roes cooked as in the last recipe and sauce them over with a moderately stiff mayonnaise. Place a few quarters of hard-boiled egg around the dish and a lattice-work of trimmed fillets of anchovy on top. Sprinkle a few capers over.

Fish

SALMON ROE

This is known commercially as *red caviar* (Ketovaya).

7.

To make red caviar. You can be your own producer of this if you live near a salmon river, for often towards the end of the season you will have had in your kitchen fish almost ready for spawning. With a little patience and some gentle working you can free much of the large-sized red spawn from the enveloping membrane. Salt this very lightly and keep it in the refrigerator, but do not freeze it.

POUTARGUE DE THON

This is the preserved roe of the tunny fish and is a commercial product. The tunny belongs to the mackerel tribe and attains to a large size, weighing sometimes a thousand pounds. This fish is an object of considerable importance to the countries bordering the Mediterranean in which sea it abounds. The flesh is used fresh, when it is supposed to resemble veal—that from the belly is the most delicate—salted and dried, marinated or preserved in oil. Tunnies appear in great shoals and their approach is perceived by the fishermen at a great distance. They apparently come to spawn in the bays around the 'foot' of Italy, notably in the bays of Sicily, and it is there in early summer that they are caught in great numbers as they have been from time immemorial. The system of taking them is an elaborate one and consists of thousands of yards of nets in the form of a lane leading to a final trap. As the fish move along the lane successive 'gates' are drawn behind them. When they reach the final netted prison from which there is no escape for the fish, a net at the bottom is drawn up and the tunnies are harpooned in the artifically made shallow water. They are hauled into the boats which surround this last enclosure and brought ashore. It is usual for several hundred fish to be killed at one time and as each may weigh from seven hundred pounds upwards it will be realized how important is tunny fishing in that part of the world.

The roe is cleaned, stripped from the covering membrane, salted, dried and pressed. It appears as a yellowish-brown sausage somewhat flattened.

8.

To serve Poutargue de Thon. Slice it in thin slices and sprinkle with a few drops of oil or of vinaigrette. At one time tunny roe was shipped in pots or little barrels in a similar manner to caviar and in that form was useful in the preparation of canapés, barquettes and tartelettes.

POUTARGUE DE MULET or BOTARGO

The preserved roe of the grey mullet is also a Mediterranean product but is held by many to be superior to the tunny roe, the smoked variety even more so. Remember to keep all preserved roe away from damp.

9.

To serve. It is served in the same way as tunny roe, in thin slices with either oil and lemon juice and a squeeze of pepper or with a few drops of vinaigrette over.

MOLLUSCA

The oyster (Ostrea edulis) occurs naturally in tropical and temperate seas. It does not flourish in water containing less than 3 per cent of salt nor will it grow in Polar regions. It is usually found on stony or shelly bottoms at depths varying between 18 and 180 feet. Dredging used to be the only method of fishing but, as the beds can be and have been ruined by over-dredging, this has given place to more scientific rearing of oysters in properly prepared areas in shallow water off the coasts of all continents. The progress of the oyster to the table may be divided into four stages. First, care of beds, i.e. by removal of enemies, pests, sea-weeds, etc., second, maintenance of a breeding stock to supply larvae; third, rearing—suitable material-cultch—placed in the water to provide a settling ground for the spat; fourth, fattening. This last may be attained by relaying the oysters on special beds where fattening occurs automatically, but there does not appear to be any safe guide as to this. Fattening grounds can only be found by experience.

Growth in the American (Ostrea virginica), Portuguese and tropical oyster is much more rapid than in the European variety. It may take five seasons to produce a British oyster of 2¾ in. but the American is said to have reached 2½ in. in seven months in South Carolina!

OYSTERS AND PORTUGESE OYSTERS

Resembling oysters are the Gryphae or, as they are commonly

known, Portuguese Oysters. These are easily distinguished by their irregular curved shell, one valve of which is less than the other. Since the culture of this sub-variety of oyster has been taken in hand commercially, there has been a marked improvement in flavour, but it does not equal that of the true oyster. Whilst we are on the subject of flavour, it is worth noting that an oyster dredged from the 'deep sea' has an indefinable something, a taste of the sea, which is not possessed by a cultured specimen.

10.

Service of oysters. Whether you get a fine fat Belon, Blue Point, Colchester, Cornish, Loch Ryan, Marenne Verte, Ostend, Portuguese, Whitstable, Zeeland or other variety of oyster, you may have to open them yourself—I have seen people attack them with a hammer! There is an American machine, which, by means of a powerful lever, drives a wedge-shaped piece of metal between the two halves of the shell, but I prefer the old-fashioned way. There are two essentials; first an oyster knife, a blade about $3\frac{1}{2}$ in. long by $\frac{5}{8}$ in. wide, tapering very slightly towards a rounded end (no point) and very stiff, inserted into a haft or handle, and second, a knowledge of where to insert it into the oyster. Take the knife in one hand and put a cloth in the other with an oyster, hinge away from you, on it. You will recognize the hinge in most oysters as being the pointed end, but in the rounded or shapeless sorts it is the point from which the growth rings radiate. Now, with the fingers of the hand holding the oyster and protected by the cloth, press the side of the knife into a point alongside the hinge, aiding this by twisting the knife backwards and forwards with the other hand. The mollusc will give up the unequal struggle sooner or later—your brute force will compel it—then slip in the knife and sever the powerful muscle which holds the shells closed and discard the flat shell. Cut the oyster from the other shell, the deep one, and turn it over. The deep shell holds all the liquor, the turning-over presents the best side of the oyster, for you may have bruised or otherwise damaged it when inserting the knife at first; and now the oyster-lover has only to lift the shell from the dish and slide the contents down his throat. The ideal to aim at is to open the oysters at the last moment, and to see that they are served cold. Serve them with their own liquor in the deep shell on a bed of crushed ice, and along with them thin slices of brown bread and butter, which may be rolled. The epicure's only additional accompaniment is a half-lemon which he squeezes as required; but for the Philistines

Mussel (*Mytilus edulis*)

you should have ready Tabasco sauce, Cayenne pepper, Shallot vinegar, Chilli vinegar and black pepper.

MUSSEL (MYTILUS EDULIS)

The mussel is a littoral shell moored to rocks, stones, even to crustaceans and ships' bottoms. It is found in all the oceans of the world, especially in temperate and colder seas. Two kinds interest us; the common mussel and the Mediterranean mussel. The former are smaller but more esteemed than the latter, though mention must be made of the giant mussel gathered at Isigny (Calvados), some of which measure nearly five inches in length, yet it only ranks as a common mussel. Both types are cultivated, and the running of mussel-beds is an important industry. The natural are easily distinguished from the cultivated. In the former the edge opposite the hinge is slightly concave; in the latter it is slightly convex. Mussels were eaten raw by prehistoric man, the sites of his former habitations abound with shells, both mussel and limpet. The life history of the mussel is similar to that of the oyster, and for centuries it has been the practice of the mussel farmer to erect wicker screens so that the spat washed in by incoming tide may anchor itself there. The mussel is considered large enough for eating when it has attained a length of 2 in., i.e. three years after the fall of spat. They, like the oyster, fatten best in a density of 1014; that of the North Sea is 1026, but mussels are more tolerant of fresh water than is the oyster. Mussels may be eaten raw, and do appear on that dish of all kinds of raw molluscs known as 'Fruits de Mer', but in general they are cooked, whether served hot or cold.

11.

To cook mussels. Cut an onion into fine rings and throw them into a pan large enough to hold the quantity of mussels you wish to open, with room to spare. Add to the onion a small pat of butter, a bay leaf, very few twiggy bits of thyme and lastly ¼ pint of dry white wine. The mussels, which have been examined (for bad ones), scraped and washed in several waters, are put into this prepared pan, the lid, which should be tight-fitting, is put on, pan and contents put on the hot part of the stove and shaken about at intervals until the mussels are opened, i.e. cooked. This will not take longer than five minutes. The subsequent use to which the mussels are to be put determines whether they shall now be removed from the shells or left in one half-shell to which they adhere.

12.

Mussel Salad (I). Cook required quantity of mussels as above and discard the shells. Allow to cool, bind them with tartare sauce (p. 108) and dress them in a glass dish. Sprinkle chopped parsley over and decorate the sides of the dish with half-slices cut from a notched lemon.

13.

Mussel Salad (II). An alternative to the above, cook the mussels with lemon juice and a little water in place of the white wine, the other ingredients remaining the same. Shell them and allow to cool. Now reduce the liquor to a syrupy consistency and allow it also to cool. Mix this with sufficient stiff mayonnaise sauce to bind the mussels, dress them as before.

14.

Mussel Salad (III). Cook the mussels as usual and when they are cold pick them from the shell and, if necessary, beard them. Mix them with a mayonnaise strongly fortified with mustard or in a mustard-cream sauce. Dish either in one pile in a glass dish or fill the largest shells with the salad as a variant.

15.

Mussels with saffron. Prepare the following souse. Chop an onion finely and allow it to cook without browning in sufficient olive oil. Add to it one clove of garlic crushed under a knife, a sprig of thyme, half a bay leaf, a small stalk of fennel (or in default a few fennel seeds), a large tomato, skinned, de-pipped and cut roughly into small pieces, a good pinch of chopped parsley, the usual seasoning of salt and pepper and lastly as much saffron as will lie on a sixpenny piece. Add a little water and bring to a full rolling boil, then throw in the mussels which you have carefully cleaned as before. Put on the lid and cook the mussels quickly. Take the mussels from their shells and put them back into the cooking liquor. When this is quite cold taste it and heighten the seasoning if required. When dressing this souse, squeeze a few drops of lemon juice over it and add a little olive oil.

16.

Curried mussels is a variant of the above. A spoonful of curry powder is added to the onions and garlic. Omit the saffron and thicken the sauce slightly. When cool dress the mussels in a border of cooked rice, and sauce over with the liquor. The rice may be decorated with slices of hard-boiled egg and half-slices of notched lemon.

17.

Moules à la Gelée. Cook the mussels in the usual way and allow them to become quite cold. Select large shells and fill them with sardine paste (p. 112), making the top surface level with a knife. On this place a fine cooked mussel, decorate it with a small leaf of parsley or chervil and by means of a brush dipped in half-set aspic jelly, q.v., give it a coating. This hors-d'œuvre looks very well when carefully prepared.

COCKLES (CARDIUM EDULE)

These, known also as Poor Man's Oyster, are found in sandy places all round the coast, but particularly in estuarial waters. By means of its orange foot, the cockle is able to burrow in sand or mud and by flicking it leaps for short distances.

18.

To eat cockles. Cockles are eaten raw in the same way as oysters and mussels or may be cooked in similar manner to the latter, i.e. in a small amount of liquid. They are apt to be very gritty and should be well washed before being cooked.

CLAMS

There seems to be much confusion in the different countries over the definition of the word 'clam'. Many species of bi-valvular shell-fish are known by this name. In England the genus Mya, which includes 'gapers' and the pearl mussel, also the genus Mactra, including many rare and beautiful species, live in sand, are universally diffused, and are known as clams—Mya Truncata being the soft clam. Scotland gives the name clam to the scallops or Pecten, an inequivalved bi-valve which is able to move in water by closing its shell with a quick movement. In the U.S.A. the term is applied to several species, but there are two broad divisions; soft-shell clams (Mya Arenaria) and hard-shell clams (Venus Mercenaria). The latter are also called Quahogs. Small young quahogs are known as 'little necks'. The Japanese little neck clam was introduced into British Columbia accidentally. There also (Queen Charlotte Islands) are situated the razor-clam beaches which support an important industry in canned clam juice.

19.

Service of clams. Clams are eaten raw or cooked; if the former, a sauce-boat of shallot sauce may be served with them.

20.

Shallot sauce. Very finely chopped shallots mixed with vinegar and seasoned with coarsely ground pepper. For clams as hot hors-d'œuvre please refer to that section.

CLOVISSES, PALOURDES, PRAIRES

These are all met in France but rarely in Britain, most probably they are species of the genus Venus, of which one hundred and fifty exist, most of them edible.

LIMPETS AND WINKLES

Use the heel of your boot to detach the former from the rock, eat and enjoy it as did your ancestor two thousand years ago. For the latter, do not forget to provide yourself with a pin!

ORMERS OR ORMIERS, OREILLES DE MER, EAR SHELLS (GENUS HALIOTIS)

This is an ear-shaped univalve found off the coast of France and the Channel Islands. It is also found off the North Pacific coasts of America and Asia and those of Australasia. This shell gets its name from the excessive amplitude of its aperture, and the flatness and smallness of its spire, when it has been likened to 'an ear'.

21.

To serve abalone. The 'foot' only of this gasteropod is used for food; it is usually soused or pickled for use cold; if hot it may be served in a sauce as poulette or even sauté. In the U.S.A. it is known as Abalone and is sliced thinly and fried.

OURSINS OR SEA HEDGEHOG

We may never be able to get a supply of these for our hors-d'œuvre table as they come from the shores of the Mediterranean Sea, at least the best ones do. Some day, perhaps, an importer may bring this delicacy to us by air. In that case you must know what to expect. The oursin looks like a round hedgehog with a petrified exterior.

22.

To eat this delicacy. You may decide to cook it in boiling salted water for ten minutes, then cool it off, or you may eat it as they do in Provence, from the shell, uncooked. In either case, snip round the shell with a pair of scissors, open it and throw away the entrails and water. The yolk-like substance (coral) at the bottom you eat and enjoy, with the help of small sippets of buttered bread or toast (mouillettes).

CRUSTACEA

This is a large and varied class of animals, including land, marine and fresh-water subdivisions; but those which interest us are few, and they are the edible ones. Reproduction in crustacea is sexual, the sexes are distinct, and the female being oviparous carries the eggs under her body for protection until they hatch. Crustacea are found in the sea at all depths, and some varieties also frequent inland fresh-water lakes and rivers. Nearly all breathe by means of gills, but there are also land crabs which are air breathers and would die if kept in water. The crustacea are scavengers and will feed on dead or living matter equally well. In fact after a fight, in which the more powerful has ripped off its opponent's claw, the victor will proceed to devour it; and since they are cannibalistic, the mature specimen is very partial to the young of its own species. The loss of a claw, however, does not worry the loser unduly for it immediately proceeds to grow another one. This second limb is never quite as robust as the one it replaces.

CRAB

This name is given to numerous species of crustaceans. The European edible crab (Cancer pagurus) is familiar to all, with its almost oval reddish-brown carapace or 'shell' and two large pincers. The under part of the body is yellowish in colour and it will be noticed that the male has a narrow pointed tail and larger claws than the female which has a broad flap as a tail. Crabs are carnivorous, and during the autumn and winter disappear into the deeper parts of the sea, returning to the rocky shores in spring. It is caught in baited traps known as crab-pots, or creels in Scotland, which are made of wicker. Another variety is the spider crab (Maia). This has long legs and a smallish, triangular-shaped body.

23.

The cooking of crabs. Crabs should be immersed in cold water and brought slowly to the boil. This is not cruelty, for the crabs will die long before the water is hot enough to cook them. If they are plunged into boiling water, as in the case of lobsters, they may shed their claws.

24.

Dressed crab. Turn a cooked crab on its back and remove the claws. Break it open by pulling the central part, which holds all the legs, away from the shell and discard the pointed, spongy, greyish organs (the gills). With a spoon remove all the soft brownish interior and rub it through a sieve; all that you find in a crab is edible except the breathing apparatus already pointed out. Mix this purée with a little made mustard, chilli vinegar (or ordinary vinegar and cayenne pepper) and salt, adding a few white breadcrumbs if found too sloppy. Now turn your attention to the shell, you will find a line marked on the under-side of the crab shell where you can enlarge the opening you have already made. Use a pair of pliers in order to break the unwanted parts of the shell off cleanly and place the crab mixture back again. Crack the claws, and take out from them the legs and the central part, all the white meat and flake it. The last part of this operation is tedious, but there is so little 'meat' in a crab that I must insist. If you will bend the end of a metal skewer over and back again, giving it the shape of the first turn of a corkscrew, your job will be much easier. Use your faithful friend the pliers for this. With the flaked crab cover the creamy part of the partly filled shell and finish the dish by decorating it with parsley, hard-boiled eggs, chopped or in slices, and serve on a papered dish, using the legs under the ends of the shell to steady it.

CRAWFISH (PALINURUS VULGARIS)

This is the French Langouste and is otherwise known as Rock Lobster or Spiny Lobster. It is generally greenish-brown in colour with splashes of orange or yellow near the tail. The crawfish differs from the lobster family (Homaridae) in having two stiff feelers and by the fact that the first legs are not provided with chelae or 'pincers'; also all the legs have six segments and the head shell is rough, quite different from the smooth shell of the lobster. It is found on the southern and western coasts of the British Isles and extends to the Mediterranean. The crawfish is usually of bigger build than the

Crayfish (*Astacus Fluviatilis*)

lobster. As to its flavour opinion is divided, in France it is certainly the more preferred.

25.

The service of crawfish. For every way of serving it except 'au naturel', the crawfish may, without detriment, be prepared and dressed exactly as the lobster.

CRAYFISH (ASTACUS FLUVIATILIS)

The crayfish looks like a miniature lobster, it rarely exceeds about 4 in. in length. This is the French 'Ecrevisse'. It inhabits fresh-water streams in Europe, generally on a chalky or limestone bottom. Other varieties of crayfish are found elsewhere in the world. They occur in the extreme north of Europe in arctic lakes and rivers; this variety extends to Norway and Sweden. Another, the Astacus Nigrescens, is found in England and in California. Rivers flowing into both shores of the Mediterranean Sea yield this little crustacean and one sub-variety found in the Danube and also in the West Indies is classed as leptodactylus on account of its long, slender pincers. Hindustan, Burma, the Molucca and Philippine Islands, Southern Asia, gener-ally, China, Japan and the islands of the Pacific Ocean from the Sandwich Islands in the north to New Zealand in the south, all have varieties of crayfish. Those found in Australia and in Madagascar are very fine and much larger than the European variety; the Tas-manian one being the size of a lobster. America has several species, notably Astacus Potamobius and Parastacus Brasiliensis.

26.

The cooking of crayfish. Prepare a court bouillon with half a bottle of white wine and a third of a pint of water. Add 4 oz. of finely sliced small onion, the same amount of carrot (which may be notched, cut into two lengthwise and then sliced thinly across), a handful of parsley stalks, a small bay leaf, a sprig of thyme and a tiny piece of garlic crushed under the knife. Season this with salt and pepper, put the lid on the pan and give it fifteen minutes' slow cooking. Take four dozen crayfish: you will notice that they have five little 'leaves' in their tails. Pull out the centre one and the intestine will come with it. Having done this, wash the crayfish under the cold water tap and throw them into the court bouillon. Cover with the lid and shake the pan occasionally, giving ten minutes to cook. Allow to cool in the liquor.

27.

Écrevisses à la Nage. Cooked as above, cooled, then served in a salad bowl or glass dish with some of the cooking liquor. This last should be tasted for seasoning before sending the dish to the table and if necessary a pinch of cayenne pepper should be added.

28.

Écrevisses en Buisson. Cook the crayfish as above and allow them to become quite cold. They are sent to the table dressed on a stand having three or four tiers of decreasing diameter. Hang the crayfish by their tails from the edge of this stand. Failing this they may be equally well dressed in a neat pile on a folded serviette.

29.

Canapés d'Écrevisses. Spread some slices of cold toasted bread with Anchovy Butter (p. 110) and cut some circles, rectangles, etc., from them. Garnish these shapes with shelled crayfish tails. As an alternative, use crayfish butter and proceed as before.

30.

Crayfish butter (cold method). An equal weight of butter and crayfish débris are pounded together. (Use for this the shells and intestines left after removing the tails.) Pass this purée through the sieve and use as required.

31.

Crayfish butter (hot method). Hot shells and trimmings are pounded as before and an equal weight of fresh butter is added and mixed well. Remove this purée from the mortar, put it into a pan with about the same volume of water and bring slowly to melting point. Strain this into a basin and put into the refrigerator or, at least, in a very cold place. When the butter has set, it may be removed from the surface of the liquid, freed from moisture and put away for future use.

A note on 'Crawfish' and 'Crayfish'

There is confusion between the terms craw- and cray-fish which need never have arisen. This, I submit, came about because those in the fish trade have been accustomed to apply the term sea-crayfish loosely to the crawfish or as it is sometimes erroneously termed the spiny lobster. This crustacean is not a crayfish and it is certainly not a lobster, for both have chelae or pincers and it has none. I appeal to my colleagues to end this etymological misunderstanding once and for all. Let us call the langouste by its real name of crawfish and the

Lobster (*Homarus vulgaris*)

écrevisse, crayfish. If you need a mnemonic to assist you in recalling which is which, suppress the first syllable of écrevisse and what is left sounds near enough to 'crayfish' to remind you.

LOBSTER (HOMARUS VULGARIS)

The common lobster is found on the European coasts from Norway to the Mediterranean. Homarus Americanus, a variety, not a distinct species, is found on the Atlantic coast of North America from Labrador to Cape Hatteras. The lobster takes a long time to come to maturity. The 'baby' of about one pound in weight is four or five years old, and it takes six to eight, possibly ten, years to arrive at that most desirable weight—from a culinary point of view—of one and three-quarters to two pounds. For this reason it is an impractical, nay too expensive, proposition for anyone thinking of lobster breeding on a large scale. But this does not hinder or affect the formation of lobster ponds, where catches are impounded awaiting the market; though this means of earning a livelihood is not without its worries, for recently in Scotland twenty thousand lobsters have disappeared unaccountably from one such pond, gone without a trace. Lobsters are caught in baited traps called 'lobster pots', or creels in Scotland, in a similar way to crabs. The first pair of legs have six segments and terminate in pincers, one of which is larger and more powerful then the other. This is a crushing claw; the other is smaller and is furnished with saw-like inner edges for cutting. The remaining legs have seven segments.

Overfishing (in America) seems to have resulted not so much in any diminution of the total yield as in a reduction in the average size of lobster caught. The world's largest recorded lobsters are in the Museum of Science, Boston, U.S.A., or rather plaster casts of them are. They weighed, when alive, 42 lb. and 38 lb. and were caught by deep-sea trawling at a depth of 600 ft. off the Virginia Capes. The larger was taken in the autumn of 1934 and the other in the winter of 1934–5. There have been stories of lobsters weighing as much as 60 lb., but these figures, unfortunately, have never been confirmed. Most countries have a minimum size fixed by law below which it is illegal to sell and in Maine (U.S.A.) a maximum size is also imposed; all lobsters above the limit must be thrown back into the sea for breeding purposes. This causes us no regrets for they are tough anyway, but the value of the protection so given has been questioned. The imposition of a close time to protect spawning lobsters has often been tried, but as the female carries the spawn attached to her body for nearly twelve months after spawning it is impossible to give any effective protection by this means. Prohibition of the capture of females carrying spawn seems difficult to enforce.

32.

How to handle a lobster. I strongly advise you to buy your lobsters alive and to cook them yourself. If lobsters are delivered to you dead send them back, for if you cook them in that state you will find when you come to cut them open later that the flesh of the tail is in crumbs and useless for your purpose. If you take them ready boiled, you are asking for trouble; you have no means of checking how long they have been cooked, and in the warmer months, when lobsters are in demand, deterioration is most rapid. They will probably arrive in a fish box packed in sea-weed, and as this is usually of the same colour as the live lobsters, i.e. a blue-black, study the mass carefully for a moment before lifting one out, in case its neighbour has been able to get rid of the lashing around its claw and is ready to greet you as a long-lost brother! Lift out the selected one with thumb on one side and fingers on the other side of the head shell. The claws cannot reach you there, but keep your hand away from the sometimes wildly flapping tail.

33.

If you wish **to cut up a lobster alive**, put it on your chopping-board with its tail extended. Using a large cook's knife, sever the claws and legs in two cuts, one on either side. Then place the point of the knife at the junction of head and tail, push through to the board and continue the cut to the end of the tail. You kill the lobster by doing so, for what amounts to a brain is the ganglia of nerves situate at the place where you inserted the point of your knife. Turn the animal end for end and make a similar cut through the head shell. You have thus cut the lobster in two lengthwise. Remove the little bag of gravel at the nose end and the intestine which shows as a black line in the tail and discard. Reserve the coral, which is black in a raw lobster but becomes red on heating, and the liver which turns green. These substances constitute the 'creamy' parts of the animal, and are most useful for adding flavour and colour to an accompanying sauce. Now crack the claws to facilitate the removal of the meat when cooked and the lobster is ready for Homard Thermidor or the raw flesh may be removed from the shell to make a soufflé.

There is a slight difference in the dismembering of a live lobster if

Lobster (*Homarus vulgaris*)

Homard à l'Américaine or Newburg is contemplated; the tail is cut across in the natural segments, but the rest of the operation is the same. These classic preparations do not come within our scope, but I felt that I had to mention them to you. Our interest, for the moment at any rate, is with cold lobster and for this we have to cook our lobster in a somewhat different manner.

34.

Cooking of lobster. After a half-century of experience of cooking I have come to the conclusion that the cooking of lobsters in a court bouillon is a mistake. Cooks are notably conservative and for them the methods in use a hundred years ago are a *sine quâ non* today; lobsters have always been boiled in a court bouillon and always will be. This argument does not make any allowance for the changes in transport which the succeeding years have brought about. Even in quite recent times I grant that it was necessary sometimes to disguise the . . . aroma; but today, when lobsters use your kitchen floor as a promenade, plunge them into boiling salted water—4 oz. of salt to every half-gallon of water—and when they are cooked I guarantee that they will have a savour that no amount of thyme, bay leaf, onion and carrot can give. Now please do not misunderstand me, I do not condemn the use of a court bouillon out of hand; like everything it has its appropriate uses; but I do maintain that one of these is not in the cooking of fresh lobsters. For a long time I have discontinued its use in the cooking of salmon, but this is, I suppose, because I live on a salmon river. It is said that only those who live on the coast know the taste of fresh fish; this is equally true of those who happen to live on the banks of a river in a non-industrialized area. Boil your lobsters in salted water for twenty to thirty minutes according to weight, and, having removed them from the liquid but before they are quite cold, rub a little olive oil over the shells, in order to give them a 'shine'. This is more appealing to the eye than the usual matt appearance of the boiled lobster's shell. When they are quite cold, and by that I mean chilled, you may proceed with:

35.

Mayonnaise de Homard. At the bottom of a large crystal dish, put a layer of shredded lettuce and over it arrange neat pieces of lobster-claw meat and débris. Do not have your pieces too small; you most certainly must not chop them. Let your dish be recognizable for what it is. Endeavour to build the shape into a dome, and cover it with neatly cut slices from the tail. Season lightly with fine salt, and cover the lobster completely with mayonnaise sauce. The decoration consists of a lattice of trimmed anchovy fillets and the squares or diamonds thus formed may have a caper, a slice of pimento-stuffed olive or a thin slice of radish placed therein. Complete the border with slices or quarters of hard-boiled egg alternating with quarters of small lettuce hearts.

36.

Lobster salad. Arrange some shredded lettuce in a salad bowl as before, but this time season your lobster meat with oil, vinegar, salt and pepper in a separate bowl and transfer it to a neat pile on the lettuce. The decoration of the dish which may consist of olives (stoned), gherkin fans, small lettuce hearts and anything which is in keeping with the dish and your fancy suggests, is kept strictly to the edge or border of the salad. A sauce-boat of mayonnaise sauce should accompany this salad.

37.

Lobster salad (II). A miniature salad is offered to you here as it is very suitable for service as hors-d'œuvre. The first spoonful destroys the appearance of a salad dressed in one pile; but if the same salad is dressed in miniature the effect is good until all has gone. Take a sufficient quantity of medium-sized tomatoes. From each one, having removed the stalk, cut a slice from the opposite end about one-third of the way down. Use a vegetable scoop (failing which a spoon) to remove the seeds and to clear out the interior. Season this lightly with fine salt and fill with a mixture of dice of lobster, cold boiled potato and dice of hard-boiled egg, bound with stiff mayonnaise sauce. Dress these on a bed of shredded lettuce, using for preference a round flat dish, and in the centre stand a head shell of lobster upright with its feelers suitably curled.

38.

Mousselines de Homard. Line the required number of small dariole moulds with aspic jelly, q.v. This is best done with jelly in a half-set condition and with moulds that have been well chilled. Fill into these a mixture of pounded cooked lobster meat passed through a sieve and pound with a quarter of a pint fish velouté (foundation sauce) to every pound of lobster meat, to which is added a quarter-pint of half-whipped thick cream and a small ladleful of aspic jelly. Verify the seasoning and, if necessary, use a few drops of carmine to heighten the colour. The flavour of this little dish is very delicate; pay due regard to this.

39.

Escalope de Homard. Take the meat from a cooked lobster tail whole, and slice it in quarter-inch slices as nearly round as possible. Glaze these with a brush dipped in melted aspic jelly and place a thin slice of truffle in the centre also glazed with aspic. When the jelly is set, mount the escalopes on half-inch slices of lobster mousseline (see above) and dress them on a bed of shredded lettuce.

40.

Aspic of lobster. This follows the usual practice of glazing the mould, decorating the top with fancifully cut pieces of truffle, filling the interior with pieces of lobster, and a final topping up with nearly cold aspic jelly. When firm, unmould the aspics on to a silver dish and surround them with either (*a*) chopped jelly, or (*b*) a thin layer of melted jelly covering the bottom of the dish.

Norway Lobster or Dublin Bay Prawn (Nephrops Norvegicus)

This variety is, like the lobster, found from Norway to the Mediterranean. It is a smaller species with long slender claws, and is of an orange colour often beautifully marked with red and blue. The tips of the claws and legs are white. The Norway lobster does not change colour on cooking. In size it is not much bigger than a crayfish, and all ways of preparing this and prawn are applicable to it; though it is less esteemed than they. It is found in deeper water than the other crustaceans and is captured by trawling, and most of the individuals so taken are males. This fish is known in France as Langoustine, and the shelled tails are well known to us as scampi.

Prawn (Palaemon Serratus)

This is the edible prawn, though the name is given to several members of the family Palaemonidae. Prawns come to us ready cooked, of a rosy pink hue and three to four inches in length.

41.

To serve prawns. (*a*) Arrange them round a bunch of parsley. By taking pains you will be able to stand them with their snouts in the air; (*b*) hang them by their tails from a champagne glass, placing a good bunch of parsley to keep them in place; (c) cut a lemon in two lengthwise and push those wicked little spears prawns carry in their noses into the lemon rind leaving their tails in the air. With a little care in sizing them and arranging them in rings, you will achieve an imposing dish reminiscent of those last-century dressings 'en couronne'. Fifty years ago when I was an apprentice we added a refinement by peeling the tails. The gourmet knew that nothing was being hidden by this, for the first thing to reveal the state of freshness in a prawn is the crispness of the shell and you would not be able to stab them into a lemon skin if they were stale. In those days everything short of actual mastication was done for the guest; there is, alas, a very different attitude to him nowadays!

SHRIMP (CRANGON VULGARIS)

This poor relation of his lordship The Prawn abounds in immense shoals on the sandy shores of this country. It is a greyish brown with spots of a darker brown which makes it difficult to distinguish against a sandy background. Many immature prawns are sold as shrimps—they can be identified by their rosy pink colour. Shrimps are usually sold cooked and shelled, but in case you have to shell them yourself, here is how to do it.

42.

Shelling of shrimps. Take hold of the shrimp (or prawn) by the head, thumb and forefinger of left hand, and tail, thumb and forefinger right hand. Bend the tail upwards so that it forms a straight line with the head, then push the tail slightly towards the body and pull apart. The shell of the tail should now come away leaving the 'meaty' part to be removed from the head. Do not throw away the débris of shrimps or prawns for they will yield a flavoursome butter if treated in the same manner as already indicated for crayfish butter (p. 42). The shelling of shrimps and prawns may take some practice before you become expert, but persevere and the knack will soon be yours. As already stated, shrimps usually reach you ready cooked—let us hope they were cooked in sea-water—and ready shelled. All you have to do therefore is to rid them of the excess salt they contain by putting them in a colander and allowing the hot water to run over them for a few minutes, then cooling them under the cold tap and draining them, squeezing if necessary. The most popular manner of serving shrimps is either as buttered, or as potted shrimps.

43.

Buttered shrimps. Blend a sufficient quantity of shrimps, freed from excess salt, with melted butter, a grating of nutmeg and a seasoning of cayenne pepper. Place them in shallow pots and when they are nearly set pour over them more melted butter.

44.

Potted shrimps are prepared by pounding in a mortar one pint of picked shrimps with a quarter of a pound of butter, half an ounce of anchovy paste and a pinch of cayenne pepper. A little ground mace may be substituted for the anchovy paste if preferred. Put into pots and cover with melted butter and keep both in a cool place.

45.

Crevettes en Mayonnaise. This is prepared in exactly the same way as others, by arranging a bed of seasoned lettuce on a dish, dressing the shelled and de-salted shrimps on it and saucing it over with a rather stiff mayonnaise sauce. Smooth the surface and decorate it with a 'quadrillage' of strips of filleted anchovy, turned olives and capers with a border of hard-boiled eggs in slices or in 'eighths' and lettuce hearts in quarters.

46.

Crevettes en Salade (I). Season your shrimps with a thinned mayonnaise (lemon juice and water) to which you have added a little made mustard. Dress the salads individually on incurved lettuce leaves and sprinkle over some finely chopped heart of celery.

47.

Crevettes en Salade (II). If preferred a more spicy dressing may be used consisting of one part grated horseradish, two parts chilli sauce, four parts catsup with a dash or two of Tabasco sauce if required and a seasoning of salt. Dress as before and sprinkle with chopped celery heart.

48.

Crevettes en Salade (III). Or a less spicy and more delicate dressing may be required. To one part of well-reduced tomato purée, add three parts of double cream and acidulate the mixture very slightly with lemon juice (and with great care also). In this salad a little grated apple will be found an improvement.

CANNED CRUSTACEA

There is a large market for all the foregoing put up into cans, and nearly every part of the world exports one or another variety of shellfish so treated. The Atlantic coast of North America from Nova

Scotia to Florida and the Bahamas even down to Brazil provides crawfish and crab. There are crab canneries in the Pacific in British Columbia, Alaska, Siberia and Japan. The U.S.A. sends special factory ships to the Behring Sea where the giant King Crab is caught by deep-sea trawling, packed into cans, processed at sea and made ready for export from Alaska. Farther south, Australia has extensive canneries, as also has South Africa and some islands in the Indian Ocean. There is an excellent pack of prawns from Batavia.

Frozen 'Tails'

The meat from crab claws, crawfish, crayfish and lobster tails is frozen and exported to this country and the U.S.A. from Australasia, South Africa and other places. This saves two-thirds of the cost of transport, but the loss of the flavour-giving other parts is a disadvantage.

49.

Use of frozen tails. Frozen shellfish meat is useful to give bulk to, for example, a lobster entrée (Américaine, Newburg, etc.) where there is already a sauce. In salads, and for bouchées, cutlets, omelettes, Coquilles Mornay or à la Crême or à la Nantua, frozen tails are an indispensable standby.

SMOKED FISH
The Smoking of Fish

A natural and very ancient method of preserving fish is to smoke it. The acids, alcohols, creosote, formaldehyde and tar present in wood smoke have a definite bactericidal action.

50.

The construction of a smoke house. It is best if one contemplates even occasional smoking to build a smoke house. This need be nothing more than a wooden box standing across the end of a ten-foot trench in the garden. A packing case will do quite well, but the joints should be papered over or otherwise made smoke proof. A hinged lid with a small tube as a vent in the centre should be provided and some means of keeping out curious persons. The trench should be about one foot in depth by one foot in width. Old paving stones or pieces of sheet iron are used to roof it over. If the trench is dug in the direction of the prevailing wind it will be an advantage.

The Smoking of Fish

51.

To operate the smoke house. Light a wood fire at the end farthest from the box, cover up with stones or iron sheets and open the lid. When there is a good red fire, rake it all to the end of the trench and put about a barrow load of oak or other hardwood sawdust between it and the box. Leave a small space as a flue and when the stones have been replaced, cover all joints with a few spadefuls of soil. The fish to be smoked is now hung on bars which have been placed across the top of the box on the inside. Close and lock the lid and it will not be necessary to inspect the fire for a period of at least forty-eight hours. The technique of smoking is to have a progressively dense smoke. Too much at first dries the fish and makes a coating that no amount of later smoke will penetrate. It is not possible to regulate the amount of smoke in our home-made smoke house to this extent but I can assure you that the smoking of salmon sides in it is possible.

52.

Preparation of fish for smoking. In general it is necessary to salt or brine the fish before smoking. This may take the form of immersion in a strong brine (holding sufficient salt to float a potato) for about twenty minutes in the case of small fish such as haddock or several days for salmon. The actual smoking of small fish varies from eight to twenty-four hours—a light smoke for haddock or a heavy one for a kipper. To prepare a salmon it is first important to scale the fish, then with small pliers or a pair of tweezers lift up small pieces of skin and slice them off with a sharp knife, leaving a bare diamond-shaped patch of flesh about half an inch in length. Do this about a dozen times on each side of the back, i.e. where the flesh is thickest and rub into each patch a pinch of saltpetre. Next fillet the salmon, cutting on each side of the fins and follow up and remove all bones, even those in the belly. Leave the stiff bone under the gill covers (collar bone) to act as a support when hanging the fish in the smoke box. Now place your salmon sides on a tray or dish and cover each with a handful of moist brown sugar, followed by a few of coarse salt. The next morning turn the sides over into the brine they have made and on the following morning wash them in cold water clear of brine, swab them dry and hang them in your smoke box. Eight hours smoking should be enough for a quick sale. I have boned a salmon early one morning and served it as smoked salmon at dinner in the evening of the next day, but if you wish to keep your smoked salmon for a reasonably long time you must salt it and smoke it longer, and keep it in a cool larder, never in a refrigerator.

Fish

53.

Smoked eel comes to us from Germany, from Kiel to be exact, and is of larger size than those taken in this country. Slice it in thin fillets and dress on a ravier with a little tuft of curly parsley.

54.

Smoked herring. (Fillets of, in oil.) An old stand-by this, especially the brand 'Au Gendarme' which depicted on the tin two gendarmes savaging a large fish with their sabres. You can make a good substitute yourself for this ready-prepared article by using kippers. Place them on the hot stove for a moment skin side down. This enables you to remove the skin without difficulty. Then ease out the bones with your fingers and store the flesh away in earthenware terrines with a bay leaf or two and a few peppercorns interspersed among the fillets. Fill up with olive oil, store in a cool place and use as required.

55.

Smoked salmon. If you have not smoked your own as suggested above, then select Scotch cured for quality, mild flavour and good colour. Place on a board, a discreet tin-tack will keep it firmly in place, and slice towards the head in thin slivers which you serve on the guest's plate with a quarter of lemon. The pepper-mill with black peppercorns should be offered at the same time. If you slice the other way—towards the tail—you are cutting with the grain and will get a ragged slice.

56.

Sigui Fumé. The fish, which is also known as the fresh-water herring though much bigger, is fished in the Swiss lakes and in France; but principally in Russia, notably in Lake Ladoga. The smoked variety comes from that country, for the Russians esteem it highly. It is usually skinned, boned, cut into thin slices, dressed on a long dish, and a sauce composed of oil, vinegar, mustard, chopped fennel, chopped hard-boiled eggs, pepper and salt poured over it.

57.

Smoked sturgeon. There are various ways of treating it, but for hors-d'œuvre it should be cut very thinly and the slices dressed overlapping one another on a ravier. A few drops of olive oil or vinaigrette sauce may, with advantage, be sprinkled over. A bouquet of crisp, curly parsley should be placed at one end,

58.

Smoked trout. Should be served as other smoked fish, i.e. sliced thinly and dressed plainly, but if small they should be skinned and served whole, leaving the heads and tails in place.

SOUSED FISH

Souse is an ancient word with an O.E. root meaning watery. Cf. the French Souchet and the Nederland Waterzooi. Souses are used for flavouring, preserving and tenderizing, and there are three broad divisions: (i) where used to flavour and incidentally to preserve (for a few days) an already cooked piece of fish, (ii) where the souse is cooked, poured over the prepared fish which may then be (*a*) put into the oven or left on top of the stove to complete the cooking or (*b*) allowed to remain for the hot pickle to continue its work. The choice here is between a thick piece of fish and a thin fillet, between a rolled boned herring and the same laid flat, and (iii) where the vinegar in the souse does the 'cooking' without the aid of heat.

59.

Pickled left-over white fish. Any white fish left over from lunch or dinner may be used. If the piece has been fried or cooked à la meunière the browned coating must be removed; if plain boiled or better, cooked in a court bouillon, arrange the fish in an earthenware dish deep enough to allow it to bathe comfortably, then take some of the cooking liquor, add a sliced onion, some aromatic herb and sliced parsley root, an equal amount of vinegar, pepper and salt if required and pour the mixture over the fish. Should there not be any cooking liquor, use a mixture of half water and half vinegar. Turn the pieces over in order to impregnate them well with the pickle and use as a variety of hors-d'œuvre, cutting them into suitably small pieces.

60.

Cold boiled salmon makes an excellent pickle when treated in this way.

61.

Sprats. These come ready smoked but it is as well to skin them before serving. Plunge them for a second into boiling water and you will be able to scrape off the skins quite easily. Cut off the heads; arrange the fish on a dish and sprinkle them liberally with white wine and allow them to soak for an hour or so.

62.

Soused herrings. (Mackerel or small trout.) Prepare a souse or marinade. There are many recipes for this, but all follow the same plan, and consist of a mixture of white wine and vinegar or vinegar and water in equal quantities flavoured with finely sliced carrot and onion (and/or shallot) in rings, a bouquet garni, peppercorns, cloves, bay leaves, salt, and sometimes mace and allspice; the whole boiled until the vegetables are cooked. This hot souse is used to cover the fish which have been placed in an oven dish, and this is then baked until the fish are cooked. The dish is allowed to become cold and served as it is, with perhaps a sprinkle of freshly chopped parsley over, and perhaps a few slices of lemon 'peeled to the quick'.

63.

Harengs Marinés au Vin Blanc. The marinade for this way of sousing herrings is composed of half a bottle of white wine and a glassful of white wine vinegar boiled together with the vegetables and aromatic herbs as mentioned above. When the vegetables are cooked the whole is poured over the scaled, gutted and cleaned herrings ready aligned in a fireproof dish. Run a spoonful or two of olive oil over the surface and place the dish in the oven to poach the fish for ten minutes. Allow to cool and serve as it is. There is a very good brand of H. Mariné au V.B. on the market which I have every confidence in recommending to you. This is 'Harengs marinés au vin blanc Capitaine Cook'.

64.

Rougets à l'Orientale. This souse of red mullet is given because it differs from the usual practice and makes use of a recipe and method which may often be employed for small cubes of white fish or for soft herring roes. For a dozen small red mullet, skin and de-pip a pound and a quarter of ripe tomatoes. Chop these, allow them to fall in oil and add two cloves of garlic chopped with a small handful of parsley, a small pinch of saffron and the necessary salt and pepper. Clean, wash, dry and pass the mullet through flour, then brown them very slightly on both sides in smoking-hot oil and arrange them in an oven dish. Pour over them the tomato sauce to which you have added a good glass of white wine, cover the dish with an oiled paper and place it in the oven to finish cooking, which will only take a few minutes. Leave the mullet to cool and serve well chilled in the dish in which they were cooked.

65.

Sledz Marynowany ze Smeitana. A Polish dish of marinated herrings but with a sour cream sauce. Use small herrings, gut them and keep them whole. Souse them as indicated above, arrange them 'tops and tails' on a flat dish when cold, and make a sauce of sour cream, yolks of hard-boiled eggs passed through a sieve, a little French mustard and sufficient of the souse to make the sauce of the exact consistency for pouring. Use this to cover the soused herrings. A little sieved yolk and a pinch of chopped fennel may be strewed over. Other fish, notably small trout, may be treated in a similar manner.

66.

Norwegian spiced anchovies come in beautifully made little oak barrels about four and a half inches in height by three inches in diameter, complete with little hoops. Open one end and hang a few of the fish over the side. Place the barrel on a dish provided with a paper doyley and a bouquet of parsley.

67.

Gaffelbitar. This is a Danish preparation of herring. It reaches us in tins. There are two varieties; one in a preparation of dill, the other with lobster sauce. I think that there used to be a third pack in wine sauce, but of this I cannot be sure. Dress these straight from the tin on to a service dish complete with the liquor. An excellent hors-d'œuvre.

68.

Bismarck Herrings. They are usually bought ready prepared, but in case you wish to make your own, here is the method. Scale, then tear off the heads from some salt herrings. Open them down the back and remove the backbone, then let cold water run over them for a few hours. This will take away the excess salt. If salt herrings are unobtainable, you may use fresh ones but must salt them slightly first. Place the boned herrings flat in crocks with sliced onions, mustard seed, a few bay leaves, peppercorns and chillies, cloves and sliced salt cucumber (agoursis) in suitable proportions between each layer. Fill up the jars with a fifty-fifty mixture of vinegar and water. Store in a cool place; they will be ready for use in a few days and if kept well covered with 'pickle' will keep for some time depending upon the weather.

69.

Roll Mops. Exactly as above, but rolled instead of being kept flat.

There is no necessity to tie cotton round them nor to skewer them if they are packed close together. Roll with them a little sliced onion and a strip of agoursis with a few mustard seeds.

70.

Sardelles seem to be immature fish treated like Bismarck Herrings, but left whole, of course. Serve as they are with a little of their own liquor.

71.

Roskilde Kryddersild. You require twenty herrings, two and a half ounces of sugar, one and a quarter ounces of salt, one and a half teaspoonsful mixed allspice and pepper, a little olive oil, some sliced raw onion and some vinegar. Clean, bone and wipe the fish. Put them in vinegar for twenty-four hours. At the end of this time take them out, drain them well and put them on a platter, skin side down. Sprinkle them with the sugar, salt and spice. After two hours, put the herrings into a crock with sliced onion and a few drops of oil between each layer. The dribbles on the platter should also be poured in, but not the vinegar. Put a board with a weight on top and leave for two days. Serve cold with new potatoes boiled with dill. Begin the preparations three days before you wish to eat the herrings and you can reckon that if the weather is not too hot, they will keep for a week.

FISH IN OIL

François Appert was the discoverer of the principle of conserving food in bottles or cans. He found that if he filled foodstuffs into wide-mouthed bottles, kept them standing up to the brim in boiling water for six hours, then sealed them with alternate layers of cork and wax, and continued boiling them for some time afterwards, spoilage of the contents did not occur on cooling. To account for the success of this simple process was not easy when no one had yet found that there were such things as bacteria. Appert's principles of food preservation were published in 1810, and it was then that Durand in England had the idea that tinned iron containers might be more suitable than glass as they were less fragile, could be made completely impervious to contact with the air by soldering and could be made in any shape or size to fit the contents. Durand took out a patent in 1810 for his tinned cans and thereafter progress in the canning industry was very rapid.

French, Portuguese and Other Sardines

FRENCH, PORTUGUESE AND OTHER SARDINES

In ancient times it was thought that they originated on the shores of Sardinia where they were, and still are, caught in immense numbers, and from whence they get the name. Sardines are really immature pilchards and shoals of them are taken off the Atlantic coast of Morocco, Spain, Portugal and France. But don't you dare call this same fish a sardine if you catch it in Britain. A famous lawsuit in 1912 established the right of the French packers to apply the name to their products. In Cornwall, when it has grown to maturity, it is a pilchard. Yet in nearly every country of the world immature young herring, brisling and even fully grown sprats may be called by the name Sardine.

The important centres of the French sardine industry are Concarneau, Douarnenez and Nantes. Ground bait in the form of salted cod roe imported from Norway is laid to attract the fish and the skill of the fisherman does the rest. The fish are brought to the canneries at the earliest possible moment where they are immediately brined (15 to 20 degrees) for twenty minutes or so. After this they are fed into a machine which beheads and draws out the guts from a hundred at a time. The sardines are now washed in sea-water and dried in a current of hot air. They are then placed on grills and fried slightly in hot oil. After draining they are packed carefully in tins, spices such as cloves, bay leaves or peppercorns may be added, the can topped up with fresh olive oil and the lid sealed on. The tins are next processed for one and a quarter to three hours according to size of can, cooled, inspected, labelled and cased.

In Spain, Portugal and Morocco, the weather being hotter, sardines are cooked in steam before being canned, oil being used to fill the cans prior to sealing. French sardines, being caught in colder waters, handled under cooler conditions and being subjected to the preliminary cooking in oil, are a superior article, the excellence of which is due solely to these factors.

The quality of any sardines wherever packed depends on the quality of the oil used. The finest olive oil is used by the world-renowned packers, but arachis (ground nut) oil or even cotton-seed oil is used for cheaper markets. All canned sardines improve with age; this is also true of canned mackerel and brisling (sprat) but not of sild (herrings). The oil thickens and darkens with age but should remain clear and sweet with a mellow flavour.

72.

Service of sardines. Sardines à l'huile may be served direct from the tin, but it is preferable to dress them fanwise, i.e. with tails pointing one way, to a good bunch of parsley, on a glass dish. In the latter case a few drops of fresh oil should be dribbled over them.

NORWEGIAN AND BRITISH FISH IN OIL

The canning of fish in Norway originated in 1873 and the Norwegian Government seeks to maintain, by constant vigilance, a high standard of size and quality. A close time is imposed from 1st January to 1st June when brisling may not be packed, so that only fish at the peak of perfection is canned. A government research laboratory works constantly in the interests of the canning industry and supervises the quality of the imported olive oil and tomato purée. Brisling containing less than a legal minimum percentage of fat are rejected for canning purposes.

73, 74.

Brisling (sprats) are canned in the summer, and **Sild** (immature herring) in the autumn and early winter. They are first washed to remove scales, passed through a brine bath and threaded through the head on steel rods to be smoked over smouldering oak sawdust, which gives the characteristic flavour. After being cooled they are decapitated and trimmed by machinery, graded and packed by hand into cans which are then filled with olive oil, and after inspection, seamed and processed at 230 deg. F. in pressure chambers. Sild are also packed 'à la française', i.e. unsmoked, but are dried slightly first in warm air.

75, 76, 77.

Mackerel, when small, are also packed in oil and mature as do sardines into a delicacy. Hard mackerel roes, less coarse and of firmer texture than hard herring roes are also packed. **Sea Lax** or smoked salmon is canned in oil and has a delicate flavour due to the use of certain aromatic woods (Juniper?) in the smoking. There is a pack of **Kipper Snacks** similar to the smoked herrings already mentioned under Smoked Fish (p. 52).

78, 79.

In this connection, mention must also be made of the British **canned herrings** and particularly of **kippered herrings** which are packed whole (differing from the Norwegian) with paper between the fish, at various ports on the East Coast from Aberdeen to Lowestoft. The new 'boneless' kipper is similarly treated.

TUNA OR TUNNY FISH

This is packed where it is caught in countries bordering the Mediterranean (see page 32 for note on tunny) and in California. There are various types of tunny, but all are equally useful as hors-d'œuvre.

80.

To serve tunny. Take the fish out of the can and drain it, slice thinly and dress the slices overlapping on a ravier or other service dish with a few fine rings of onion in graduated sizes on top. Dribble a few drops of fresh oil over before sending to table.

ANCHOVY

Next we have anchovies in both salt and oil. The anchovy swarms in the Mediterranean Sea off Italy. It is also caught off the coasts of Sicily, France, Spain, Portugal and Holland, but those most esteemed are taken in the Gorgona area, in fact the name has become a trade one. The heads and guts are removed and the anchovies packed in salt. Anchovy paste and essence are made directly from anchovies so exported. The fresh anchovy is not likely to come your way, but the salted ones should be soaked in cold water to de-salt them, then rubbed gently with a cloth to remove the scales. Open them length-wise carefully and discard the backbone. Now store them away in olive oil in a cool place. You can get Spanish or Portuguese anchovy fillets which will save you the trouble.

81.

To dress anchovy. With a sharp knife trim the prepared fillets and cut them in full lengths about one-eighth of an inch wide. Arrange them in the form of a grille on a ravier and decorate the dish with a few capers, a little sieved yolk and white of hard-boiled egg, chopped parsley and lobster coral.

82.

Alternative dressing. Arrange the narrow fillets alternately with strips of pimento. In both cases finish with a spot or two of olive oil on the anchovy. Anchovies are also prepared rolled with capers, which may be considered a waste of time according to whether you have a use for them or not. There must be a market for such a pack.

Fish

There is also a pack known as 'Hors-d'œuvre in Oil' marketed by Portugal, which consists of broken sardines, pieces of tunny with vegetables, tomato, spices and seasoning.

83, 84.

Smoked cod roe is canned in Norway. **Pilchards** are packed in oil or tomato sauce in both Cornwall and California. All the above have uses in the preparation of hors-d'œuvre.

SALADS OF FISH

85.

Anchoiade Languedocienne. A slice of tomato, a ring of hard-boiled white of egg and a fillet of anchovy rolled to take the place of the yolk. Arrange these three ingredients in the order given in little piles neatly on your service dish, sprinkle with vinaigrette dressing and strew the sieved yolks over.

86.

Médaillons d'Anchois. Lay a quarter-inch-thick slice of cooked potato on a similar slice of cooked beetroot slightly larger in diameter. Put a fillet of anchovy round the potato and fill the centre with stiff mayonnaise. Sprinkle the surface with paprika pepper.

87.

Filets d'Anchois Chavette. For this salad you require anchovies, de-salted, scaled, boned and trimmed as already explained. Prepare a salad of finely cut lettuce seasoned with vinaigrette and dress this on a service dish. Arrange the anchovy fillets on this and decorate the border with tiny piles of seasoned dice of potato and beetroot alternating. The dice must be cut very small and very even. Complete the dish with yolk of hard-boiled egg pushed through the sieve and with chopped parsley.

88.

Anchois Madrilène. Prepare a fondue of tomatoes by cooking in oil tomatoes, onion, garlic with salt and pepper and passing the resultant purée through the sieve. When this is cold dress it on a dish, arrange your fillets of anchovy on top, garnish with thin slices of lemon (peeled and de-pipped) and decorate with finely sliced rings of sweet pepper.

89.

Anchois Gastéréa. This time prepare a salad of julienne of celeriac and truffle bound with mayonnaise and on this arrange your anchovy fillets. Over them put a line of finely sliced tomatoes—down the centre for preference—and a border of sieved hard-boiled egg.

90.

Aspic de Crevettes. Chill the small dariole moulds as instructed under Aspic de Foie Gras and line them with aspic jelly at near setting point. Now fill with picked shrimps which have been washed under hot running water and then under cold (in order to get rid of the excess salt). Fill the moulds with more half-set jelly and allow to set in a cold place. Unmould on to a dish covered with shredded lettuce.

91.

Aspic de Homard. This is made by substituting dice of cooked lobster for the shrimps in the above, and may be unmoulded on to a thin slice of tomato set on seasoned shredded lettuce.

92.

Aspic de Filets de Sole. Pieces of cold cooked sole or of any cooked white fish may be prepared similarly to the above or the fish may be coated with a sauce chaud-froid, decorated with details of truffle, etc., then covered with aspic jelly at near setting point, before moulding. It is not necessary to go to much trouble in preparing the small quantity of sauce chaud-froid required for this variation, a few spoonsful of jelly added to a good fish velouté enriched by the addition of a little cream will suffice.

93.

Salade de Poisson. Use left-over fish of firm texture for this salad. Cut the fish into small cubes if firm enough otherwise flake it. Add the same amount of cubes of cold boiled potato and a few pieces of peeled, seeded tomato. Bind with tomato mayonnaise to which has been added a few drops of Worcester Sauce. Use small incurved lettuce leaves to line a dish and pile the fish salad in the centre.

TWENTY-THREE OTHER SALADS OF FISH
94.

Open some clams. You do this by putting either water, wine or fish stock into the pan with them, clamping on the lid and heating; they will soon respond! Take out the fish, reserving the liquor, and cool. There is an alternative method of opening a can of course. Arrange a border of sliced cooked potato round a dish, put the clams in the centre and sauce over with piccalilli dressing, q.v., let down if necessary with some of the reserved cooking liquor.

95.

A round of lettuce cut out with a one-and-a-half-inch-diameter cutter, on which you place a round of cold cooked potato cut out with a one-inch-diameter cutter. On this base place a piece of cold left-over kipper, sauce it over with piccalilli juice mixed with a little mayonnaise sauce and let down further, if necessary, with vinegar, and on the kipper put a skinned section of orange. Sprinkle the merest dusting of finely chopped chives on top.

96.

Make a salad of flaked cooked kipper, dice of cooked potato, pieces of tomato flesh and well-drained piccalilli (roughly chopped). Mix some tunny fish paste, q.v., with mayonnaise and thin down with vinegar for use as a dressing. Arrange slices of cold cooked potato on a service dish and pile the mixed salad in tiny heaps on these.

97.

Cut Bismarck herring, celery and raw apple into strips, not over long, and make a dressing of freshly shredded coco-nut mixed with French mustard dressing, q.v.

98.

Make a julienne of gendarme herring (or raw boned kipper), raw apple and cold potato. Sprinkle with a pinch of finely chopped raw onion or chopped chives and season with vinaigrette.

99.

This salad is composed of cubes of cooked carrot, potato and Bismarck herring with the addition of a little finely chopped onion and seasoned with oil and vinegar. It may be dressed in small heaps on slices of pickled beetroot, or the dish may be sprinkled with chopped débris of beetroot and the salad dressed thereon.

100.

Cut Matje herring into convenient sized pieces and soak them in red wine. The lees of a decanted bottle are quite suitable for this purpose. Dress with sliced raw onion over and a dusting of chopped parsley.

101.

Cut a cooking apple into small dice and do likewise with an equal amount of smoked herring in oil—kipper snacks, gendarme or your own filleted kipper in oil. Add a small teaspoonful of finely chopped onion, and season with a spoonful of white wine, two spoonsful of olive oil, a turn or two of the pepper-mill but no salt. Mix this intimately together and dress in a neat pile on the service dish.

102.

Arrange little piles as a salad as follows; a round of lettuce, a spot of mayonnaise, a slice of skinned tomato, a spot of mayonnaise, a slice of prawn (cut one in half), mayonnaise, a round slice of cooked potato, all surmounted by a slice of stuffed olive. Vinaigrette dressing over all. Endeavour to decrease the diameter of the various layers as they mount upwards.

103.

For this salad, dice of pimento, round slices of prawn, preserved nasturtium seeds, slices of celery and a few cubes of potato are bound with French mustard dressing, q.v.

104.

Halve some prawns lengthwise and use them to cap some piles consisting of slices of cooked potato, agoursis and tomato. Sauce with a dressing of French mustard dressing and mayonnaise mixed.

105.

Cut a few outside leaves of lettuce into a fine julienne and make a bed of this on the dish you are to use for the salad. Dust lightly with salt and arrange slices of hard-boiled egg on this bed. On each slice of egg place a piece of skinned and boned sardine with a thin slice of small braised onion thereon—left-over onions from a garnish are suitable. Use French mustard dressing as a seasoning and sprinkle chopped parsley over all.

106.

Make a julienne of raw carrot, turnip, cabbage and onion seasoned with salt and pepper and dressed with orange juice and sardine oil. A few tiny heaps of this are placed on the dish, each with a sardine on top sprinkled with grated cheese and decorated with a thin slice of a small tomato.

107.

A slice of cooked potato; a round of sardine purée with a smaller round of stiff cottage cheese on top. Make little heaps of these three ingredients and arrange these heaps in rows on a dish. Sauce them over with tomato mayonnaise, q.v.

108.

Take a slice of tomato on which place a blob of stiff French mustard dressing. On this arrange a slice, or slices if small, of banana and pipe these with sardine butter from a star tube—stars, curls, Cs, Ss or what you will and decorate with a caper or two.

109.

Shred some cold cooked salmon carefully and sprinkle it with wine vinegar. Mix together potato and cucumber dice and blend with the shreds of salmon using mayonnaise sauce to bind.

110.

Scraps of tunny fish made into a paste with cottage cheese, then rolled out and cut into rounds. Place each round on a slice of tomato, a slice of pickled walnut on this and a slice of pickled gherkin to finish. Mix some thinned French mustard dressing with fines herbes and cover each with it.

111.

On a slice of tomato place a slice of hard-boiled egg covered in mayonnaise. On this place a flattened ball of tunny fish paste, with a round slice of pickled gherkin on top. Arrange these slices in decreasing diameters so as to display the different colours to advantage.

112.

On a slice of tomato place a round of hard-boiled egg. On this place a round of tunny fish paste and sauce completely over with French mustard dressing. To decorate place a thin slice of stuffed olive on top.

113.

Any scraps or débris of tunny should be flaked and added to an equal volume of skinned flesh of tomatoes and the same volume of cooked rice. Season with vinaigrette.

114.

Take some of the sliced onion left over from Bismarck herrings and chop it roughly. Mix with it some skinned and de-pipped tomatoes which have also been roughly chopped and some flaked tunny fish débris. Season this mixture with a vinaigrette containing chopped fennel and dress on chopped lettuce.

115.

Small cubes of cold, cooked fish may be placed on tiny lettuce leaves or on nasturtium leaves and sauced over with tomato mayonnaise. Decorate with two blanched leaves of tarragon placed cross-wise.

116.

Cut the tender green part of celery leaves into a julienne, flake some cold cooked fish and chop (concasser) about one-third of this volume in agoursis and another third in chopped tomato flesh. Mix together lightly, season with mayonnaise and dress in small individual piles on whatever base you may fancy or have available.

2. Flesh and Fat

THE PRESERVING OF MEAT

The date when the first leg of pork became a ham will never be known, for it is lost in the mists of antiquity which surround the earliest essays into the preserving of meat by salting. Success in smoking, salting and drying must have been achieved by a process of trial and error; for technical knowledge in the days when it was first practised was nil by modern standards. We do know, however, that the curing of meat as we understand it was successfully performed by the Romans. For no less a person than Cato has recorded the method in use in his day, *circa* 200 B.C., which by the way, differs very little from the salting of bacon as carried out by the ordinary farmer of today. The market for the salted bacon and hams of former times is a dwindling one, for the machine age has had a two-fold effect upon it. By lessening the 'sweat of the brow' it has diminished the demand for salty and fatty foods, both of which are required by the heavy manual worker. The increase in the class of sedentary workers has had a like effect. The mild-cured hams and bacon now the rule are the direct result of this decrease, and of mechanical refrigeration which has made it possible to cure pig-meat all the year round instead of only in the colder months of the year. This requires less salting, for the old cure, to last probably six months, carried about five times as much salt as does the factory one of today, made for quick consumption. Further, fat meat is easier to cure than lean, and a pig to be really fat must be large, a fact which may have accounted for those enormous sides of bacon and gargantuan hams we used to know. We, as cooks, may deplore the passing of delectable chunks of larding bacon but fashion is against us and there is nothing we can do about it.

The method of preserving used must be one that will hinder, if it cannot stop altogether, the growth of unwanted bacteria and moulds. As putrefactive bacteria require moisture for their growth and development, the simplest, and incidentally, the oldest method of preserving meat is to dry it.

Low temperature helps in the battle against spoilage by putrefaction; meat will keep any length of time if frozen, and many cooks will have cause to bless the advent of 'deep freezing'. My experience of this way of keeping stocks of meat, game and poultry is that after a certain time there is marked drying out of the tissues; and I have found that by smearing the breasts and legs of poultry and game with olive oil and then wrapping the bird in oiled paper, this drying is to a large extent avoided. The subsequent thawing by immersion in cold water, whether of meat or bird, will bring the object back so nearly to normal that it is indistinguishable from fresh.

Smoking is another old way of preserving meat, and is now generally allied to salting. If prior salting is not done the operation becomes a very laborious one. Wood smoke provides tars, acids, etc., which help in the preservation of the meat, but the prime object is the added flavour. Fir, larch, green juniper all give odoriferous smoke, whilst a good smoke is obtained from beech and oak. In terminating the fumigation by aromatic smoke, a distinctive taste is given to the meat. For this, bay, and its leaves, rosemary, coffee beans, incense, liquorice, cloves, juniper berries, dried fruits and many other woods or roots are used in the various countries.

The use of chemical substances known as 'preservatives' in food is controlled by the Public Health Regulations (1925 and subsequently) on the matter. It is illegal to add boric acid, benzoic acid, their compounds or derivatives, formaldehyde and in certain circumstances sulphur dioxide to food offered for sale. This reduces the curing ingredients to a small number which includes the products of wood smoke, alcohol (in beer, wines and spirits), sugar, saltpetre and common salt—the most important of all—for without it curing could not be successfully undertaken. The preservation of meat by curing, as it is understood today, consists partly in drying and partly in getting a solution of common salt and saltpetre, with, in some cases the addition of sugar, at a concentration of sufficient strength to inhibit the growth of putrefactive bacteria, into the meat fluids and fibres.

117, 118, 119.

Curing may be divided into three methods; but it is rare that one only is followed, except in the case of the dry salting used generally by farmers and others who kill a pig for home use. Usually a combination is employed of dry and wet methods. Curing, then, is carried out by (a) **the dry method of curing**, which consists in rubbing the surface of the meat with a mixture of salt, saltpetre and perhaps sugar and then bedding it in a mixture of these, making sure that the meat as it shrinks is always in contact with the salt. Some curers add an aromatic note here by mixing with the salt, juniper berries, cloves, thyme and bay leaves or other similar substances; (*b*) **curing by brine** consists of immersing the pieces to be dealt with, with or without prior dry salting, in a salt solution containing from twenty to twenty-five per cent of salt and a small proportion of saltpetre and sugar. The length of time that the meat is left in contact with the salt or in the brine is determined by its thickness rather than its weight or size; (*c*) **curing by the injection of brine**. This consists in introducing a brine containing about thirty-three per cent of salt and one per cent of saltpetre into the meat. This is done by means of a pump and hollow needle or a type of syringe. The cuts of meat are afterwards brined and this method is the most speedy of all, but is only practised by the large packing houses and bacon factories. Saltpetre has the effect of hardening the meat, and sugar, which has the reputation of keeping cured meat soft, may have been introduced to counteract this.

HAMS AND CHARCUTERIE

HAMS AND BACON

After salting or brining, hams and bacon are well washed to remove excess surface salt, as this may prove to be a source of trouble in attracting moisture, and drying begins. Most hams and some bacon are smoked after salting, some much, some little, the type and quality of the smoke helps in determining the resultant flavour. Certain changes, not properly understood, take place in a matured ham which give it the flavour of cured meat.

Almost every country has a type of ham, some indeed have several. Among the French hams those of Bayonne enjoy the highest reputation. Those of Rheims are a good second, followed by those of Bordeaux and Angers. The districts around Paris yield the well-known Jambon blanc de Paris, which has a very light cure (demi-sel) and consequently more of the flavour of boiled pork than true ham. Germany has her hams from Mainz, Hambourg, Stuttgart and the Westphalian area; the latter being the most renowned, along with those from Bayonne already mentioned and the hams from Parma in Italy, for slicing very thinly, raw, for use as hors-d'œuvre. Hams which are in general served raw carry much salt, and it is a strange thing that this is only apparent after cooking.

For cold boiled ham it is advisable to use a variety of cure famous for its qualities when cooked. Here our vote must be given to the

York hams which have been famed throughout the world for more than a century, so much so that the term 'York' has long since been given to the cure and not to the product of the county.

For a ham to be served hot, my preference goes to the Prague hams. They are small in size, weighing about five or six pounds each, and therefore admirable for carving, also they have an exquisite flavour unsurpassed by any. American hams are similar in cure to the York, and boil very well. There is a variety of American ham known as 'tenderized'. This term may signify that the meat has been partly pre-cooked, for the instructions on the wrapper enjoin one not to soak the contents prior to cooking. All one has to do is to strip off the paper covering, immerse the ham in water and the cooking commences at once.

120, 121.

Hams from other countries do not interest us, as hors-d'œuvre, very much. There is one exception; the Spanish ham, from the Asturias, served as **Jamon dulce huevos hilados**. The curing of this ham is begun dry, i.e. by rubbing with salt to which has been added a small proportion of saltpetre and sugar, and is continued after a few days in a pickle containing a proportion of sherry. It is then smoked lightly with the smoke from smouldering aromatic plants. This process gives a ham which is sweet, full of flavour and lightly salted. It is braised in the ordinary way, removed to another pan, covered with a bottle of sherry, returned to the stove and the cooking continued under a close-fitting lid until the wine has almost disappeared. The bones are then removed and the ham pressed until cold. It is then dressed on a long dish and the required number of slices cut and left in position. The garnish placed around the ham and its slices consists of **oeufs filés** made from egg yolks beaten slightly and passed through a type of strainer having a number of tubes. This instrument is moved slowly over a shallow pan containing simmering sugar syrup at 240 deg. F. so that a thread of egg, something like vermicelli, is left to poach in the syrup. A certain amount of skill is necessary to accomplish this operation successfully. The threads of egg are lifted out of the sugar solution with a skimmer and put into cold water and then drained. Jamon dulce huevos hilados is completed by a decoration of aspic jelly.

122.

Bath Chaps. The lower jaw of the pig may be divided into two and each half becomes a 'chap' when cured.

Flesh and Fat

123.

Cornets de York. These are made from triangles of very thinly cut lean York ham (cold boiled). Put them just inside a cream horn tin and give them a touch of aspic jelly to hold them in place. Then chop some aspic jelly evenly and add a very little melted jelly, mix, fill into a forcing bag and pipe into the cornets. When set, remove them from the tins and dress them on a service dish or ravier with a sprig or two of parsley. Success with this very simple hors-d'œuvre depends on three things: (*a*) having a really good well-flavoured aspic; (*b*) in not chopping it too small, and (c) in not making it sloppy when adding the melted jelly. See that this last is not hot.

124.

Mousseline of Ham. For this you require one pound lean cooked ham free from gristle or skin, which you pound until fine in the mortar. Nowadays the use of the mortar is out of fashion, but if you have access to one you should consider yourself lucky. One reason for the superiority of the old-fashioned cooking over that of the present day is that whereas now everything is passed through the mincer, in those days everything was pounded in the mortar and passed through the sieve with a resultant gain in texture in the finished article. A partial return to the former state of affairs has come about by the appearance in this country of machines modelled on the Waring 'Blendor' or the John Oster Mfg. Co. 'Osterizer', both of the U.S.A. At the bottom of a glass container, a series of knives driven by a powerful little electric motor at a fast speed pulverize almost everything that is fed into the machine. The machine works very well with very dry substances or with those in a semi-liquid state. With meat alone or with any material liable to clog, it is not successful. Nevertheless meat can be made into a fine purée. To continue: add to the ham one-third pint of well-reduced Béchamel sauce and one-quarter pint melted aspic jelly. When these are well blended together, add two-thirds pint of half-whipped cream. Take the required number of small dariole moulds which have been previously masked with jelly and decorated on the bottom with fancifully cut pieces of sliced truffle or with a line of cooked green peas round the bottom, and fill them with the above mixture. When set in a cold place, dip the mould and contents boldly into hot water, dry at once on a cloth, give a shake and unmould on to a prepared dish. The temperature of the water and the length of immersion can only be found by experience.

125.

Cold Ham Soufflé may be made from the same mixture by placing a collar of stiff paper inside some small paper soufflé cases, or porcelain ones if you have them, and filling them half an inch above the top of the soufflé (hence the collar). When set decorate the top surface to your fancy and run a little aspic jelly over it. Remove the paper collars before serving.

SAUCISSONS AND DRIED SAUSAGES

126.

Casings. In the average pig there are about twelve to fifteen feet of large intestine and roughly four times this length of small intestine. the former is used for andouilles in conjunction with parts of the stomach or for large casings; the latter for sausage skins. Containers or skins for sausages, both fresh and dried, are also furnished by other animals and thus we have large and small beef and sheep casings. Prior to the war the bulk of casings in this country came from the Continent and U.S.A., and when this source of supply dried up, casings made from cellophane or similar material appeared on the market.

The preparation of the intestines is a long and laborious job. They are first freed from all membranes and fat and then turned inside out by means of a small stick, washed and scraped until nothing remains but the transparent skin so well known. The large intestine is treated according to the use intended for it. After trimming the outside it is either slit or turned inside out and the inner, mucous, lining scraped away with a blunt knife. The parts of the stomach intended for use are similarly treated. The intestines must be well washed in salt water (water acidulated with vinegar is used in some parts) and if they are not to be used at once, they must be drained and packed in plenty of dried salt.

The products of Continental 'charcuterie' or pork butcher's art are quite as important as the better-known cuts or cures of pork flesh. Of prime importance to us are the saucissons or dried sausages.

127.

Saucissons de ménage are generally made from a mixture containing twice as much lean meat as fat, the lean being provided by the cheapest cuts of pork, such as the neck and shoulder. Seasoning is added at the rate of one part ground pepper, one part spice, twenty parts salt and one part saltpetre (this last in order to keep the pink colour in the meat), to five hundred parts of the chopped fat and lean mixture. The addition of finely chopped garlic is optional. After being well mixed this preparation is filled into small beef casings, the extremities tied with string and the saucissons are suspended in a cool part of the kitchen so that they may dry. At the end of a few days remove the saucissons from the kitchen and hang in a cool, but airy larder where they will keep for several months.

128.

A variant of this is **Saucisson de ménage fumé**. Take the required amount of pork, having more lean than fat, and chop it roughly. Add seasoning at the rate of twenty parts of salt, three parts ground pepper, one part peppercorns, one part spice and one part sugar to every five hundred parts of the chopped fat and lean mixture. Garlic should be included this time and the mixture chopped again and finally pounded in the mortar. Fill the preparation into beef casings of the desired length, tie the ends with twine and hang the saucissons in the smoke chamber until they have a brown-yellow colour. The smoke chamber in the country districts of France being the chimney. Next stab them with a needle and cook them for forty-five minutes in boiling water and allow them to become cold in the liquor. Wipe them dry on removing them from it.

129.

Probably the best known of the dried sausages are the **Saucisson d'Arles**, the *Saucisson de Lyon* and the *Salami di Milano*. For the first of these take two hundred and sixty parts chopped ham, one hundred parts pounded beef, sixty parts of fat bacon cut into small cubes. To this mixture add seventeen parts of salt, four of ground pepper, one of peppercorns, one of spice and two of sugar. Fill this preparation into large beef casings, pressing it in well to avoid any air pockets, and hang the sausages in a cool, airy place. When the filling has shrunk a little and the casing become dry and hard, it is time to begin the stringing. First the ends must be re-tied and in so doing the meat should be squeezed together and away from the ends as much as possible. The shrinkage is considerable. Next tie the lengths of string from end to end and then proceed to wind a continuous length tightly around at about half-inch intervals. This enables you to undo and re-wind the string if the further shrinkage of the filling makes it necessary. When the sausages are ready for use, which will take about six months, they will be covered with a whitish powdery scale. They are eaten raw, being cut into very thin slices.

130.

The manufacture of the **Saucisson de Lyon** is in all respects similar to that of the above, but this time beef is not used. The recipe is as follows: To four hundred parts finely chopped and pounded ham add fifteen of salt, two of sugar, one of pepper, one of spice, and one-half part of peppercorns. Mix this intimately together and finally add sixty parts of fat bacon cut into small cubes. Fill into casings as before as tightly as possible and follow the same procedure during drying.

131.

The Italian **Salami di Milano** saucisson gives us another variant to our recipe. For this take: One hundred parts of lean pork, one hundred of veal and chop these two meats finely then mix in fifty parts fat bacon cut into small cubes and fifty parts pigs' blood. The seasoning is: ten parts salt, three of ground pepper, three of ground ginger, three of ground nutmeg, three of ground cinnamon and one-fifth of a pint of white wine. The mixture is then filled into pigs' bladders which are bound carefully with string as before. After drying for several days the saucisson is smoked over branches of juniper, then rubbed with olive oil and kept hanging in a dry cold place until ready for use.

132.

Mortadella is another renowned Italian saucisson. Bologna has the reputation for these, but Lyon, Strasbourg and even Paris have made substitutes worthy of our consideration. The manufacture of Mortadella dates back to the Middle Ages, and was originally made whilst the flesh of the pig was still warm, that is to say, soon after the slaughter of the animal. A recipe which dates from the 'nineties is as follows: Lean pork, one thousand parts, salt, forty parts, saltpetre, two parts, red colouring, sufficient. Chop the meat roughly, mix in the seasoning and allow to lie until the next day. Then chop very finely and pound in the mortar. Complete the mixture and the seasoning by adding: fresh pork fat, one hundred and twenty parts, ground white pepper, three parts, whole black pepper, three parts, cardamom, two parts, one clove of garlic pounded, one glass of Italian white wine. Work the mixture well and fill it into pigs' bladders. Tie firmly and bind it with twine, then hang it in the larder or any place where it will dry. This preparation is served raw, but it may be served cooked. For this, place the mortadella in a pan with sufficient cold water to cover it and bring slowly to the boil. Allow to cook gently for forty minutes. Remove from the fire and leave to cool until the following day. Wipe dry before cutting into thin slices.

133.

Mortadella (II). A modern recipe is as follows: To two hundred parts of lean pork and one hundred parts of fresh pork fat chopped together very finely add one hundred and twenty-five parts of salt pork fat cut into small cubes and a seasoning of ten parts of salt, two parts of saltpetre and two parts of peppercorns. Mix these together well and allow mixture to drain on a cloth for about twelve hours. Then fill into pigs' bladders, string it as before and place in a pickle composed as follows: four and a half pints of soft water, four and a half pints white wine, four and a half pounds of salt, four ounces saltpetre, two ounces of spice and two ounces of carbonate of soda. The water, salt, saltpetre and soda are brought to the boil and the wine and spice then added. The pan is removed from the fire and the contents allowed to become quite cold. Filter the brine into an earthen-ware jar which is kept for the purpose. This pickle is Italian, the cost of the white wine is not prohibitive there, and is the one used for curing the Modena ham. After immersion for about thirty days, the hams or other pieces of meat are either smoked if to be used raw, or put into a pan of olive oil if to be served cooked. Our mortadella is left in the pickle for ten days, then taken out, dried, and smoked for four days. Finally it is cooked for three hours in boiling water and allowed to become cold before use.

134.

Salami di Bologna has a renown from ancient times, that from Milan has, seemingly, ousted it from popular favour. There are different varieties of this dried sausage and mention must also be made, in

135.

passing of the **Hungarian Salami**.

Enough has been written to give an idea of this extensive field but it must be remembered that all those mentioned above must be matured before being consumed; eaten fresh they are, one and all, detestable. It will be noticed towards the end of the first week of the drying period that a saucisson, if all is going well with it, becomes covered with whitish spots. These spread gradually until the whole surface is covered with them. They are evidence of the presence of certain micro-organisms of the yeast or ferment family which will prepare a suitable medium for the later development of other mic-robes which in turn assure the transformation of the meat and the development of the distinctive flavour. At least a month is necessary some indeed require six, for this maturing during which time the saucisson loses nearly half its initial weight. For this reason saucis-sons are never cheap.

Andouilles and Andouillettes

136.

These products of French charcuterie are typically good hors-d'œuvre, and are made from the large intestine of the pig, and in some districts, part of the stomach of the animal, the small intestines being used as already explained for sausage casings and for the manufacture of boudins, or black puddings as they are known over here. The parts intended for use as andouilles are first cleaned, soaked in running water for twenty-four hours, turned inside out and scraped carefully. For the outside envelope or 'robe', a suitable length about eighteen inches of the gut is chosen and put on one side. The rest is macerated with salt, pepper and spices for about six hours. At the end of this time cut this gut into strips about an inch wide and of the length of the intended andouille. From this point on, the various regional recipes diverge, but for the renowned **Andouille de Vire** it is continued as follows: the maceration is continued for twenty-four hours in all, also sliced onions and crushed garlic are present to add their flavour to the meat during this time. A piece of shoulder pork, cut into a long strip about one inch across is also marinated with the other lengths. When the time comes to assemble the andouille, free the strips from onion, etc., and drain them well, then arrange them on the table with the lardoon of shoulder pork in the middle. Tie them with a length of string, pass this up the middle of the reserved outer envelope and pull the 'filling' into place. Cut and remove the string and smoke the prepared andouille slowly in smoke-box or chimney with smoke from hardwood roots mixed with oak sawdust until the exterior is dry. String the outside tightly with strong string in a spiral and cook the preparation slowly for about four hours in water to which the same aromatic note has been added as was present in the marinade. Undo the string, re-roll it around the andouille and allow it to become cold.

137.

Andouillettes, analogous to chitterlings, are very similar but on a smaller scale. They consist of several lengths of carefully cleaned bowel pulled inside one another, with or without strips of tripe. Sometimes the partly cooked intestine is cut into small cubes and filled into the reserved 'robe' and sometimes they are plaited depending on the local custom. The preparation is next cooked slowly in seasoned water and allowed to become nearly cold before being pressed until quite cold. They are then 'glazed' with a mixture of lard and veal fat or mutton and veal fats, and are cut into lengths of about eight inches. They are then ready for final treatment for the table; being incised with a sharp knife and grilled gently. They are usually served with mashed potatoes and strictly speaking are light entrées and not hors-d'œuvre, though they can be used to begin a meal.

FRESH SAUSAGES AND CRÉPINETTES

These come to the hors-d'œuvre as cooked ones left unused after the breakfast, or other service; but a note here of the different varieties may be of interest to you. The fillings are very much alike, lean pork, fat pork, salt, pepper and spice appear in every recipe, with sometimes the addition of beef or veal but never, except in this country, soaked bread or rusks. The main differences are in the size, seasoning or in the treatment of the sausage after filling.

One distinct variety of sausage not very well known in Britain is the crépinette. This is a product of Continental charcuterie, and instead of being filled into casings, is shaped into a small flat cake about an inch thick and then wrapped in a piece of crépine, the light membrane which envelopes the intestines of the pig. Here fancy may let itself go! All shapes, round, square, oblong, triangular and oval are made from all kinds of meats, poultry and game, but in general these are used in the form of salpicon enclosed in an outer layer of sausage meat or farce and the little parcel wrapped up in crépine. Where dice of truffle have been used in the inner filling it is customary to place a slice of truffle on top of the crépinette before wrapping it in the outer covering of crépine.

138.

It is usual *to serve* the **Crépinettes** as follows. They are passed through melted butter and freshly made white breadcrumbs before being gently grilled.

Crépine or caul is used in the manufacture of faggots in this country.

139.

Note on Spice in Saucissons. I have referred to spice in the recipes given for saucissons. By this is meant what is known in France as 'quatre épices', the name given to the fruit of the myrtus pimenta, or as we know it Jamaica pepper or allspice, because it unites the aroma and properties of pepper, clove, cinnamon and nutmeg. This spice may be bought ready for use, or a well-known formula is:

Fresh Sausages and Crépinettes

seventy parts Jamaica pepper, ten parts nutmeg, ten parts cloves and ten parts cinnamon, to which may be added one part thyme, one part bay leaf, one part marjoram and one part rosemary. These are pounded well, passed through a fine sieve and kept in a closed tin.

THE SERVICE OF DRIED SAUSAGE AND OF RAW HAMS

For the service of all dried sausages, i.e. *Saucisson de Ménage, Saucisson de Ménage Fumé, Saucisson d'Arles, Saucisson de Lyon, Salami di Milano*, slice them thinly and dress the slices overlapping on a ravier, the small diamond-shaped salad dish, or if larger numbers are to be catered for, use the rectangular porcelain dish, and do not forget a small bunch of parsley in the centre or at the side.

Mortadella, Andouille de Vire. These should be sliced slightly thicker and rolled on account of the larger diameter.

Garlic Sausage, Leberwurst, Liver Sausage. Thicker slices because of the softer consistency.

Boeuf Fumé de Hambourg, Smoked Fillet of Pork, Smoked Tongue, Brunswick Sausage. Sliced as for dried sausages, the first-named very thinly.

Bayonne, Parma, Westphalia Hams are usually clamped in a special stand which holds them rigidly in the best position for carving into very thin slices—raw, of course.

SCOTS SMOKED SAUSAGE

A relic of days long past, and probably carried along with a bag of oatmeal by every man on those long tramps across moor and hill, cf. the Arab's dried meat and dates. A piece of beef was salted for a few days then minced very finely with half of its weight in suet and seasoned highly with pepper, salt and mixed with chopped onion. The Scots still have a predilection for spices (cf. their liking for gingerbread, black bun—which contains pepper as an ingredient), so it is quite possible that ground ginger, ground cloves or other spices would find their way into the mixture. This was filled into a well-cleaned ox gut, tied into suitable links and hung in the open chimney to dry and smoke.

140.

To serve. The sausage was boiled as required but, if you find any in the remote Highlands or the Hebrides, you may use it as it is, sliced thinly, as hors-d'œuvre.

77

Zampino or Zampouni

141.

This is a product of the Italian pork-butcher's art (charcuterie Milanaise): pigs' feet boned, stuffed and smoked. Soak them in cold water for a few hours, scrape the skin side, prick with a knife here and there, tie in a cloth, cover with cold water, bring to the boil, remove to a cool part of the stove and finish cooking slowly, allowing a good half-hour per pound. When quite cold dress as usual in thin slices with a décor of parsley.

Rillettes and Rillons

142.

Similar products, usually made in the country districts of France when 'le Monsieur' has been killed, a great day that! Pork belly, neck or trimmings cut up into small dice or pieces (not chopped) is allowed to cook very slowly, five or six hours or so, in its own fat with the addition of lard and/or water and seasoning. When the mass is uniformly brown in colour and the water evaporated, the fat is strained off and the remains—crushed in the case of rillettes, left whole for rillons—are cooled slightly then mixed with some of the half-set fat and put away in pots. If a good layer of the same fat is run over the top later, this useful hors-d'œuvre will keep for months. There are many varieties of these, in some districts goose or rabbit with or without pork is used.

PÂTÉS

Foie Gras and Its Not So Rich Relations

In 1782, Marshal de Contades was appointed military commander of the province of Alsace and took with him his Norman cook, by name Jean-Joseph Close (also written Clause), who had already given proof that he was clever at his work. Close was cook and pastry-cook so what is more simple than that he should make a pie or pâté containing a foie gras, a material ready to hand, enveloped in a kind of farce. This he did and his master's table became renowned for this dish. In 1788 the marshal was relieved of his command and Close entered the service of the Bishop of Strasbourg, but shortly after opened a shop where for the first time were sold the marvellous pâtés which used to grace the exclusive tables of Bishop or Marshal. Then came the Revolution and, in the disturbed state of the country after it, there was swept to Strasbourg another cook named Doyen. He was young, intelligent and ambitious. He began in a small way, as a pastrycook. The pâté of Close interested him greatly; he thought it lacked something, so he added to it the Périgord truffle and thus was invented the pâté de foie gras truffé which we know so well. Other towns than Strasbourg are famous for their foies gras; Nancy, Périgueux and Toulouse are quite reputed. Charles Gérard, the author of *L'Ancienne Alsace à table*, writes: 'The goose is nothing, but the art of man has made of it an instrument which gives a marvellous result, a kind of living hot-house where the supreme fruit of gastronomy grows.' Fat livers from ducks are also very good eating, but as they apt to melt somewhat and give up some of their fat on cooking, they are, therefore, not so much sought after for the various culinary preparations.

The house of Feyel of Strasbourg say that foie gras may be served as (*a*) hors-d'œuvre; (*b*) as an entrée; (c) as a dernier plat, or (*d*) in sandwiches. Now this firm know as much as anyone about foie gras as you will agree on studying their display every Sunday at their business address in Strasbourg. Read what the Académie des Gastronomes has to say on the matter, 'Le foie gras doit être aimé pour lui-même. Il doit être dégusté en hors-d'œuvre au début de repas avec un appétit frais et joyeux. . . . C'est une erreur de le servir avec la salade. . . . C'est une erreur encore pire d'en fourrer partout, dans la viande, dans le gibier, dans la volaille, dans le poisson et jusque dans l'entremets.'

May the voice of an insignificant cook here be raised in protest to this august body against so sweeping a statement as that contained in the last paragraph. What of our garnitures Impériale, Régence, Rossini, Talleyrand and even Strasbourgeoise, and of our Faisan en cocotte Souvaroff?—to name but a few of the appearances of that fairy—a slice of foie gras which can transform otherwise ordinary dishes into feast for the gods. These garnishes are confirmed by long usage, they are traditional, they are the classics of the kitchen, and I fear it will take more than the fulminations of the Académie des Gastronomes, whoever they may be, to make any alteration.

Foies gras come to you as a pâté, slightly taller than wide; this is the form of the original pâté en croûte as invented by Close nearly one hundred and seventy years ago; or in terrines.

143.
The Service of Foie Gras. First of all, it must be served very cold;

it must never be exposed on the table before the commencement of the meal, as the heat of the room will destroy the consistency of the livers and the subtle aroma of both liver and truffle will evaporate.

For service, the pâté en croûte is best cut into wedges and each wedge divided into two by cutting across. Terrines are best served as coquilles, which are made by using a spoon with as sharp an edge as possible, and, having dipped it into hot water, scooping out neat spoonsful of the foie gras. These may be arranged on a folded serviette in a pile or on a silver dish with a layer of madeira-flavoured aspic set on the bottom and decorated with diamonds, cubes, stars, half-moons, etc., of the same jelly cut from the solid. Endeavour to give your guests as representative a portion as possible, i.e. one that has a fair share of the contents of the pâté or terrine, liver and truffle. There are also foies gras in tins from whole livers, for use in the kitchen as escalopes or for making aspics of foie gras, down to spreads or pastes ready for use in sandwiches or on croûtes.

Excellent raw fat goose livers used to arrive from Czechoslovakia and Hungary. If you can come by any of these you may care to prepare your own.

144.

Foie Gras en Terrine. Here is a recipe I have found easy and good. The night before you are to use them, take the required livers, remove the gall if necessary, the green mark left by it and the sinews, then season. Next day make a sausage-meat farce with one quarter more fat pork than usual, i.e. one part lean pork, one and a quarter parts fresh pork fat, with seasoning and condiments as usual. Next 'clouter' your foie gras (*clou*=nail) with truffle, i.e. make an incision with a sharp-pointed knife or trussing needle and push in wedge-shaped pieces of truffle. If you can obtain fresh truffles so much the better. Wash, brush, peel and season them with salt and spice, then sprinkle them with madeira and cognac. At the bottom of your terrine place one bay leaf, cover bottom and sides with larding bacon then a light layer of farce to insulate the foies. Now arrange your prepared foies and cover each one with more farce until the terrine is full. Finish with a slice of larding bacon and cook 'en bain marie', i.e. in a pan with water reaching halfway up the sides of your terrine, in a slow oven (see page 82 for timing). On withdrawing, fill up with melted goose fat or lard. For all hot dishes of foie gras use goose livers; duck livers are best used in cold preparations.

Here is a good dish of goose liver I met in Prague.

Foie Gras and Its Not So Rich Relations

145.

Foie Gras en Hérisson. Prepare fat goose livers as above but use filleted or strip almonds instead of truffle and leave half of each almond sticking out, giving the appearance of a hedgehog. Braise the livers in a good stock and when they are cooked, remove the fat from the braising liquor, making sure that the latter is gelatinous enough to set, arrange your livers on a service dish and run the strained liquor around them. When quite cold they will form a welcome addition to your cold table. If imported foies gras continue to be difficult to obtain you will find several recipes for hot pâtés in the section on hot hors-d'œuvre.

146.

Aspic de Foie Gras. Take the required number of small dariole moulds measuring 1¾ in. in diameter at the bottom, 1½ in. in diameter at the top with an overall height of 1¾ in. or thereabouts. These are the sizes of the ones I have found most satisfactory for this work. Chill these moulds thoroughly, then pour in some aspic jelly at about setting point and pour out again. This will line them with a coating of jelly. Place a circle of truffle at the bottom, setting it in jelly. In this prepared mould place a neat piece of cold cooked foie gras and fill the mould with jelly. You have now a delightful hors-d'œuvre which you should serve very simply by unmoulding it on a dish and surrounding it with chopped jelly.

147.

Liver Paste. Put through the fine plate of your power mincer twice (don't attempt it on a hand machine for it will reduce you to tears) 10 lb. liver, calves', pigs', chickens', ducks', or what you have, 6 lb. fresh pork fat, 1 lb. onions. Place the resultant purée in the mixing bowl (machine) and add 1 lb. flour, salt and pepper to taste. (Sorry! It is essential that you taste this repulsive-looking mess in order to verify the seasoning.) Then dissolve in a tablespoonful of milk as much saltpetre as will lie on a shilling and add to the mixture. Mix well in the machine and divide into three or four casseroles. Level the top surface, put on the lids, and cook 'en bain marie' in an oven at 300 deg. F. for about two hours. When cooked sufficiently allow to cool slightly, then run either melted pork fat, bacon fat or lard on the top to a depth of about three-eighths inch. This liver pâté will keep six months, if in a cool place of course; but it is not necessary to freeze it.

Flesh and Fat

TERRINES AND PÂTÉS

After many years, I am unable to distinguish any point of difference between the two. To my knowledge, there is no pâté which could not equally well be made and served as a terrine. In fact, considerations of service will most certainly incline you to the view that terrines are superior to pâtés. In general the crust of a pâté is not eaten, indeed I have a recipe which says that the paste is not in the proper sense of the word comestible and that its only use is to protect the filling during cooking! In a terrine, on the other hand, all is eatable, the contents can be allowed to become cold whilst being pressed under a small board with a weight on top and this weight may be graduated according to the texture one wishes in the finished article, i.e. an open texture with plenty of jelly separating the elements of the filling, or a compact one. Such a course could not be followed with a pâté.

This last is the method used when the terrine is to be kept for a long time, say a month or two in cold weather. You must turn out the contents of the terrine when it is quite cold, and remove all the jelly carefully. Remember it is the jelly which in souring spoils the whole. Having put the block of meat back into the terrine, cover it completely with melted lard and when this has set place a sheet of paper on the top to exclude the air. Store in the dark.

148.

Filling of Terrines and Paté. First place a bay leaf in the empty dish, then line the interior with a thin slice or slices of larding bacon, failing that with the fattest bacon at your disposal. Then cover this with a layer, half an inch thick, of the prepared farce to be used, making it slightly thicker at the bottom. Your terrine is now ready for alternate layers of the chosen filling and farce until full. Endeavour to avoid air pockets and make the last layer one of farce. Cover this with a final slice of larding bacon, place the lid in position and cook the terrine in a water-bath in the oven as recommended for liver paste. The time required depends on the nature of the principal filling and on the thickness of the bulk; a large terrine only half full will take less time than the same weight of material in a smaller but deeper one. The safest guide is the state of the liquid in the terrine, when this ceases to be cloudy and becomes fairly clear, then the terrine may be removed from the oven. In general a terrine measuring $11\frac{1}{2}$ in. by 9 in. by $4\frac{1}{2}$ in. will take two hours. A further guide is to insert a trussing needle into the middle of the filling, and on withdrawing it, test the heat of it on your lip.

A further point in favour of terrine is that you can cut a thinner, neater, slice from it than from a pâté—no untidy crumbs about—even though in deference to British taste you have roofed it over with a covering of puff or other paste, and thin slices are what you desire in your service of hors-d'œuvre. Of course, if the terrine is for immediate use, do not remove the jelly. Instead, when it is taken from the oven add more stock made from its own trimmings and bones, in which an odd leaf or two of good gelatine has been dissolved.

149.

Terrine Bonne Femme. This is a most useful dish. Take pork, veal, hare, pigeon, chicken, game, or what you have in any proportion—the more mixed the better—cut into pieces the size of a filbert and give them a preliminary tossing in the frying-pan to stiffen the meat but not to cook it. Next strew it with chopped onion, parsley, mixed spice, a little thyme and broken bay leaf, salt and pepper and mix well together. Put into a terrine, sprinkle with a little madeira and a glass of white wine and put aside until next day. Then cook with its own liquor in the oven, covered, and finished with a well-flavoured jelly.

150.

Terrine of Minced Hare. For this you may use a mountain hare. Select a freshly killed white hare and bone it. Chop the meat with 1¼ lb. of lean veal, 1¼ lb. fresh lean pork, ½ lb. beef suet. Season with salt, chopped parsley and chives with two cloves of garlic, thyme and bay leaf minced fine, pepper and ground cloves. Line a terrine with larding bacon, mix ¾ lb. streaky bacon in dice with the above mince and fill a terrine with it. Pour a glass of brandy over it and cover with more larding bacon. Put on the lid and seal it with a flour-and-water paste. Cook in a cool oven for four hours. When done, cover with a jelly prepared from the carcass of the hare if to be used at once; if not, drain off all liquid and cover with melted lard as already advised. Serve from the terrine.

PIES IN PIE DISHES

These do not differ much from those we have just reviewed. The main difference lies in the fact that they do have a lid or covering of paste. Further, as they are generally made for immediate consumption, the 'gravy' or jelly surrounding the filling is an important part of the whole. It is not the general custom to line the dish with farce though I consider this a refinement which certainly adds to the quality of the finished article.

151, 152.

Veal and Ham Pie (Pâté de veau et jambon). Bone the veal, trim it, cut it into lengths and macerate these in cognac. Next prepare a **Farce Fine de Porc** consisting of one-quarter lean pork, one-quarter lean veal, one-half pork fat chopped separately then pounded together with $\frac{1}{2}$ oz. General Seasoning (p. 86) to every pound and lastly the cognac of the maceration. Pass the mixture through the sieve, and then spread half-inch layer of it on the inside of the pie-dish. Commence the building up of the interior of the pie by putting alternate layers of macerated veal and quarter-inch-thick slices of ham. In the middle arrange a line of hard-boiled eggs and sprinkle chopped parsley between each layer. Finish with a layer of farce. Egg-wash the rim of the pie-dish and cover the top with a very thin sheet of short pastry. Egg-wash this covering and on it place the lid of puff pastry. Trim the top edge and gimp it with the back of a knife. Egg-wash the surface and arrange a decoration of pastry leaves on top. Make two or three holes through the pastry to let out the steam during cooking. Allow the prepared pie to rest for twenty minutes before baking. On removing it from the oven fill it up with prepared gravy made from veal bones well seasoned.

153.

Chicken Pie (Pâté de volaille). Proceed as above, but replace the ham by a few lardoons of salt belly pork, i.e. long strips about half an inch square cross-section, mixed with boned chicken.

154.

Hare Pie (Pâté de lièvre). Remove the fillets from the hare, bone the legs and macerate all the flesh, seasoned with spiced salt, in cognac and madeira. For this pie you add to the farce the finely chopped liver—remove the gall bag, very small but sufficient to cause trouble —lungs and heart, together with the blood and a little more spice.

155.

Game Pie. As above, remove as many sinews as possible, or pound the meat from the legs in the mortar, pass through the sieve and add it to the farce. In this as in the last, make the stock for the gravy with the débris and bones.

156.

Venison Pasty. Cut lean venison into thin slices. Season, then arrange them in a pie-dish with a sprinkling of finely chopped onion and parsley between each layer. Fill up the dish with good, clear venison stock, place a metal cover on the dish and bring the contents to the boil. This done, put the dish with its cover in a moderate oven and cook until the meat is well stewed, adding more stock if required. Next morning remove the fat and cover the pasty with either a short crust or puff paste lid and bake. When ready, pour off all liquor and verify the seasoning, adding a leaf or two of soaked gelatine and a spoonful of either madeira, marsala or sherry. Return this to the pasty, and allow to cool thoroughly and set before serving.

Raised Pies

These are nowadays usually baked in a tin-plate mould, which is hinged to facilitate removal. One seldom sees a genuine raised pie, for those which pose as such have had the assistance of a paper band around their middles during those first critical minutes when the heat of the oven softens the paste and so many otherwise fine, upstanding ones spread flat. The art of making a raised pie stand up without any aid from without seems to be lost, or is simply not practised.

157, 158.

Pork Pie (Pâté de porc). For this I advise you to use a long mould 14 in. by 3¾ in. by 3½ in. high. This will give you twenty good slices, if you wish to serve it as such, but more than twice that number if used as hors-d'œuvre. This mould is held together by pins forming hinges at opposite corners, and is therefore easy to remove from the pie when the latter is baked. I further recommend you to use a special pie paste, namely **Hot Water Paste**. Weigh on to the marble slab 1¼ lb. flour and make a bay. Measure 7 oz. of water into a pan and add to it 9 oz. of lard and ¼ oz. of salt. When these last are boiling, pour them into the bay and with a stick make into a smooth dough. Allow this to cool slightly, put on one side about one-sixth of the bulk and use the rest to line your mould, which you have placed on a level baking sheet (the mould has no bottom). I find it best to put the paste into the mould and then work it upwards with the fingers; if you attempt to roll it out and cut off bands with which to line the mould, you are asking for the trouble you will surely get when the joints begin to leak during baking. Fill the interior of the pie with pieces of pork—cooked for preference—about the size of a filbert. You can of course use raw pork or a mixture of American chopped pork luncheon meat and raw sausage meat. In each case an admixture of cooked ham about one-eighth is permissible, as is also a discreet amount of finely chopped sage. By the way, you notice— I hope—that I recommend you to use chopped sage instead of rubbed sage; the leaves from the garden are infinitely superior to the dried kind.

159.

General Seasoning. Season with a mixture of four parts salt to one part pepper with one-sixteenth part of ground mace if liked. When this has been well sieved together use half an ounce of it to every pound of meat.

The paste you have put on one side is now used to make the lid for the pie and the trimmings, the leaves for decorative use, not forgetting the 'roses'.

160.

Raised Grouse Pie. Use a round pie mould, $5\frac{1}{2}$ in. in diameter and 4 in. high, hinged as before. One and a half pounds of the above paste will be required for the lining and the lid. Again make sure that there is no seam or crack which may cause trouble later in the baking. Having completed the lining of the mould to your satisfaction adorn the interior with rashers of streaky bacon minus the rind. The four old grouse that decided you to make a pie earlier in the day will have been dealt with as follows: the meat from the breasts put to soak in a glass of whisky, the meat from the thighs and the livers finely minced and added to $1\frac{3}{4}$ lb. of pork sausage meat, to which a small onion finely grated is also added. Now proceed to fill the mould, putting a thin layer of the prepared sausage meat over the bacon first. Next a row of grouse fillets at the bottom, with a layer of sausage meat over it. Continue until the pie is full, making the last layer one of sausage meat filling. If you can give the top a dome, so much the better for the final appearance of the pie. Cover the top with a thin sheet of the same paste, sealing it to the sides with a pinched border. Decorate the top with a few pastry leaves and glaze with beaten yolk. Bake in a moderate oven for about two hours, remove the tin and varnish the sides with yolk of egg. When the pie has cooled somewhat fill it carefully with a gravy made from the carcasses and giblets, making sure that this will set well by adding $1\frac{1}{2}$ oz. gelatine to the pint.

GALANTINES

A useful and economical addition to your cold table or hors-d'œuvre in that there is no waste—it slices to the very end and the last one is as good as the first—an old bird can be used, is indeed preferable to a young one, and lastly a galantine is a very good standby and yields excellent stock.

161.

Galantine of Chicken. Bone a fowl—not a difficult operation, far more easy to show you how to do it than to describe it to you. Start by making a cut through the skin all the way from the back of the neck to the tail, and remember that this is the only time that you cut through the skin! With your knife ease off the flesh from the bones and take out all the toughest sinews. When you come to the legs cut round the bone, then scrape the flesh downwards and finally pull the skin of the legs inside and cut off. You will have most difficulty in removing the cartilage on the ridge of the breastbone from the skin without breaking the latter, but with care it can be done. Spread out the skin, with the attached flesh, on a clean pudding cloth slightly bigger than the boned fowl, on the table; you should have a rough square, and distribute the meat as evenly as possible without detaching more than is necessary from the skin. Now take some 'farce fine de porc' (see page 84) and spread a layer of it over your boned fowl, with strips of tongue of about half an inch square section here and there and a sprinkling of pistachio nuts. Next add a few drops of sherry or madeira and roll up the galantine in the cloth. Tie the ends securely and add two more strings in the middle, then put on to cook in a boiling stock which you have prepared from the bones, etc., and a few vegetables. Simmer gently allowing twenty minutes to the pound of galantine. When cooked let it cool slightly, take off the strings, roll up again tightly as there will be considerable shrinkage and tie afresh. Place on a long dish with a piece of board on the galantine and a weight on top. Not too heavy or you will squeeze out some of the flavour-carrying juices. Allow to remain thus until cold, then unwrap, remove any fat or jelly from the surface with a clean cloth, and glaze.

162.

An alternative method of making a galantine is to skin the bird completely and without holes, please, then bone the carcass and cut the meat thus obtained into fingers. Pound that from the legs and add it to the farce. Then garnish the skin with a layer of farce and on it spread the fillets of chicken, strips of tongue, ham, fresh fat pork, sprinklings of pistachio nuts and chopped truffle. Complete with another layer of farce and roll up as before. Cook in the same manner.

163.

Galantine of Veal. Use breast of veal for this and proceed in similar fashion, substituting gherkins of a good green colour for the pistachio nuts. Chaufroiter a galantine and it gives a background for your artistic skill. With a few scraps of tomato skin and a long strip of cucumber peel you can make a bunch of 'poppies' on this even surface which will help enliven the hors-d'œuvre table.

164.

Boar's Head. This is a variety of galantine, the same principles and methods are used with slight variations. There is nothing very difficult about the preparation and cooking of this substantial and decorative centre piece for your cold table, and you will find it very useful during the Christmas and New Year celebrations and the ball supper season. See that the head is cut as long as possible in the neck, then having soaked it in running water and scraped it clean you bone it carefully, beginning at the under-side. When you reach the ears, cut them out deeply and cleanly for they will need to be cooked separately, ready for the final setting up of the piece. Take great care when boning the top of the skull, for any slitting of the skin there may spoil the looks of the head. The bones and gristle at the end of the snout should be sawn through so as to leave that easily recognizable feature of the porker intact.

It is now necessary to salt the head. For this you require twenty parts salt, one part saltpetre, one part brown sugar, one quarter part ground pimento, one eighth part ground mace, one eighth part powdered marjoram and one clove of garlic crushed. Mix these ingredients well together and rub the head with them every day for ten days or a fortnight, leaving the head well covered with the salt mixture. If the weather is very mild it may be advisable to pickle the head in brine after the first day's rubbing. Take about two gallons of water, put it in a tub and add sufficient coarse salt to make an egg float, add four ounces of saltpetre and a pound of brown sugar and any spices you may fancy. You may require a board with a clean stone on top to keep the meat under the pickle. A week's immersion should be sufficient. Drain the now salted or pickled head, having washed it free of brine and sponged it as dry as possible.

Place the head, skin side downward, on a cloth with its nose at the middle and pointing to one corner. You will require 5 lb. of farce de porc (page 84), 1 lb. of fat salt pork cut into half-inch-sided cubes, one skinned boiled ox tongue trimmed down and the trimmings cut into dice and added to the farce, a handful of blanched pistachio nuts, three cloves of garlic chopped with a handful of parsley, a small tin of truffle peelings and 3 oz. of general seasoning. Mix all this except the whole ox tongue, together with two eggs and spread a layer on the skin. Place the ox tongue in position, pointing to the snout, and build a layer of the stuffing around it. Pull the skin across from the two sides, giving the head its former shape approximately. Put a dinner plate on top and tie the four corners of the cloth above it. With tape bind the snout so that it will keep its shape during boiling. Cook the stuffed head in stock for about six hours at simmering point, then remove, re-roll and re-tie, and hang it up snout down until next day. The ears should be cooked in the same liquor but do not require more than forty minutes. At the end of this time take them out—it is simplest to hang them in the stock-pot at the end of a string—and stuff them with something to keep their shape until cold. When the cloth is removed trim up the base of the head, enlarge the place where the ears are to be and make a paste of these trimmings to shape the head into a more lifelike resemblance to the original. Place the ears where they should be, fix them in place with short skewers and plaster round the base with some of your paste.

The glazing is done with a strong jelly, gelatine and water, coloured dark brown with caramel or gravy browning. Do not forget to add a spot or two of red colouring to attain the exact shade and I urge you strongly to use some meat glaze for the sake of flavour—one of your guests may eat some of the glaze and if it tastes of nothing but gravy browning, your reputation will suffer. It used to be the practice in days not so very long ago to use nothing but meat glaze, but now few of us are able to make sufficient stock for daily use, and certainly not enough for boiling down to a glaze. It is customary to insert glass eyes and tusk bought from the taxidermist, but you can simulate these quite well with cooked white of egg and truffle, and pieces of white cardboard for the tusks, or if you are very clever you may carve some from pieces of bone which will last you for your lifetime. It is usual to decorate the glazed head with creamed butter piped from a paper cornet and you may let your decorative skill have full rein here. If the head is not to be shown on the cold buffet, there is no need to spend the time necessary for the glazing and decoration upon it, merely cover the outside with breadcrumbs and the ears could be cut into dice and added to the stuffing. A head weighing about 14 lb. will give you 18 lb. of finished boar's head.

165.

Hure de Sanglier. A similar product from the French kitchen, and one that must be included in this répertoire. The preparatory work of cleaning, scraping, soaking and boning is identical with that already outlined. It is the custom in France to remove the tongue and fleshy parts of the head and cut these into dice, adding them to the stuffing, not forgetting to skin the tongue. Farce is composed as follows: $2\frac{1}{4}$ lb. lean cooked ham, $2\frac{1}{4}$ lb. skinned ox tongue of a good red colour, $2\frac{1}{4}$ lb. fat pork, $2\frac{1}{4}$ lb. boned, skinned chicken, 10 oz. peeled pistachio nuts, one tin of truffle peelings and 7 lb. farce fine de porc with the necessary spices and salt. This stuffing is well mixed together, adding four eggs and a glass of brandy. The head is now stuffed with the above mixture, enveloped in a cloth and cooked as before. One main point of difference between the two methods is that in the French one the head is not pickled in brine although it may be macerated with sliced vegetables, salt and pepper for about twelve hours prior to the stuffing. The final treatment is in all respects similar to that recorded above.

166.

Alternative method. The French charcutier sometimes bones the head completely and moulds it in a long mould with a curved top, after cooking it as usual. This for economy's sake, for the meat may then be sliced to the end. When this is practised it is general to salt the head slightly, say for three or four days. For the stuffing, pigs' or calves' tongues are used, each being wrapped, after skinning, in a thin slice of larding bacon before being placed in position in the skin. An effort is made to give as much of a marbled effect as possible, this is of course helped by the presence of the green pistachio nuts and the black truffle. When the head is in position in the mould a board with a weight on top is placed to press the hure and assure cohesion between the various elements. When the hure is quite cold it is taken out of the mould and covered with jelly, which is usually made from the stock or liquid in which it was cooked.

167.

Ballotine. This is a variant of the galantine, generally served hot, but may be served cold. The meat, usually red meat, is rolled and bound with string, and braised on a bed of sliced vegetables which may or may not have been those used in a prior marinading of the piece in question, with stock, wine or marinading liquor alone or in any proportion. So-called 'white' meat—veal and lamb—may be treated similarly. If the meat is to be served cold, it is glazed with meat glaze, dressed on a flat dish and surrounded with croûtons of aspic jelly. Ballotines of poultry and feathered game are treated as galantines, and here I wish to suggest to my colleagues that in order to make a stand against this laxity of description which has crept into kitchen language, we define a galantine as a boned, stuffed meat which is cooked in a stock and a ballotine as a similar preparation which is cooked by braising under cover in the oven with a relatively small amount of liquor, and either may be served hot or cold. For

168.

the sake of clarity we may also regard a **Roulade** as a ballotine. In the ancient kitchen a roulade was a large slice of meat, flattened, and upon which a layer of farce has been spread prior to rolling and subsequent cooking on the spit.

POTTED MEATS

These we have had with us always, or so it seems, for who does not remember that fragrant potted beef of those youthful high teas? Other almost forgotten dainties come to mind—potted char, potted herrings, potted salmon, potted cheese, but who can remember them all? They belong to an era which is fast receding into the dim distance.

169.

Brawn, Potted Head, Fromage de Tête de Porc. The method is substantially the same whether ox, sheep's or pig's head is used. Trim, clean, remove eyes and brain, and scald the head. Then put it on to boil slowly in sufficient water, with salt, pepper and 'aromates', until the bones leave the meat easily. Take out the tongue and skin it, then chop up the remainder of the meat. Verify the seasoning and the setting properties of the stock, adding gelatine if required, and fill up your moulds, putting the tongue in the centre or dicing it along with the other meat as you wish. (Note: Ox tongue is not usually put into brawn.) A fair amount of stock may be used, and you may press the preparation lightly or not as you wish. A plate with a one-pound weight is sufficient. Next day you may turn out the now solid mass on to a dish, and if you have provided this with a loose piece of wood between brawn and dish, you will be able to slice away thinly enough.

170.

Potted Hough. An old Scottish variant of the above. Take about three or four pounds of hough (shin of beef) with sufficient water, pepper and salt and simmer gently until done. Then cut the meat up fairly small, return it to the pan, rectify the seasoning, add some of the liquor, boil up well, stirring the while, and put away to cool and set in a basin. This is apt to eat stringy if the meat is not cut up fine enough.

171.

Potted Beef. Similar to the above, is sometimes flavoured with essence of anchovies and is put through the fine plate of the mincer twice. Finish with a little melted butter on top.

172.

Potted Ham, Tongue, Chicken—alone or in combination—are prepared in the same way, with, in some cases perhaps, the addition of a little gelatine to assist in the setting and a spot or two of red to heighten the colour.

MISCELLANEA

There are still many hors-d'œuvre which do not come under any of the foregoing heads, but which rightly should be included in this section devoted to derivatives of 'flesh . . . and fat'. With your permission I propose to deal with these under the above heading. First we will select those of beef or mutton.

MEAT

173.

Pressed Beef. Salt brisket of beef may be bought from your butcher, and all you have to do is to boil it gently until cooked, then press it in a rectangular mould, taking care to have the grain of the meat running the same way, for ease in carving later. If you wish to pickle a piece of brisket, it is first necessary to prepare the brine which may also be used for pickling ox tongues. To every gallon of boiling water add 4 lb. of common salt, 4 oz. brown sugar, 2 oz. saltpetre and a sprig of thyme, a bay leaf or two and, if desired, some mace and cinnamon. Bring these to the boil and allow to become quite cold before immersing the brisket. It is advisable to remove the bones from the piece and to rub it well with salt for two days prior to putting it in the pickle. See that the meat is kept under the brine by means of a board with a weight on top and allow eight days in mild weather or ten days in colder, turning it every day.

At the end of the time wash the salted beef well and put it into boiling water with a few peppercorns, allspice and cloves tied in a little bag to accompany it. Proceed as above, making sure that the meat is well cooked. Pressed beef may be glazed and decorated with aspic jelly, or it may be left unadorned except for a sprig of curly parsley. In either case it is a valuable addition to your cold table and cannot be surpassed.

174.

Langue de Boeuf à l'Écarlate. Fresh ox tongues, having been soaked in cold water for several hours to rid them of as much blood as possible, are pricked all over and rubbed with a mixture of salt and saltpetre. Only a small percentage of the latter is used; not more than five per cent of the total weight of salt. They are rubbed with this mixture twice at intervals of two days, then covered with salt well pressed down for a further ten days. The tongues are then washed and allowed to soak in cold water for four or five hours, then hung by a string through the tip to drain thoroughly before being smoked for twenty-four hours. When smoked they should be of a pale yellow colour.

The tongues are then cooked in water at simmering point for a period varying from two and a half to four hours according to the size of the tongue. Some cooks add to the water an aromatic note of thyme, bay leaf, cloves, etc., but this is not necessary. When cooked the tongues should be skinned, trimmed and allowed to cool. Prepare a suitable length of ox-gut by tying one end of it on the inside. Wrap the tongue in a thin sheet of larding bacon (bardes de lard gras) and insert it carefully, pointed end first into the gut. Tie this at the other end, leaving a loop by which to hang it. Now prick the gut all over and immerse it in a bath of water at simmering point containing red colour. The object of this is merely to poach and colour the gut so the time required is only a few minutes. It is possible to do this poaching in plain water and to paint on the carmine at the end of the time. Hang the tongue to dry and when nearly cool rub it with a cloth dipped in oil or lard to give a brilliant gloss.

175.

Pigs' tongues may be treated in a similar way without the smoking, but only require to be pickled for four days, hung for two days, soaked in running water for two hours, and boiled for two hours. Subsequent treatment is the same as for the ox tongues.

176.

To serve tongue. Both the above are served cold cut into slices, not too thin, as hors-d'œuvre. The dish may be decorated with a few gherkin fans.

177.

Museau de Boeuf, Palais de Boeuf. Both these may be purchased ready for use, but you are a cook by interest or inclination or you would not have read so far, and therefore you will wish to know how to prepare them for yourself even though you may never do so.

178.

To make a blanc. First you must make a 'blanc' in which to cook them, i.e. to every quart of boiling water add one heaped spoonful of flour made into a cream with cold water, salt, two spoonsful of vinegar, and lastly, in the case of meat (such as this for example), a 'garniture' consisting of an onion stuck with a clove, a bouquet garni and the museau or palais blanched, trimmed and scraped. You then put in sufficient kidney suet to form when it is melted a layer, half an inch thick, of fat on the surface of the liquid to prevent the contents making contact with the air. That is the reason why a 'blanc' is used in cookery: to keep a substance which would darken on contact with the air, free from that contact. It is more generally used when cooking celery, sea-kale, salsify, etc. Museau de boeuf will require about seven and palais de boeuf about four hours of gentle cooking. Allow them to cool, then drain them and wipe clear of the cooking liquor. When they are thoroughly cold, they should be sliced very thinly and dressed on a service dish with graduated rings of onion over them. Dribble a few drops of oil and vinegar on them and a sprinkle of chopped parsley.

179.

Calves' feet, Pigs' feet, Sheep's trotters. These are all treated in much the same manner, i.e. blanched to facilitate the removal of the hair in the first and last and any remaining fine bristles in the case of the second. They are then cooked in a 'blanc' as detailed above, except that pigs' feet are always split into two lengthwise and bound to little boards with broad tape or a bandage of medium width, cut side down, in order to keep them from deforming during cooking. It must be remembered that there are several classic ways of serving pigs' feet (Sainte-Ménéhould, etc.) which oblige us to use this method. Perhaps the only way of serving feet cold is **Pieds à la Vinaigrette** or

180.

à l'Huile and this is not strictly speaking cold, for the foot is hot but the sauce (which in some houses is poured over) is cold. Anyhow, I shall have more to say to you about feet in the section devoted to hot hors-d'œuvre. The thing to remember is the method of cooking them outlined above.

181.

Salade de Pieds is similar to the last. The feet are taken cold and cut into a fine julienne, mixed with one-third of their volume in finely sliced onion and a seasoning of oil, vinegar, salt and pepper, with a mere dusting of cayenne pepper. Having dressed this salad, you should strew over the surface a liberal dusting of chopped chervil, then eat and enjoy.

182.

Pigs' Ears, Jellied. (Oreilles de porc en gelée.) Take well-cleaned pigs' ears, singe and wash them well. Put them to cook in a deep pan with sufficient cold water to cover them and plenty of pork skin (couennes) to make a jelly. Add a few cloves and a bouquet of thyme and bay leaf with a few peppercorns and a handful of salt. Allow them to cook slowly for about one and a half to two hours. At the end of this time remove them to a flat dish, cover them with some of the cooking liquor and press lightly. Allow to cool until the next day when they should be set in some of the clarified jelly in which they were cooked. Served dressed on a bed of green salad with a sauce boat of Sauce Vinaigrette.

183.

Beef Cornets. Cut thin slices of cold boiled beef. Pipe in the centre a blob of whipped cream flavoured with finely grated horseradish and seasoned with salt. Roll these into cornucopia and dress on a bed of chopped lettuce.

184.

Boiled Beef Salads (I). Cold boiled (or roast) beef may be cut into strips and marinated in oil and vinegar. Place a neat border of slices of cold cooked potato round a glass dish, drain the strips of beef and pile them in the middle. Sauce over with vinaigrette dressing.

185.

Boiled Beef Salad (II). Cold boiled beef from the stockpot may be cut into thin slices, and laid on a dish with layers of sliced hard-boiled egg alternating. Sauce over with French mustard dressing (page 121).

186.

Boiled Beef Salad (III). Slices of cold boiled beef—again from the marmite—alternating with slices of cold potato and tomato arranged on a service dish. Seasoned with vinaigrette containing chopped raw onion and a good amount of chopped parsley.

187.

Salade de Boeuf. Cut cold boiled beef into a 'grosse julienne', skinned and de-pipped tomatoes into pieces, cold boiled potatoes into slices and onion into rings which you then halve. Bind this with thinned mayonnaise and dress in one pile, decorate the sides with slices of tomato and sprinkle chopped parsley over all.

188.

Salads with Ham or Bacon (I). When a ham is being carved, there is always a surplus of fat—no one seems to wish to eat this, the best part of the ham. Fat of any kind is never wasted in a good kitchen of course, and ham fat is like gold to a larder-cook or hors-d'œuvrier. Here is an unusual little salad which may help reduce the surplus: Cut some ham fat into small dice, mix with it an equal amount of chopped pimentos and half the amount of chopped mango chutney. Pile this on to slices of hard-boiled egg which have been placed on rounds of nasturtium leaf and seasoned with French mustard dressing.

189.

Salads with Ham or Bacon (II). Cut into a julienne some well-boiled ham skin, not from a smoked ham, and mix with shredded lettuce and a julienne of hard-boiled white of egg. Add a little finely chopped onion, mix well and season with vinaigrette dressing.

190.

Salads with Ham or Bacon (III). Make left-over cooked bacon into a julienne. Cut some cooked beans into halves and chop a small quantity of piccalilli. Mix these ingredients and season them with piccalilli dressing.

191.

Salads with Ham or Bacon (IV). Prepare some thin slices of cold ham about 2 in. by 1½ in. and on them spread a smear of savoury yellow butter (page 111). Sprinkle with grated cheese and roll. Arrange the rolls on the service dish and put a few drops of vinaigrette over them.

192.

Salad of Turkey Stuffing. There is a left-over which more often than not finds its way into the pig's pail—cold turkey stuffing. If you have any surplus, cut it into small dice and take the same amount of cold boiled potato also cut into small dice. Bind these with French mustard dressing and dish them on rounds of lettuce, or of nasturtium leaves or of the tender inner leaves of cabbage.

POULTRY

193.

Smoked Goose Breast. If you must have fat goose livers, what do you suppose becomes of the rest of the bird? The thrifty French certainly do not waste it and apart from confit d'oie and its derivatives, cassoulet, alicot and the rest, here is one way of using up what might be a potential source of worry. Smoked goose differs from the sister preparation of confit in that it is not cooked slowly in its own fat as is the latter. Further, the quarters of goose destined for confit are lightly salted for twenty-four hours whereas that part intended for subsequent smoking is salted for a week at least. Afterwards it is smoked gently over oak sawdust or hardwood roots mixed with aromatic plants. Smoked goose breast (Poitrine d'oie fumée) is a commercial product and is furnished by Alsace and also by Germany. It is eaten cold, sliced very thinly in exactly the same way as raw smoked ham. Smoked Breast of Turkey, so much pushed latterly, is merely an adaptation of this older method.

194.

Stuffed Goose Necks. These are usually prepared at the same time as the confit. We are not likely to have that to do, so I offer you an adaptation of the original recipe. Make a cut the length of the neck and remove the bone. Now prepare a stuffing from the débris of the bird, the gizzard and heart, some ham and belly pork, seasoned with salt, pepper and spices, add sausage meat for bulk if required. Spread this on the skin and treat it like a galantine, i.e. roll it in a cloth and cook in stock. (The ancient recipe says sew the skin together, tie the ends tightly and cook the stuffed neck in the fat along with the confit.) When ready, remove the neck from the stock, allow it to cool slightly, then roll it up again tightly and press until cold. Serve as you would galantine.

195.

Grattons, Frittons or **Gratterons.** These are a by-product of the

G 97

melting of goose fat for the confit d'oie and consist of the residue after the clear fat has been decanted. This is salted whilst still warm and is eaten as hors-d'œuvre when cold. The rendering of pork fat gives a similar product; grattons must not be confused with Rillettes (see page 78).

3. Herbs, Condiments and Spices

These are the most important helps to the hors-d'œuvrier, they heighten the taste of a dish or salad and without their aid cookery would be reduced to a sameness and insipidity too frightening to contemplate. Their use must be learned by experience for no instruction can help you here—your pinch of thyme may be bigger than mine—all that can be done is to indicate what is usual and leave it to yourself to find out how much or to discover new and exciting combinations. Train yourself, when tasting a dish prepared by some skilful person unknown to you, to 'dissect' the flavour then endeavour to repeat this yourself. In this way you will learn much.

Salt, the most important of all condiments, is best crushed by hand from coarse cooking salt. As it is slightly hygroscopic it must be kept dry. If it becomes even slightly damp it will 'cake' on drying and require re-crushing. The much-advertised free-running table salts should be frowned upon in the kitchen as they contain an admixture to help keep them dry and free from lumping. This reduces the saltiness—'the salt hath lost its savour'—and therefore its usefulness as a seasoning.

Pepper, white or black, comes from the same plant. The pepper plant bears its berries in clusters something like tiny grapes; they are bright red when fully ripe but are gathered green and put out to dry in the sun, where they turn black and shrivel. This gives us the black variety. The white is made from this by soaking the peppercorns in lime and water, when the outer covering can be removed by hand. The finest berries are naturally used to make white pepper, which, in addition to the handling cost, probably accounts for the higher price. The white pepper is not quite so pungent as the black.

Cayenne Pepper is a powder prepared from the fruit of several varieties of the Capsicum (an annual originating in the East Indies), a few of which have been induced to grow in this country. The best Cayenne pepper however is made from the variety Capsicum Baccatum or bird pepper and is produced in the West Indies.

The **Cinnamon** tree is a native of tropical climes, is a member of the laurel family and grows to a height of twenty to thirty feet. It is the inner bark which forms the cinnamon of commerce.

The **Clove** tree, another native of hot countries, bears large quantities of flowers on the ends of the branches. These flowers, at first white then green, finally become red and hard. The unopened flowers are gathered and dried, turning yellow in the process and later assuming the familiar dark brown hue. Cloves yield an abundance of aromatic oil, about twenty per cent, but a remarkable thing is that the flowers themselves do not have any scent nor are the fruits in any way aromatic.

Allspice or **Jamaica Pepper** is also the product of a tree grown in the West Indies and South America. It is a berry gathered green then dried, turning black in the process. As its name implies, the flavour resembles a combination of spices and does not strike a distinct note.

Bay Leaves, although not a native of this country, can nevertheless be grown here if the tree from which they are gathered is given a little shelter. I had a bay tree growing for many years—it is probably still there—along the outside wall of a greenhouse facing south. Many translators 'qui ne sont pas du métier', when transcribing French recipes into English, make 'feuille de laurier' into laurel leaf, but you will be wiser than they.

Mace is the inner part of the outer covering of the nutmeg. When dried as we know it, the colour is yellowish-orange. It has similar properties and flavour to nutmeg, for which it is often used as a substitute. It is generally sold finely ground.

Nutmeg, the kernel of the fruit of the nutmeg tree, is well known to all. It is best to buy it whole and grate it the instant it is required as in this way the maximum flavour is obtained. Ground nutmeg is apt to deteriorate if kept too long.

Balm and **Borage**, those two herbs which used to be of prime importance in the mixing of claret cup, cider cup and the rest, and now seem to be under something of a cloud, may yet achieve popularity again when it is remembered that the former has a pronounced lemon perfume and the latter is a useful addition to salads.

Basil, an essential for certain Italian dishes, but certainly worth a trial as an unusual condiment by an enterprising hors-d'œuvrier.

Chervil, which I consider of greater importance to us than parsley, can easily be grown if you have a small garden. Sow a few seeds and after you have made use of the green aromatic leaves all through the season, allow a plant or two to go to seed. The leaves, after the little white flowers have set, become a beautiful purple and you will soon distinguish the seeds which you should allow to sow themselves. Thereafter you will never lack this most useful herb, for even the coldest, snowiest winter has never, in my experience, killed all the plantlets.

Tarragon must be cited after chervil as these two are inseparable in the kitchen or nearly so. Tarragon grows well with me in Scotland and I advise you to ask your nurseryman to provide you with a root or two. You will be sure then of having the genuine type and I do not think you will experience any difficulty as to future supplies of this useful herb. In the late summer if you will pick a handful or two of the leaves and put them in vinegar, you will have both tarragon vinegar and a supply of the herb for your Sauce Béarnaise throughout the winter. The plant sends out long 'runners' which will in turn bear the tall stalks, sometimes nearly four feet in height, and I advise you to chop off one or two of these roots and replant them if you wish to be sure of succession in your herb. Although tarragon does not seem to require a particularly good soil, it is nevertheless advisable to give it a change of locality.

Chives, those tiny onions whose green tops are so useful in the spring, as at all other times, for the fines herbes mixture, are easily grown in any odd corner of the garden. When they become too crowded lift a few to another spot. They will occasionally throw up a flower stem bearing a bud in the form of a small purple onion, which will break out into a purple flower something like thrift. Be ruthless! Rip this stalk out for it is as tough as wire and will spoil your mixture in fines herbes.

Onion you all know, but you are not perhaps aware of the trouble it gives to the gardener to keep away that pest of pests, the onion fly. If you have a garden my advice to you is not to waste your time on onions but to grow shallots.

Shallots. These are free from the attentions of the onion fly, and except for their smaller size have every advantage over the onion.

Tree onion is an interesting variety from both practical and horticultural standpoints. Not only do you get bulbs below the ground but the plant also bears a cluster of reddish-skinned onions as a 'fruit' on a true onion stalk two feet above the ground.

Welch onion to an amateur like myself appears to be a large-sized edition of our friend the chive. Take a sharp knife with you into the garden and cut off the top three inches or so of the leaves if you wish something to flavour your marinade; or later dig up a few of the bulbs for your navarin if the crop of 'petits oignons' is a failure.

Herbs, Condiments and Spices

Garlic is an essential ingredient in most dishes, or in the preparatory work for them and the supposed aversion to it held by many people is not a fact. They object not so much to garlic as to the evidence of its presence when coming from other people. In any case not many can recognize it after long cooking. It grows quite well here, likes a fairly moist situation and a rich soil, and will withstand our normal winters. It helps to make large heads if you twist and make the leaves into a knot as they do in the Midi of France. This is done when the plant is fully grown and probably has the effect of conserving the sap in the cloves.

Mint is a most useful herb and the most flavoured kind is, I have found, the variety known as Lamb's Mint. The leaves of this plant are rounder and more hairy than those of the more common sort, but the flavour is infinitely superior. Unfortunately it has the habit of straying all over the garden, and if allowed to do so unchecked, will choke any other plant in its way.

Mustard you all know, whether as a fine powder or as seed with not quite the same pungency but none the less an indispensable ingredient of certain pickles or marinades. The same seed when sown thickly on damp sacking, covered up until it germinates and then put into a light place in the kitchen will soon give you the mustard half of mustard and cress—it is best to grow these separately—and no one will appreciate better than yourself how useful it is to have a supply of this little salad on tap so to speak.

Marjoram is a useful ingredient in many so-called Italian dishes. Please do not misunderstand me, marjoram is used in Italy. As a plant it will grow in the South of England, but I fear the northern winters are sometimes too much for it.

Origano. Any nurseryman will tell you that this is wild marjoram, but what they do not and cannot tell you is why it tastes so different when used in Greece as it is on almost every dish.

Rosemary is another plant which prefers the comfort south of the border. Northerners may encourage it to thrive by giving it a sheltered corner in a garden, but should be prepared for disappointment.

Thyme, common, don't bother with the others. Lemon thyme, to you as a cook, is of little interest because you can get the same combination of flavours in a different manner and variegated thyme should be allowed to grace your rockery untroubled by thoughts of utilitarian employment.

Sage. Stick your finger in the ground and fill the hole thus made with sand. Push a twig of sage from a friend's bush in the centre of

102

this sand, and for ever after enjoy the extra fragrance of fresh sage as opposed to that foul dried substitute for it.

Savory is a useful herb, especially in the cooking of broad beans in Italian cookery generally, or where in a French recipe one would use sariette. The variety in my garden must, I think, be the Winter Savory for it seeds itself all over and grows in the paths and tightly wedged between stones. It is very hardy and even after the severest of winter weather fresh growth can be seen on plants self-sown in unlikely places.

Parsley is too well known to need any recommendation from me. It appears so regularly as a flavoursome ingredient or as a decorative adjunct to many dishes that its appearance is taken for granted. Parsley is easy to grow; the seeds take a long time to germinate and the seedlings do not seem to object to being transplanted, especially if a little lime rubble is incorporated in the soil of their new habitat. A few plants may be transferred to a frame in the late autumn in order to ensure a supply during the winter months. Parsley seed is useful as a flavouring should all else fail, and the roots indispensable in certain Russian or Polish dishes.

Celery seed, too, is acceptable should supplies of the plant fail. The green leaves are as much use to us as hors-d'œuvriers as any other part of the plant. Shredded, their flavour in a salad is often appreciated though their presence may not be obvious.

Nasturtium and its near relation **Tropaeolum** are more useful to us than is admitted. The leaves of the former act as a base for our Salades Mignonnes—if they are too large they can easily be reduced in size by means of a suitable cutter—and the seeds of the latter if picked small enough are a very good substitute for capers. All you have to do is to go round your plants at regular intervals with a bottle containing vinegar and pick off suitable seeds and drop them into that vinegar; your supply of 'capers' for the winter is thus assured. Nasturtium flowers are mentioned elsewhere in this book both as a decoration and as a flavour. They are of course edible. It is said in Scotland that Tropaeolum will not grow in soil which does not contain peat and that it must face north.

Fennel, Caraway, Dill and **Coriander** may all be grown in your herb garden and if you do not get the seeds to ripen you have the tiny groups of flowers which form the umbels to give a flavoursome, intriguing decoration to salads. For instance, the flowers of fennel (common) are yellow and about the size of a pin's head but are borne in a group the size of a sixpenny piece, many of these groups form the flower head. A line of these down a salad of beetroot or a scalloped border around the edge of the dish gives the same effect as a delicate lace insertion in a dark red velvet gown. The chopped feathery leaves of fennel are used in some Russian dishes.

Saffron is the dried stigmas of the Saffron Crocus (Crocus Sativus). It has many uses medicinally and was formerly used in dyeing, but our concern with it is solely as a condiment although its properties of giving a rich orange-yellow colour are not to be despised. One grain of saffron rubbed to powder with a little sugar and water, imparts a distinctly yellow tint to ten gallons of water! Saffron is chiefly cultivated in Spain, France, Sicily, on the lower spurs of the Apennines, in Persia and Kashmir, and was at one time grown in England (cf. Saffron Walden) but its cultivation there was gradually extinguished about 1768. Vast quantities of the flowers are required to make a small amount of the herb, hence the price, which has risen to fantastic heights.

Horseradish, of which the root scraped and grated is of much use in the kitchen, will establish itself only too readily if given the chance in your garden and defy all your efforts to keep it within bounds. The tall-growing leaves are of no use in a culinary sense. A mixture of grated horseradish and chopped cooked beetroot is known in Central Europe variously as **Chrane** or **Krane**. It is prepared with vinegar and spices but need not present any real difficulties to anyone interested enough to prepare it for himself. It is a welcome 'raw material' in the preparation of many little salads.

Paprika (Capsicum annum) comes from Hungary, or at least the best variety does, and it has come to be recognized as the national Hungarian spice, yet a century ago it was not generally known and used in that country. It would appear that the Paprika plants were introduced into Europe simultaneously from East and West in the sixteenth century. Columbus brought paprika into Spain from Central and South America, that is the large, fleshy, mild variety known as Spanish or sweet pimento. When the Turks overran Hungary, they planted for their own use the smaller-podded variety of varying sharpness and characteristic aroma which is indigenous to India. There are different qualities of Hungarian paprika; that known as sweet or rose paprika being the best. It is garden grown, bright red, mildly piquant and sweetish. Great care should be taken in the cooking of it by frying, for the natural sugar it contains is easily caramelized and both colour and flavour spoiled.

Curry. I have made reference here and there in this book to curry powder. I am fully aware that no self-respecting Indian cook would use any made-up powder but would himself grind the ingredients according to his fancy or the requirements of the dish in hand. These ingredients include Red Chillies, Turmeric, Cayenne Pepper, Black Pepper, Caraway, Coriander, Cardamom and Mustard Seeds, Ginger, Cloves, Cumin and Poppy Seeds, Garlic and Fennugreek. We are not, however, concerned with Indian cookery as such and the use of a small quantity of a reputable brand of curry powder is therefore permissible in our case.

4. Sauces, Dressings and Seasonings

SALAD SEASONING

196.

Some hints on seasoning a salad. A word about the seasoning of a salad. No doubt many people are put off from seasoning a salad, or given a feeling of inferiority when contemplating such an adventure, by reading in one of those cookery books written by dear old ladies that 'the perfectly seasoned salad should have no liquor at the bottom of the bowl'. Lettuce and other saladings, especially the early frame or glasshouse ones, are so delicately fragile that you are most likely to ruin your salad by overmixing than by adding too much oil and vinegar. What is easier than to season your salad in one bowl and transfer it to another one for the table? The waiter's trick of mixing French mustard with salt, pepper, vinegar and oil in a spoon and then using the mixture to season the salad is not practicable in the kitchen. There, a slightly different technique is practised. Sprinkle on a few drops of oil—then tumble the leaves over—a few drops of vinegar—again a few turns, and then, and then only, dust from a height of about eighteen inches or so a little salt and a turn of pepper from the pepper-mill on to the wetted leaves. Do not give your salad a bath in the dressing, use discretion, but above all do not be afraid. Avoid if possible washing the lettuce. The outside leaves can be used for other purposes, soup or, when well washed and shaken as dry as possible in the salad basket, for shredded lettuce. From the inner leaves, any specks of grit can be removed with a dry cloth.

SALAD DRESSING AND SAUCES

Salad dressings need not be complicated, nor need they be as numerous as in America, where the tendency seems to be to rely too much on the adventitious aid brought by the dressing rather than upon the inherent flavour of the salad. Dressings should emphasize not dominate.

197.

Vinaigrette (1) dressing is made by measuring three parts of olive oil to one part of vinegar (French wine vinegar for preference, but if not available then a reliable brand of brewed malt vinegar, which may have to be diluted with cold water if too acid), adding salt, pepper and fines herbes, i.e. finely chopped parsley, chives, chervil and a little tarragon. Stir these vigorously together before using.

198.

Vinaigrette (II) or Ravigote (sauce for use with calves' head or feet, pigs' feet and sheep's trotters). Two and a half parts of olive oil to one part vinegar and in addition to the fines herbes add a small onion very finely chopped and a spoonful of capers, pepper and salt. If the capers are the small 'nonpareilles' variety they may be used as they come from the bottle, but if of one of the larger varieties they should be chopped.

199.

Mayonnaise sauce. For use in the salads to be described later in this work, I suggest you make a stiff mayonnaise as a base; this you may then let down to any desired consistency with cream, vinegar, piccalilli juice, orange or lemon juice, tomato juice, water, or as advised. Take four yolks, put them in a basin and add a good pinch of fine salt. Work this well together with a whisk and you will notice that almost immediately the yolks become stiff. Have the vinegar bottle at hand and at once add a spoonful to thin the yolks to their original consistency. Now begin to add the oil, carefully at first, whisking well between each addition. When you notice that the sauce has 'taken' you may add the oil by spoonsful at a time, still continuing to whisk the mixture well between each addition. If you find the sauce is becoming too stiff then the addition of a few drops of vinegar will put matters to rights. The four yolks will take a pint of olive oil. If you will follow these instructions carefully you will succeed with your mayonnaise not once but every time. There are two points which you must watch. First the addition of the salt to the yolks and second the temperature of the oil. Contrary to the advice usually given in the cookery books to make your mayonnaise in a cool place, my experience has been that it is easier to prepare it in a hot kitchen. Please note that I do not advise you to have the oil hot, less than blood heat is the ideal. But if you are faced with cold or congealed oil, 'thaw' it by standing the container in luke-warm water. Have the oil for mayonnaise at the temperature of the kitchen. Lastly you must verify the seasoning and add the necessary freshly ground pepper. Notice that it is not required to add either dry or made mustard. Do not add too much vinegar at this stage, for reasons already given you desire your sauce to be as firm as possible.

200.

How to bring back a 'turned' mayonnaise. In spite of all your attentions sometimes the sauce will 'turn' or 'curdle'. The oil separates out of the emulsion because you have added it too quickly, or because you have added a bigger quantity than the yolks will take, or, most likely, because it was too cold. The remedy, fortunately, is simple. Put a few drops of very hot water into another basin, then add a mere dribble of the faulty sauce, whisking the while. Continue the addition little by little, stirring vigorously and when you notice that the mixture has become smooth again, you may add the curdled sauce more quickly until all is in. If you feel expert enough to tackle the job another way, you may put a few drops of water in at the side of the first basin and, using a small flat whisk, stir in the same spot until the sauce 'takes' again, then widen the arc of movement gradually until you have the whole bowlful 'brought back'. The first method is the surer one.

201.

Tomato mayonnaise. To one-quarter of its bulk in fine tomato purée of good colour, add the requisite amount of stiff mayonnaise sauce, and a little paprika pepper. Whisk well together.

202.

Sauce Rémoulade. Put a spoonful of French mustard into a basin, and using a whisk, blend with it about ten times its volume of your stiff mayonnaise, Chop finely some capers, gherkins, parsley, tarragon and chervil. Add these and finish with a few drops of anchovy essence. I advise you to add the mayonnaise to the mustard gradually, for if you do it the other way round you may 'turn' the mayonnaise.

203.

Sauce Tartare. This is a mayonnaise made with the yolks of hard-boiled eggs. Make the yolks of four hard-boiled eggs into a smooth paste with a good pinch of salt, the same of freshly milled pepper and a few spots of vinegar. Squeeze a finely grated onion in the corner of a clean cloth to extract the juice and use this juice and three-quarters of a pint of olive oil to make a sauce in the same manner as a mayonnaise. Garnish this sauce with a handful of chives cut excessively small. If you are the lucky possessor of an old-fashioned mortar you may use it to make this sauce, using green onion tops pounded and passed through the sieve.

Salad Dressing and Sauces

204.

French Mustard Dressing, or 'F.M.D.'. Put a spoonful of French mustard into a basin, add the yolk of one egg and season with salt and pepper. Whisk well together, then add olive oil until fairly stiff and finish with vinegar to the desired consistency. You will find that this dressing does not tend to separate out, and is a most useful stand-by.

205.

Now come two dressings which are very similar: **Sour Cream Dressing.** Let down ordinary sour cream with a little lemon juice and thin to the desired consistency with cold water. Add salt and use paprika instead of pepper. This will give a beautiful pink dressing

206.

which you may use very effectively. **Cream Cheese Dressing** is made very simply by letting down cottage cheese with either orange juice or pineapple juice to the required consistency. Vinegar and/or water may also be used.

207.

Piccalilli dressing is simply stiff mayonnaise reduced with the liquor from piccalilli.

208.

Spiced vinegar. Put $\frac{1}{4}$ oz. of each, allspice, cinnamon bark, cloves, root ginger, mace and black peppercorns into the mortar and bruise them slightly. No mortar? Then use a rolling-pin on the table. Tie these spices in a piece of muslin and infuse them in one quart of vinegar just off the boil. Use a well-tinned saucepan when boiling the vinegar.

209.

Marinade à la Grecque. Take a quart of water, the juice of four lemons, four tablespoons of olive oil, enough salt and crushed peppercorns to season, a few coriander seeds, a little thyme and bay leaf, a quarter of a root of fennel and half a root of celery. Boil these together and cook in the resultant 'cuisson' whatever you wish to cook 'à la Grecque'.

5. Flavoured Butters, Pastes and Spreads (Beurres Composés et Fromages)

The rôle played by flavoured butters used to be an important one. The pounding together of the different elements and the forcing of them through the 'étamine' or tammy-cloth, made the texture of the resultant 'butter' so fine that the presence of minute particles could not be detected in the final sauce or soup— they were used in both. This means of heightening the flavour was a great advantage to the conscientious sauce- or soup-cook. It is true that a decline has set in and except for the use here and there of Beurre Maître d'Hôtel, Lobster or Shrimp Butter and perhaps Beurre Montpellier, not many are used or even remembered; too many cooks have come to rely on artificial colours in bottles for their effects. Many of the 'butters' formerly used do not interest us as hors-d'œuvriers; we shall confine our notes to those which we can use for decoration or finishing-off, and to those which are simply a purée bound in butter. As for the fromages (or pastes) these had more 'body' due to the Gruyère cheese which formed part of the mixture, and although they were thinned down with cream, still never had that oily appearance —the unfortunate lot of the true 'butter'—however long they had to remain in a hot room.

BUTTERS

210.

Anchovy butter. Skin by wiping them with a cloth, bone and de-salt a dozen anchovies (Gorgona) and pound them with two and a half times their weight in butter. Then pass the mixture through a sieve, this is the classical way, you can achieve approximately the same result by adding anchovy essence to the required amount of softened butter. Best quality margarine may be substituted for butter and if you do not have a mortar to use, rub down fish, fat and seasoning on the marble slab with a rolling-pin.

211.

Green butter. Take four parts spinach, two parts chervil, one and a half parts tarragon, one part parsley, one-quarter part finely chopped shallot, blanch them, drain them well and pound them. Add sufficient of this purée to your butter to obtain the desired shade of green, mix well and pass. The task will be easier if you soften the butter first and it may be necessary to incorporate the yolk of a hard-boiled egg in order to bind the mixture. (Note: This is **not** Beurre Montpellier.)

212, 213, 214.

For **Red butters** you have a choice of several: (*a*) **Paprika butter.** Cook a little finely chopped onion in lard without browning, then mix with a teaspoonful ($\frac{1}{4}$ oz.) of finest Hungarian paprika—this has a most brilliant colour—when cool, stir it into $\frac{1}{2}$ lb. of butter, and sieve as usual. (*b*) **Pimento butter.** Roast and remove the outer skin from some red pimentos, reject the seeds and pound the flesh with about two and a half times its weight in butter (or use canned pimentos, draining them well first) and pass through the sieve. (c) **Tomato butter.** Rub together three hard-boiled yolks, six ounces of butter and two tablespoons of well-reduced tomato purée—cold of course. Canned 'double concentrated' tomato purée is excellent for this purpose though some brands are an abomination as they carry far too much colour. Pass all through the fine sieve and add paprika pepper if the colour is not pronounced enough. Season with salt and, if required, with cayenne pepper.

215.

Yellow butter. Take the yolks of six hard-boiled eggs and rub them down in the mortar with four ounces of butter. Season and finish with a few drops of olive oil.

216.

Beurre de Foie Gras. Equal parts of butter and foie gras rubbed together and passed through the sieve.

217.

Herring butter. De-salt, skin and remove as many bones as possible from two salt herrings and pound them. To the resultant purée add about half a pound of butter, mix well and pass through the sieve. Fresh herrings do not make as good a butter as the salt ones.

218.

Beurre de Homard ou de Langouste. The procedure has already been detailed under crayfish butter on page 42. There is also **Lobster**

111

Flavoured Butters, Pastes and Spreads

219.

Oil made in a similar manner, i.e. pound the débris of lobster or crawfish, coral, eggs or creamy parts in the mortar. When you have reduced the mass to a pulp add the oil slowly, also a few grains of paprika, rubbing the pestle round and round the sides of the mortar. Turn this purée on to a sieve and rub as much as will go through with the 'champignon'.

220.

Mustard butter. If English mustard is used, mix one tablespoonful of the made-up mustard to twelve ounces of softened butter (en pommade); but if you are using French mustard, take two table-spoonsful.

221.

Sardine butter. Bone a dozen sardines and pound them in the mortar with twelve ounces of butter. Season with salt, pepper and a dash of Tabasco and rub them through the sieve. Keep the butter in a cool place and use as required. Brisling, sild or the large Portuguese sardines may be used quite successfully for this butter. It may be advisable to bone the fish and remove the scales from the last named.

222.

Crayfish butter. See page 42.

223.

Shrimp butter is made exactly as Crayfish butter.

224.

Smoked salmon butter. Pound some scraps of smoked salmon with about twice their weight in butter, season with a speck or so of cayenne pepper and pass through the sieve.

225.

Horseradish butter. Grate some cleaned horseradish finely, take a little of it in the corner of a cloth and squeeze a few drops of the liquid into some softened butter. This is one way of making horse-radish butter, but if you are the fortunate possessor of one of the high-speed rotary knife electric chopping machines, you will be able to reduce the horseradish to a fine pulp and mix it with the butter. Do not add too much as it is very pungent.

PASTES

226.

   Grouse cheese paste. Pound 6 oz. of cold grouse débris with the same amount of gruyère cheese, add 2 oz. of butter, season with salt and cayenne pepper and pass through the sieve. Finish with two tablespoons of double cream. Should gruyère cheese not be available some new Cheshire or Cheddar may be substituted.

227.

   Kipper cheese paste. As above, and you will find that, if you make this paste into a suitable sized block and keep it in a cold place, you will be able to cut slices from it, arrange them on toast, grill them and serve as an excellent savoury.

228.

   Salmon cheese paste. Pound 4 oz. of cooked salmon débris with the same weight of gruyère cheese. To this mixture add 1 oz. of butter and stir in well. Season and pass through the sieve, and, should it need to be thinned, add not more than two spoonsful of thick cream.

229.

   Tunny fish paste. This mixing is identical with the last, except that the butter may be omitted.

SPREADS

   These may be prepared from any potted meat or fish by thinning them down to 'spreadable' consistency with cream, or olive oil and cream. Exact quantities cannot be given as they must be determined by the requirements of the moment. Remember to verify the seasoning after making the spread.

230.

   Chicken spread may be made by pounding débris of chicken with a pinch of celery seed, thinning with cottage cheese and seasoning with a spoonful of French mustard in addition to salt. Rub through the sieve in order to trap any of the celery seeds which have survived the pounding, and to ensure the smoothness of the texture. If preferred, sweet cream may be used in place of the sour cream cheese, but the latter gives an added piquancy to the resultant spread.

231.

   Chicken and ham or **tongue.** A combination of chicken with either ham or tongue or with both, the amount of chicken predominating, may be made on similar lines to the above.

232.

Chicken liver spread. Cook slowly in chicken fat some chicken livers and rub them through the sieve. Make into a paste with fromage blanc and débris of hard-boiled eggs also passed through the sieve. Season with pounded caraway seeds, salt and cayenne pepper, add a squeeze of onion juice and if required in a more liquid state, add chicken fat.

233.

Mushroom spread. Take some well-reduced Duxelles, add a spoonful of Sauce Demi-glace to bind it and allow to cool before use.

234.

To make **Duxelles**, take the required amount of mushrooms and chop them very finely (as they are to become a spread). Then chop equally finely one-quarter of the amount in a fifty-fifty mixture of onion and shallot. Allow the latter to 'fall' in butter and oil, then add the chopped mushrooms and reduce carefully until the liquid has evaporated. I am against squeezing the mushrooms dry before cooking them as is done in some kitchens. Why waste the valuable mushroom liquor? And most certainly do not peel them or remove the stalks. Season the Duxelles with salt and pepper with a touch of cayenne. Cool before making into a spread.

235.

Variant of Duxelles. You may add some potted meat or game to vary the flavour or pound a few chicken livers which have been 'sauté', in chicken fat for preference, and make into a workable consistency by adding a spoonful or so of Demi-glace sauce.

236.

Potted Stilton. Trim the outside from a crust of Stilton cheese, and pass the usable part through the mincer. Mix this with butter in the proportion of one-quarter butter to one pound of Stilton purée. Add a pinch of powdered mace and a glass of brandy. Mix well and press into little pots. This potted cheese is delicious and is helpful in many hors-d'œuvre.

6. *Pickled Fruits, Fungi and Vegetables*

PICKLED FRUITS

For these I use the American type of sweet-sour pickle. I find that guests are pleasurably surprised to discover an odd dish of this type of hors-d'œuvre with the more orthodox kinds. The most popular one is pickled grapefruit skin. Here it is:

237.

Pickled grapefruit skin. Take halves of grapefruit skin, the pulp of which has been used for grapefruit cocktail or other uses, and soak them in cold water for at least twelve hours. At the end of this time, boil them in slightly salted water, until they are soft enough to be pierced easily with a skewer. Rafraîchissez! or allow the cold water to run on them. Meantime prepare the pickle. This consists of two pounds of sugar (brown or what is known as Scotch moist for preference) with one pint of ordinary brewed malt vinegar and an aromatic note of six cloves and a two-inch piece of stick cinnamon boiled together. Strain the grapefruit skins, remove some of the white pith and cut the remainder into pieces about one inch square. Add them to the pickle, boil until the skin becomes clear and put away in a jam jar for use.

238.

Pickled watermelon rind. This may be made in similar manner, but in this case it is advisable to drain the syrup next morning, boil it up and pour over the melon again. Repeat this on two further mornings just as though you were making candied peel. I also advise your reducing the strength of the vinegar by taking half water, half vinegar in the quantities given in the preceding recipe. Further, if you will always use stick cinnamon and whole cloves in place of the ground kind, you will have a clearer, brighter syrup. Ground spices tend to make the syrup dark in colour.

239.

Pears, peaches, nectarines, plums and **cherries** may all be pickled

115

on the lines indicated above. The general recipe is two pounds of fruit, one pound of sugar, half a pint of vinegar and spice (cloves, allspice, mace, cinnamon and nutmeg) to suit individual fancy. The first four fruits mentioned above should be blanched and skinned and then cut into convenient sized pieces or if small left whole. Cherries may be stoned or not and if preferred may be left with a short length of stalk as for brandy cherries.

FUNGI

240.

Mushrooms are an excellent hors-d'œuvre when cooked (pickled) according to one or other of the following methods. Wash button mushrooms rapidly in running water, but do **not** peel them, in fact you will be very clever if you can peel mushrooms no bigger than a shilling, with a good many no bigger than a sixpence. *Method (a)*. Acidulate the water with lemon juice, add pepper and salt and a pat of butter. Cook your mushrooms in this, with a buttered paper over them, for five minutes by the clock. Then clear them away in a terrine with the liquor and the same buttered paper on top until they are cold.

241.

Method (b). Take half a pint of wine vinegar, one-sixth of a pint of olive oil, thyme, bay leaf, a crushed clove of garlic, a few coriander seeds, and peppercorns, a piece of fennel root and a root of parsley and lastly salt. Place the button mushrooms in a terrine and after having boiled the above 'cuisson' for a few minutes, pass it through a strainer on to the mushrooms, cover and clear away in a cool place until wanted.

242.

Method (c). Pass the mushrooms in hot oil, then cook them in white wine, vinegar, salt, cayenne pepper, a pinch of sugar, a little finely chopped celery, and a few grains of coriander seed. Allow them to cook thus for an instant, then clear them away in their liquor and serve them when cold.

243.

Method (d). This is very suitable for the cold display. Chop finely one medium-sized onion and with it two cloves of garlic, allow this to 'fall' in a little oil and add three skinned, de-pipped and roughly chopped tomatoes. Cook together for a few moments and add a minute pinch of rubbed thyme and a seasoning of salt and pepper. Now add this to some mushrooms cooked by *Method* (*a*) and put away to cool. To serve: dish up in an earthenware or porcelain oval dish and add a few drops of olive oil and a sprinkling of chopped chervil, or failing that, parsley.

244.

Chanterelles. Those of you who live in the country will be able to collect for yourselves a delicious little 'mushroom', especially if there are any beech woods in the neighbourhood. They are known in France as chanterelles or jaunottes and in appearance resemble a tiny umbrella that the wind has blown inside out. They are yellowish in colour and have fins or gills up the outside like the ribs of the out-turned umbrella. Cook them very slowly under cover with a little butter and finish with a spoonful or so of thick cream. When they are cold, you may thin down the sauce with either lemon juice or wine vinegar, dress them and sprinkle a little chopped parsley over all. (Note: they must not be washed.)

PICKLED VEGETABLES

245.

Pickled gherkins (small). Put small gherkins in a cloth with coarse salt and rub them together. This removes part of the very tough skin and makes it easier for the pickle to penetrate. Now put the gherkins into a basin and cover them with vinegar. Measure this vinegar, and to every quart add ¼ oz. black peppercorns, 1½ oz. bruised ginger, two blades of mace, one bay leaf, some coriander and fennel seed. Bring this to the boil and strain it over the gherkins. The next day the vinegar must be boiled again and poured over the gherkins. When cold transfer to jars, cover and store in a cool place.

246.

Large gherkins, of about three or four inches in length, should be put into jars and covered with a strong brine—half a pound of salt to each quart of water—and stored for a month at least. They can be used sliced in salads, etc.

247.

Small cucumbers or **gherkins salted** (Agoursis). These may be salted in the Russian way. Use a deep butter crock to hold them and a layer of leaves at the bottom. Oak leaves, vine leaves or those of the cherry tree may all be used. In some parts horseradish leaves or a little grated horseradish is used for flavour. On the layer of leaves, place one of washed cucumbers, then sprinkle some aromatic herbs such as fennel, tarragon, parsley and a few peppercorns, though I do not think these last are needed if horseradish is also used, and cover with a layer of coarse salt. Continue thus until the crock is nearly full and finish with a layer of leaves. Fill the crock with boiled water which has been allowed to cool, place a board on top and a clean stone heavy enough to keep the cucumbers under the liquid. Keep the crock in a cool place, and the salt cucumbers (Agoursis) should be ready for use in about ten days, but depending on the weather they may take three weeks. These salted cucumbers are particularly good with cold meats.

248.

Dill cucumbers (fermented). The method for these is slightly different as they are fermented. Place a layer of vine leaves and sprigs of dill at the bottom of the crock and on these lay the cucumbers. Halfway up the crock place another layer of vine leaves and sprigs of dill, and continue with cucumbers until the vessel is full, leaving room for a layer of dill and finally vine leaves. Boil together 1 pint of vinegar, 2 gallons of water and 1¼ lb. of coarse salt. When this pickle is cold use it to cover the contents of the crock. Place a wooden cover which fits easily inside the vessel, with a weight on top of the cucumbers, and stand the crock in a warm place so that fermentation may begin. Allow six weeks for this to be completed, and during this time replace the water that evaporates and skim off the scum which forms on the surface two or three times a week. If you wish to can this pickle, the procedure is as follows: pack the cucumbers into the cans and add a sprig of dill, then fill up with boiling brine in which the pickle was fermented, and seal.

249.

Pickled red cabbage. Select firm cabbages of good colour. Remove the hard mid-rib of the outer leaves and discard, then shred the remainder finely. Sprinkle the shreds with coarse salt and leave them for a day. Next drain them thoroughly and pack into jars. Cover with cold spiced vinegar. A few juniper berries may, with advantage, be added. The red cabbage is ready for use at once and may be served drained, with a dressing and chopped parsley over, or as it comes from the jar.

250.

Green tomato chutney. Take 5 lb. of green tomatoes, 3 lb. of green apples, 1 lb. brown sugar, 1½ lb. chopped onions, 1 quart of vinegar, ½ teaspoonful cayenne pepper, salt to taste, and a small muslin bag to be boiled with and removed later from the chutney containing half a teaspoonful each of cloves and crushed peppercorns and a one-inch piece of stick cinnamon. Slice the green tomatoes or if very tiny cut them in four, mix coarse salt with them and leave them for twenty-four hours. At the end of that time drain them well, put them with the peeled and cut apples and the rest of the ingredients into a pan and boil until soft. The chutney should be boiled until it is of the consistency of jam and then bottled. Green tomato chutney makes quite a good variety of hors-d'œuvre and should be served as it is.

251.

Pickled pimentos. This is best done when they are beginning to turn red or yellow, according to variety. Split, take out the seeds and pack them into a jar. Cover with vinegar, drain it into a measure and to each quart allow one teaspoonful of salt, a quarter-teaspoonful each of ground mace and ground nutmeg and six chillies. Boil this vinegar and allow it to cool before pouring it over the pimentos and sealing the jar. Forget them for a month.

7. Aspics, Moulded Creams, Royales

ASPIC JELLY

There are two kinds of aspic jelly, meat and fish; but the principle remains the same in both cases. The object is to extract gelatinous material from meat or fish bones, flavour it and if necessary to add best quality gelatine to aid the setting-power—see also glossary.

252.

To make aspic jelly: (a) Meat (grasse). This jelly is made from a good meat and bone stock to which have been added a few blanched calves' feet or fresh pork skin and the necks and feet of any available chickens. After sufficient cooking skim this stock, strain it and allow it to become quite cold. If not set, decant it and estimate how much gelatine will be required to bring the aspic to the required consistency—more than eight or ten leaves to the quart should not be needed. Clarify in the usual manner, i.e. with whites of eggs, minced lean raw beef, the normal garnish of carrot, leek, turnip, celery, crushed peppercorns and salt. When ready to strain add a few bruised leaves of tarragon and a glass of madeira. Pass the jelly through a soup cloth or jelly bag and store away.

253.

To make aspic jelly: (b) Fish (maigre). The jelly should be prepared from a gelatinous fish stock such as is made from the bones, skin and trimmings of a turbot. Proceed exactly as above but do not add madeira.

254.

A substitute aspic jelly. If there is not time to prepare an aspic jelly properly, i.e. from a good stock, it may be made from the following: 2 quarts water, $\frac{1}{4}$ pint mixed tarragon and wine vinegar, $\frac{1}{2}$ lb. of best quality leaf gelatine soaked for an hour in a further quart of water, add crushed peppercorns, salt and a few drops of caramel colouring. Whisk six egg whites well and add to the mixture, bring to the boil slowly and whisk occasionally until the moment of coagulation arrives. Then pull the pan to the side of the stove and allow the clarification to proceed. When well off the boil, pass the contents through the cloth. (Note: If you have to use powdered gelatine, this varies so much in quality that you should make a small test to discover the amount required to set a given quantity of liquid.

We have already made Aspics of Foie Gras, and of Lobster, Shrimps and Sole, which you will find under the appropriate headings. There remains:

255.

Aspic of chicken. These should be made in the same moulds as those referred to on page 81, when making Aspic de Foie Gras. Coat them with jelly as described and set a few green peas at the bottom, fill up with diced chicken then pour in aspic at near setting point to fill the moulds. A vivid touch of colour can be given to this little aspic by setting in the centre of the ring of green peas a round piece of pimento cut out with a suitable cutter.

MOULDED CREAMS

256.

General method of moulded creams. Pound 4 oz. of débris of any one of the following: smoked salmon, tunny fish, cooked shellfish or white fish, cooked chicken, game or veal. Blend with two spoonsful of thin Béchamel sauce, adding at the same time three spoonsful of whipped cream and lastly two spoonsful of jelly. Use the small moulds already mentioned and either mask them with aspic jelly or oil them with a drop of olive oil. My experience has been that if you are rushed you should oil your moulds, but for a better job, and especially if you have any decoration of the moulds to consider, then mask them with aspic jelly every time.

ROYALES

Royales are similar in many respects to moulded creams except that cream may be absent and the liaison is by egg and egg-yolk instead of by jelly; and of course the mixture is cooked 'en bain marie' in the oven or may be steamed. Take care that the preparation does not boil or your Royale will be as full of holes as honeycomb. Use small dariole moulds again and butter them this time.

257.

Foundation Royale as used to garnish soups, in particular clear ones, is very easy to make. Beat up three eggs, season them with pepper and salt, add one-third of a pint of consommé, strain this into a charlotte or other mould previously buttered, place a buttered paper on top and stand the mould in a pan containing hot water. Bring this water to the boil and at once place the pan and contents into a moderate oven. When a clean skewer or the blade of a knife inserted into the Royale comes out clean the mixture is cooked. Allow it to cool before unmoulding and cutting. This as you will have noticed is nothing more than a Crême Renversée or a Baked Custard with about twice the usual number of eggs. The reason for this is that, whereas in a custard it is desirable for the sake of delicacy in eating to use only the minimum number of eggs that will hold the preparation together when cooked; in a Royale the mixture must be well bound because of the subsequent cutting into cubes and other shapes. Nothing looks worse than a Royale which has disintegrated in a plateful of otherwise enticing clear soup.

Our use for this article, i.e. cold as a variety of hors-d'œuvre, is more in the nature of a Pain de Légumes or vegetable loaf and does not require to be quite so firm as that used as a garnish in soup. In general you may use two eggs and one yolk for each half-pint of well-reduced purée bound with Béchamel sauce and/or cream.

258.

Tomato Royale. Take some concentrated tomato purée, add a spoonful or two of Béchamel sauce, season and pass through the tammy-cloth (nowadays a hair sieve may be used), then measure and add egg in the proportion above mentioned. Fill the greased dariole moulds and poach in the usual way. When cooked and quite cold, they should be unmoulded on to a suitable base; a tiny cooked artichoke bottom or mushroom. They may also be dressed on a bed of lettuce or cress.

259.

Spinach Royale. Bind sufficient well-reduced spinach purée with a spoonful or so of Béchamel and rub it through the hair sieve. Add proper amount of egg to the measured purée, mould and poach in the usual way. The tomato and spinach ones look well dressed together.

260.

Pistachio Royale. This is a more luxurious one than the last. Pound about four ounces of blanched (that is to say skinned) pistachio kernels and when they are a fine pulp add a dessert-spoonful of Béchamel sauce. Heighten the colour with a few drops of spinach greening and add two spoonsful of thick cream. Bind with an egg and two yolks and finish in the usual way.

261.

Chicken Royale. Pound two or three ounces of cooked white chicken meat and when fine enough add two dessert-spoonsful of Béchamel sauce and one of thick cream. Pass through the sieve, bind with one egg and two yolks, and finish in the usual manner.

262.

Game Royale. Pound two ounces of game débris, free from sinew and skin, with a spoonful of good brown sauce containing some meat glaze and verify the seasoning. Stir in one egg and two yolks and pass the mixture through the sieve. Put the purée into a basin, if you have a spoonful of dregs of madeira add it and lastly a good spoonful of thick cream. Stir carefully, fill your buttered dariole moulds and poach them in water in a baking-tin in the oven in the usual way. Cut a left-over cooked head of celery across in quarter-inch slices and use these to make a border on a toasted canapé in the centre of which you unmould the now cooled Royale.

Note. I advise you always to test a little of any of these mixtures to prove its setting properties before you cook off the whole batch. It is impossible to give a recipe which will give perfect results every time owing to the varying moisture content of the purée, etc. Some mixtures may need a little more egg, others a little more cream, and of this you can only be sure if you make a small test.

263.

Green Pea and Carrot (Mixed) Royale. In the season you can do a little mystifying by cooking an equal number of darioles of green pea purée (made from peas very new and freshly cooked à l'Anglaise) and of carrot purée (likewise from the first new carrots). In both cases follow the usual procedure as laid down above. When these are thoroughly cold unmould them carefully on to a clean cloth and cut each vertically in four. Put a few drops of aspic in each mould and reassemble the purées, this time putting in two of each colour. If required run another drop of aspic on top of the filled moulds to make certain of the contents holding together when turned out again. If you wish you can unmould your little mixed Royales a second time, cut them across in half, re-mould but give one half a 90 deg. twist, thus bringing carrot under green pea and vice versa.

8. Vegetables

Vegetables may be prepared in a variety of ways and if we ever have to consider seriously a vegetarian diet, this would accord-ing to some be a benefit. One thing is certain, if more vegetables were eaten raw a change for the better in the general health would take place. At present our business is only with vegetables which have been cooked or pickled and allowed to cool; the consideration of them in the multitude of ways they may be cooked and served hot does not now concern us. Uncooked vegetables follow on page 134.

COOKED VEGETABLES

264.

Agoursis, or **Russian salt cucumbers** (see under Pickling) should be sliced and served with a little of their own pickle. They will appear in many of the salads to be detailed later, either as ingredient, accom-paniment or as finishing touch. Dill cucumbers prepared and sold in this country are usually overgrown and in consequence have a tough skin; remove this and they are a good substitute for the real article with its more tender skin, although they (dill cucumbers) may have a hollow middle.

265.

Another way of serving Agoursis is to take slices of them, rounds of hard-boiled egg and slices of small tomato, all of as near the same diameter as possible and arrange them overlapping, alternating the colours in a circle in a porcelain egg dish. Sauce them with a mayon-naise thin enough to show the colours through.

266.

Artichokes. If ever you have the chance of getting any of those tiny globe artichokes that gardeners sometimes have for disposal, seize it, for you have the opportunity of preparing one of the finest

267.

of hors-d'œuvre, namely **Petits Artichauts à la Grecque.** Trim them

124

and blanch them in water acidulated with lemon juice or, failing that, vinegar. Cool them under the cold water tap and drain them. Then plunge them into a 'cuisson à la Grecque' as given on page 109, and give them about thirty minutes to cook. Keep them in the liquor in which they were cooked in a cold place and serve with a little of the same liquor.

268.

Asparagus. Two-inch lengths of asparagus tips can be arranged in little piles of three or four on fingers of toast and sauced over with a thin mayonnaise. Decorate with a thin strip of pimento as a band or with a thin fillet of anchovy, and sprinkle some sieved yolk over. Alternatively, short lengths of asparagus may be rolled in mayonnaise then in sieved yolks. Serve on fingers of brown bread.

269.

Asparagus tips or **Pointes d'Asperges.** For use in salads or as decoration, these should be dealt with as follows: Take some sprue, hold each stick in turn by the thick end in your left hand, and, with the thumb and forefinger of the right hand, bend the stick almost at right angles. Keeping the stick bent, start near your left hand and slide your fingers towards the tip. The stalk will snap off at the point where it becomes tender. When you have broken all, tie the tender pieces in small bundles with a strip of raffia as this is better than string because it is easier to cut when the asparagus is cooked and so less likely to cause damage to the fragile stalks. They should be tied at a point one inch from the heads which are all nicely levelled. Now cut across them at a point one inch on the other side of the raffia and you will have little bundles of two-inch lengths of pointes d'asperges. The pieces of varying length which you cut off should now be assembled and cut into half-inch lengths. Remember that they are all tender and when cooked in slightly salted water along with the bundles will form part of a salad or a garnish later. As for the tough ends of the stalks, these may be used as the foundation of asparagus soup.

270.

Salade d'Aubergines is a Turkish or Eastern Mediterranean dish. Take equal quantities of aubergines and poivrons. The latter should be either grilled or placed in a hot oven for a few minutes to facilitate the removal of the tough skin which covers them. The aubergines should be cooked slowly in a moderate oven until thoroughly soft. Then remove the pulp from the black skin and allow it to cool. Chop it roughly and season it with oil, vinegar, salt and pepper. Dress it on a service dish and decorate it with strips of the cooked poivron.

271.

Beans. Salade de Haricots Verts et Tomates. The haricots verts for this admirable salad must be very young, and not much longer than a match stick. Cook them in the usual way and cool them. Dress them in a salad bowl and decorate with about half their volume of firm ripe tomatoes cut in slices or in 'eighths' and sauce over the whole with vinaigrette.

272.

Salade de Haricots Blancs. Soak the white haricots for twelve hours and then cook them in plenty of water, slowly and regularly, with a garnish of a carrot cut in four, an onion stuck with two cloves and a small bouquet garni. Season with salt after an hour's cooking. Allow them to become quite cold, drain from the liquor, add some finely chopped onion and a seasoning of olive oil and wine vinegar, with, of course, salt and pepper. Dress on a service dish and sprinkle chopped parsley over.

273.

Salade de Haricots Flageolets. These are the green haricots and may be treated exactly as above.

274.

Salade de Haricots Rouges. Cook as white haricots with the addition of red wine (the unwanted remains of several decanted bottles) and a chunk of salt belly pork.

275.

Beetroot. Beetroot may be either boiled or baked in the oven like a baked potato. The latter course is preferable as some varieties which 'bleed' very easily lose nearly all colour if boiled. Whichever way you cook them you may slice them or cut them into a julienne or in dice and season with plain oil, vinegar, salt and pepper. If you decide on dice, you may dress alternate heaps of diced beetroot and diced cucumber for colour effect. Remember always that the beetroot stains everything with which it comes in contact and for this reason is best kept out of mixed salads. A border of fancifully cut beetroot round the dish is very effective and may be served along with the salad it decorates.

276.

Beetroot shapes. If you select the long type of beetroot, you will be able to cut off suitable lengths, push a crimped pastry cutter over them and use a round vegetable scoop (as used for Pommes Parisienne) to hollow out the centre. Macerate these shapes for a time with aromatic vinegar, then fill them with a suitable fish or vegetable salad. You need not confine yourself to round shapes, boats or rectangular boxes may also be fashioned and the trimmings need not be wasted.

277.

Cassolettes de Betteraves à la Collioure. Proceed as above, then fill them with a mixture of small dice of fillets of anchovies, hard-boiled egg (i.e. a salpicon), seasoned with oil, vinegar, mustard and fines herbes with a few capers. Chill before serving.

278.

Salade de Betteraves. A neat little salad of orange sections and a short julienne of beetroot may be arranged on incurved lettuce leaves and sauced over with French mustard dressing.

279.

Cabbage leaves. Take some cold boiled rice and mix with it some grated Parmesan cheese and a little butter. With this preparation stuff some small-sized cabbage leaves which have been previously blanched and cooled. Make these into small balls and give them a further braising for about ten minutes. When they are cold, dress them on a dish and sauce them over with French mustard dressing mixed with tomato catsup.

280.

Carrots in wine. There is a variety of early carrots which is nearly round in shape. Take of these the required quantity and peel them by scraping, then blanch them in slightly salted water for half an hour. Meanwhile prepare the following 'cuisson'. Equal quantities of white wine and wine vinegar, a bouquet garni, a crushed clove of garlic, salt and pepper. Drain the carrots and put them on to cook slowly (mijoter) in this until they are done. Before you clear them away, pour a spoonful or two of olive oil on the surface. Keep on ice if possible, but serve cold.

281.

Carrots with peas and rice. With a small vegetable scoop, make some balls of cooked carrot the size of a pea and mix them with an equal amount of cooked green peas and twice their volume of pilaff rice, page 131. Season with vinaigrette dressing. (Note. If you do not have a vegetable scoop of the size mentioned cut the carrot into small cubes—the effect is not so good.)

282.

Cauliflower Vinaigrette. Cut off the flowerets from a cauliflower and cook them as usual in salted water. (The centre stalk should be cooked and used separately.) Season these with vinaigrette dressing and allow them to macerate for a time, then arrange them on the service dish and pour over them a little of the dressing.

283.

Céleris à la Grecque. Use small heads of celery, strip off the outside leaves and use only the white hearts. Cut them into halves or quarters according to size, blanch them and cool. Then put them to cook in a marinade à la grecque, page 109, and allow them to cool in the liquor. Serve very cold with some of the 'cuisson'.

284.

Cucumber salad. Peel a cucumber and slice thinly, cut in two lengthwise to extract seeds if these are old and hard. Then sprinkle with salt and put on one side, later pour off the salty liquid and drain well. Then season with vinegar, pepper, and a few spots of oil only. Arrange the slices on a glass dish and sprinkle with chopped parsley or chopped chervil on serving. British taste generally prefers crisp cucumber salad. (In all probability you will be told that your salad is stale if you serve this limp one which has been salted and drained, though this is gastronomically correct.) Therefore slice your cucumber and arrange it on a glass dish, at the last moment sprinkle it with vinegar (leave out the oil this time) and dust it with salt and pepper.

285.

Barquettes de Concombres. (*a*) à la Danoise. Prepare your boat-shapes by cutting slantwise across a rather thin cucumber and paring to shape. Blanch them carefully in acidulated water as above and macerate them in oil and vinegar. Then garnish them with the following mixture: Pass the yolks of three hard-boiled eggs and the fillets of a marinated herring through the sieve and season the purée thus obtained with oil, vinegar, salt and pepper (careful with the last two), adding a little chopped chives and grated horseradish, also a dash of French mustard. When the barquettes are filled and the surface has been built up to a ridge and smoothed over with a palette

286.

knife, sprinkle a little sieved cooked white of egg over. (*b*) à l'Ecossaise. Prepare the boat shapes as before, and garnish them with a little finely shredded cold cooked salmon, bound with sufficient stiff mayonnaise sauce.

287.

Cucumber creams. Remove the seeds from some half-inch-thick slices of cucumber. Season the cucumber cases with salt, allow them to stand for a while then drain them well. Pass some cooked chicken through the fine plate of the mincer and mix it with half cream, half mayonnaise. Fill the prepared cucumbers with this chicken cream and dress them, then sauce them with a thinned mayonnaise.

288.

Leeks: Poireaux à la Grecque. Cut the white part of the leeks into three-inch lengths and blanch them well. Finish cooking in the marinade à la grecque (page 109) as for celery. Serve very cold in a little of the liquor and sprinkle with chopped parsley.

289.

Stuffed leeks. Cut off the roots—the next one and a half inches is the bit you want—blanch it well. Then macerate it in a mixture of oil and vinegar or cook it à la grecque. Take out the centre and stuff the little case you have left with anchovy or sardine butter, q.v., or with a macédoine.

290.

Coeurs de Poireaux à la Russe is a more elaborate version of the above. Blanch as before for about ten minutes and macerate for a few hours in aromatic vinegar. Then drain and stuff with the following mixture: Pound two or three spoonsful of pressed caviar with the same number of hard-boiled yolks of egg and rub through the sieve. Season with a pinch of finely grated horseradish and bind with a little stiff mayonnaise, to which with advantage a few drops of aspic (maigre) may be added. Serve very cold.

As a variant, use the same mixture as in Barquettes à l'Ecossaise.

291.

Lentilles en Salade. Treat lentils, the true lentils not the Egyptian variety, in the same way as white haricots.

292.

Maize (Corn) salad. Drain a can of corn. Make a dressing by mixing a little mustard and finely chopped onion (or onion juice) in an ordinary French dressing, i.e. three parts oil to one part vinegar, with salt and pepper. You will find it easier to mix the dry mustard

I 129

with the vinegar before adding the other ingredients. Season the drained sweet corn with the mixed dressing and arrange the salad in one heap on a dish previously garnished with crisp young lettuce leaves.

293.

Stuffed onions. Roast some medium-sized to smallish onions in the oven. When they are cold, peel and squeeze them gently and the centres will come out. Cut off the root end and replace this as a plug. Now fill them with débris of pickled fish, or any highly seasoned filling, and dress. A few drops of vinaigrette should be sprinkled over them.

294.

Onion salad. The insides which you squeezed out should be cut into slices, put on a dish and sauced over with vinaigrette. A border of slices of hard-boiled egg should be placed round the dish and a few rings of pimento on top to decorate.

295.

Pimentos or Poivrons, Capsicums, Sweet Peppers. These may be stuffed and braised. First grill them slightly to remove the outer skin, then make a cut across the stalk end and take away the seeds. Now stuff them with a riz pilaff, re-form them and braise them in a good stock. When cold dish them and sprinkle with a little oil.

296.

Poivrons à la Roumanie. Take green poivrons, grill them and peel off as much of the outer skin as possible. Pack them closely into an earthenware oven dish, put on the lid and cook them in a slow oven. Then marinate in oil, lemon juice, salt and pepper and serve from the dish in which they were cooked.

297.

Potato salad. Steam the potatoes in their jackets, and when cold peel them and cut them up either into slices or cubes. Then pour over them a ladleful of cold consommé or water and allow to stand for a while. You will find that the prepared potatoes have soaked up all the liquid yet remain 'free' and in this state will require much less of the dressing now to be mixed with them. The choice is either oil, vinegar, salt and pepper with fines herbes or mayonnaise sauce thinned with weak vinegar, and mixed with very finely chopped onion or chives.

Cooked Vegetables

298.

Salade de Pommes de Terre à la Parisienne. A luxurious variant of the above. Use a non-floury variety of potato, shape them to a regular size and slice them warm. Pour over them (2½ lb.) about half a pint of dry white wine and allow them to macerate. At the last moment season with oil, vinegar, salt and pepper with chopped chervil and parsley.

Rice is an excellent admixture in salads. For this you may use any cold boiled rice you may have left over, but it is preferable to use:

299.

Riz Pilaff. Chop an onion finely and allow it to 'fall' in oil. Now measure the required amount of Patna rice (for preference), a cupful, a bowlful, or whatever amount you require and add this to the onion, stirring so that the grains become coated with the oil. Allow it to fry gently for a minute or two and then add *twice* the volume of white stock, season and bring to the boil. It is most important that you are careful about this measuring. If you are using one measure of rice, then take two measures of stock. Cover the surface with a buttered paper and the pan with a close-fitting lid—to hinder the escape of steam—and put the pan into the oven, 400 deg. F., where you leave it for twenty minutes by the clock. At the end of this time take it out and you will find that all the liquid has been absorbed by the rice, which is perfectly cooked. Change the now cooked rice into another pan—to stop any drying of the contents—and use as required, cold for your salads of course. Pilaff rice is even better than boiled for use in salads because of its more compact texture, and may be used up to fifty per cent of the total bulk.

300.

Rice salad with pimento and peas. Cut some cooked or canned pimentos into dice and mix with them an equal volume of cooked green peas. Prepare some pilaff rice as above and take of it about the same amount as pimentos and peas together. Bind this salad with mayonnaise and dress it in small incurved lettuce leaves, individually.

301.

Salad of rice, tomato and pimentos. Pilaff rice two parts, ripe tomatoes cut into 'eighths' one part, julienne of pimento one part (for contrast the last item may be of uncooked green pimentos) seasoned and mixed together with the following dressing: chop a small onion and reduce to a fine pulp a small clove of garlic with a branch or two of parsley. Mix with this two parts of oil and one part of vinegar and add to the salad, seasoning with salt and pepper. This salad looks well if piled high on a glass dish.

302.

Rice, kohlrabi, agoursis and beetroot. Make a julienne of kohlrabi, agoursis and lettuce. Add to this about half the volume in cooked rice. For the dressing, mix the dill pickle with sour cream until of the right consistency. Place rounds of pickled beetroot on the service dish and make neat little heaps of the salad on them.

303.

Rice and chicken salad with truffle. There is a simple salad, but none the less recherchée, which consists of a julienne of white chicken meat and cooked rice in equal proportions. Season with French mustard dressing and sprinkle the surface with finely chopped truffle.

304.

Rice and chicken with asparagus tips. As a variant of the above, add a few asparagus tips.

305.

Salade à la Russe. There are two kinds, (*a*) **grasse.** Cut and cook separately in boiling salted water a jardinière of carrot and turnip, haricots verts in lozenge shapes and green peas. These four items should be in equal quantities. Add lesser amounts according to your taste of cooked potato in dice, cooked cauliflower buds, small dice of mushroom, either dice or short julienne of truffle, short lengths of ham and tongue, dice of lobster, slices of agoursis and of saucisson, dice of anchovy fillets and capers. Bind with mayonnaise, dress the salad in a dome and decorate it with all the above-mentioned elements together with hard-boiled eggs cut into quarters or sixths, trimmed fillets of anchovies, capers, diamond or other fancy shaped pieces of cooked beetroot and caviar. The other variety is (*b*) **maigre,**

306.

and made as above but with all meat such as ham, tongue and saucisson left out.

In the old days when there was time and the artistry to do these things, the preparation of this salad was a veritable chef d'œuvre. The carrot, turnip and potato were either cut with a column cutter or lifted with a vegetable scoop. Asparagus tips, small artichoke bottoms cut 'en paysanne' and a julienne of chicken have disappeared from the present-day recipe. The various elements of the salad were dressed in separate 'bouquets', the surface levelled off then covered with mayonnaise which was then decorated with a reserve of the underlying vegetable. The centre held a bold bouquet of cauliflower also sauced with mayonnaise and decorated. The sections of hard-boiled egg were placed around this and finally a contrasting border was placed around the edge. An alternative method was to set the salad in a special mould, the top of which had a double curve terminating in a point. This mould was usually coated with aspic jelly and decorated and the salad in the interior was mixed with mayonnaise 'collée', that is to say with a small proportion of jelly to set it. Another way was set the salad in a tall charlotte mould, the one used for Brioche à la Parisienne was just right, coated with aspic and decorated with the vegetables and truffle cut out with a cutter. This was kept in the ice-box and when required was unmoulded on to a border mould similarly filled but with the addition of caviar. If you make a vegetable salad or a salade de légumes, please do not call it Salade à la Russe; a vegetable salad may be anything, but a Salade à la Russe must contain both meat and fish, excepting of course the one served on the fast days imposed by the Church, when maigre ones only are permitted.

307.

Macédoine Niçoise. Cut into julienne equal quantities of cold boiled fowl, Gendarme herring, mortadella and lean boiled ham. Cut also in pieces as near a julienne as possible, but in half the above quantities, white of hard-boiled eggs, beetroot and apple. Add one-quarter of the quantity in julienne of celery. Now take some slices of cold boiled potato and pile on them the above salad, then place each of these on a neat in-curved leaf of heart of lettuce. Decorate the top with a few rings of stoned olive and a slice or two of seeded and skinned poivron. Then sprinkle over the whole a sauce rémoulade and serve.

308.

Salade Algérienne is a simpler edition of the above. Make a julienne of peeled and de-pipped tomato and poivron and add one-quarter of the volume in sliced raw onion. Season with a plain dressing of oil, vinegar, salt and pepper.

309.

Spinach: Salade d'Epinards en Branches. Cook your spinach in the usual way and leave it unchopped. Cool it and season it with a plain dressing of oil, vinegar, salt and pepper. This salad is, to my palate, the best of them all, if you add a few 'chapons'. If you cannot easily get French roll, the crust of which is generally used for chapons, use cold dry toast and rub the clove of garlic on that until it disappears, and then cut it into pieces, and mix with the spinach salad.

UNCOOKED VEGETABLES

310.

Cabbage salad. Slice the white heart of a cabbage on the 'mandoline' (the vegetable slicer), but do not attempt it unless the heart is really compact. Season it with mayonnaise dressing.

311.

Salad, using cabbage stalks. You may also use the pith of cabbage, cauliflower or broccoli stalks if you shred them finely on the 'Wonder Shredder'. Take care to remove the woody exterior before you do so.

312.

Carrot. Grate the red outside of carrots on the No. 1 vegetable shredder. This will give you an excellent julienne. Take balls of cottage cheese about the diameter of a shilling and roll them in the grated carrot. Dress these on rounds of lettuce or nasturtium leaf.

313.

Carrot salad. Shred some raw carrot as above and mix it with a plain French dressing—mayonnaise seems to make it so clogged and lifeless. Dish in one heap and decorate with the yellow-green leaves from the heart of a lettuce.

314.

Celery. The white heart of celery, cut into two-inch lengths is then cut lengthwise into julienne. These little sticks are seasoned with a rémoulade sauce (page 108), and dressed in a neat pile.

315.

Stuffed celery. Sticks in two-inch lengths may be stuffed with tunny paste, q.v. merely plastered into the hollow—and mounted on cocktail sticks.

Variant of above. Use potted Stilton or Rocquefort cheese.

316.

Celeriac or turnip-rooted celery should be peeled and cut into julienne, if old it is advisable to blanch it and drain it well. Bind the strips of celeriac with a light mayonnaise well reinforced with French mustard. Dress this salad in one heap.

317.

Coeurs de Palmier. These are strictly speaking the terminal leaf-buds of a species of cabbage palm and each palm has of course only one such bud. They reach us in Britain as a canned product from the French Ile de la Réunion. Palm hearts to be served cold should be drained well and dried in a cloth. They may be either sliced or left whole and should be dressed with mayonnaise or vinaigrette.

318.

Green peppers may be chopped and mixed with tomato catsup.

319.

White pickled onions—cocktail onions—covered with tomato and French mustard dressing, make an easy variety if one is hurried.

320.

Radishes. The rosy kind are washed well and scraped slightly to remove the rootlets and are left with about an inch of the green top. They should be dressed with a few small blocks of ice. **Black** radishes

321.

are peeled or scraped, sliced thinly and sprinkled with salt. Later they are drained well of the water they have given up and seasoned with vinegar and a squeeze of pepper, with a few drops of olive oil dribbled over just prior to serving.

322.

Tomatoes: salad. Remove the stalk from a tomato and put this end down on your board, and starting at one side slice downwards thinly. Arrange such slices overlapping on a dish, sprinkle with chopped chives, or place graduated onion rings on top with a dusting of chopped parsley over all and season with a few drops of olive oil and vinegar and a sprinkling of salt and pepper. This method of seasoning is to be preferred to that of using ready-mixed vinaigrette dressing because the latter has 'body' and thus does not find its way between the slices so well. Perhaps I'm fussy.

323.

Tomato baskets. Select small tomatoes of even size. Remove the stalk then make two cuts down from the other end each a little to one side of the centre and reaching about halfway down. Now make two more cuts at right angles to the others from the sides and remove the pieces. Next hollow out the flesh and seeds and you will have little baskets, the interior of which you should marinate with a few spots of oil and vinegar until wanted.

The above baskets may be filled with cooked green peas bound with mayonnaise.

324.

Tomates Monégasque. Make a filling for the baskets composed of small dice of tunny fish (in oil), dice of hard-boiled egg, mixed with chopped parsley, chives, tarragon and chervil and bound with mayonnaise.

325.

Cherry tomatoes. Covered with sour cream dressing, q.v. (Note. Cherry tomatoes are a special small-sized tomato not larger than a shilling.)

TOMATO SALADS

326.

Tomato baskets may be filled with a mixture of dice of tomato flesh, dice of peeled and de-pipped orange, and roughly chopped pickled walnut. A speck or two of salt is the only seasoning required. Prepare the oranges by cutting off the peel and white pith in one operation. Then cut the sections free from the membranes which divide them, remove any pips still left on the now bare sections and cut these latter as required. This process is known as 'peeling to the quick'.

327.

Tomatoes, either as baskets or as 'dog-toothed' halves, may be hollowed out to receive a filling of flaked lobster claw meat mixed with very small torn pieces of lettuce and bound with mayonnaise to which a little grated horseradish has been added.

328.

Tomatoes or tomato halves may be hollowed out then refilled with a mixture of dice of pickled walnut, a julienne of hard-boiled white of egg, and dice of the firmest bits taken from the insides of the tomatoes, seasoned with salt and bound with mayonnaise.

329.

Make a julienne of ham and of tomato flesh in about equal quantities and add a few cooked green peas. Make a dressing by working some vinegar and chutney juice into some crowdie (Scots for cottage cheese or fromage blanc). Mix these ingredients together and pile the salad on small lettuce leaves or on rounds of tender cabbage or nasturtium leaves.

330.

On a slice of tomato place a small heap of chrane (an excellent Czechoslovakian pickle mixture of beetroot, horseradish and spices).

On this place a thick round of tunny paste, q.v., and sauce over with thinned French mustard dressing.

331.

Cut out rounds of lettuce with a convenient-sized cutter and place a slice of tomato on each. On this put a blob of mayonnaise with a round of cooked potato over it. Now place a piece of Bismarck herring with a slice of agoursis on the potato and finish by saucing with vinaigrette dressing.

332.

Place a leaf of nasturtium on the service dish. It is a good plan to stack a pile of say ten of these leaves and to cut them all at the same time with a round pastry cutter about one and a half inches in diameter, this evens the size and makes the arranging of them on the dish so much easier and neater. On this leaf put a blob of mayonnaise to fix a slice of tomato. Next put a rectangle of corned mutton on the tomato with a blob of rémoulade sauce anchoring a small slice of pickled walnut. When all are in place, you should get eight or ten of these little salads on an oblong dish; sauce them over with thinned French mustard dressing.

333.

Button mushrooms cooked in white wine, mixed with dice of tomato flesh and seasoned with tomato mayonnaise make a pleasing variety.

334.

Prepare a julienne of cooked duck. Peel 'to the quick' an orange as described above, and remove the sections without the dividing membranes. Cut these pieces of orange into smaller pieces and take about the same volume of tomato flesh also in small pieces. Now add about twice the amount of diced cold potatoes and a few green peas. Bind this salad with mayonnaise sauce and dress it tastefully in individual heaps on a previously prepared bed of chopped lettuce.

9. *Eggs*

We used to take eggs very much for granted and our concern in those days was not so much the supply as the 'weight per long hundred' and the precise distinction between the trade terms 'new laid' and the merely 'fresh'. I need not remind you how invaluable eggs are in cookery; for the hors-d'œuvrier they are indispensable.

335.

Hard-boiled eggs. The best way to hard-boil eggs is to put them (of irreproachable freshness) into a wire basket and plunge them into a pan of boiling water of sufficient quantity to submerge them completely. From the moment the water comes to the boil again, count nine minutes. Then plunge the eggs into cold running water and leave them until they are cold. Take off the shells and keep the eggs under cold water until required for use.

336.

Poached eggs. To poach an egg successfully a few hints must be borne in mind. First and most important, only use the freshest eggs. Secondly, prepare a pan of water salted, acidulated with vinegar and of sufficient dimensions to allow the number of eggs you intend to cook to bathe freely and unimpeded in it. Thirdly, break your eggs carefully, even dipping your finger-ends into the water to allow the egg to slide gently into it. Fourthly, never allow the water to boil fiercely; a gentle simmering is all that is required. Your eggs will take six minutes to cook. At the end of this time, take them out with a skimmer and keep them in reserve in cold water.

337.

Oeufs Mollets can best be described as hard-boiled eggs half-cooked. The whites should be hard-cooked, but the yolks should remain fluid. The method of cooking is to plunge the eggs into boiling water and when they come to the boil again, pull the pan from the fire, cover it closely and give the eggs six minutes to cook, after which cool and shell them.

Variants of Hard-boiled Eggs

338.

Scrambled eggs. Put a knob of butter into a sauteuse and allow it to melt whilst you break the eggs into a bowl. It is advisable to crack each one separately into a cup to assure oneself of its state of freshness before adding it to the bulk. Season the eggs with salt and pepper and break the grain of the yolks with a whisk. Now pour them into the sauteuse and stand the pan on a moderately hot part of the stove and stir gently. As soon as the eggs reach a creamy stage remove the pan to a cooler part of the stove. A properly scrambled egg should consist of small lumps bound in a creamy mass of egg. This is attained by a not too vigorous whisking, rather by letting the egg set and then scraping it off the bottom of the pan so to speak. If the egg is stirred too quickly a mass resembling a custard will result. In one place where I worked, we were not allowed to use a whisk for scrambling an egg, only a trussing needle or a skewer was permitted. At all costs avoid over-cooking; that mass of dry, crumbly stuff which is too often served as scrambled egg is a disgrace to the cook.

When the desired state of creaminess is reached, change the eggs into another casserole as a thick-bottomed sauteuse holds the heat and may go on cooking the eggs long after you have taken it from the fire. An optional but desirable addition to the eggs when scrambled is a spoonful or so of thick cream.

339.

Oeufs à la Mayonnaise. This, the first dish of hard-boiled eggs which comes to mind, is an old friend and is very popular with all who come to be served at the hors-d'œuvre table. Slice the hard-boiled eggs into rings (a most useful tool for this job is one of those gadgets which cut the egg by means of fine wires). You may prepare a bed of finely cut lettuce or not as you wish. Arrange the rings of egg overlapping one another and use up much of the débris of hard-boiled egg you will have accumulated thus far. Season very lightly with salt and pepper and cover with mayonnaise sauce (thinned slightly). To decorate, use blue anchusa flowers placed in a line across the dish—these flowers are quite edible—or you may use a vivid orange nasturtium. Whatever you decide, do not as most cooks, leave your egg mayonnaise looking out on life with the placid pallor of a bladder of lard.

Variants of Hard-boiled Eggs

340.

A variant of the above is to coat the sliced egg with cream cheese dressing (page 109) and relieve the dead whiteness of it by a judicious décor of sieved lobster coral (cooked) and finely chopped black truffle.

341.

Dress alternate slices of hard-boiled egg, tomato and spring onion, these last in very thin slices. Use a white porcelain egg dish or fish dish and have the slices overlapping neatly. Sauce over with French mustard dressing and sprinkle with fines herbes.

342.

On neatly incurved leaves from the heart of a lettuce arrange alternate slices of hard-boiled egg and slices of tomato. Keep the diameter of the tomato roughly the same as that of the egg slices, and use about three of each. You will have cup-shapes of lettuce holding your egg and tomato slices, but in order that they may do this successfully you should cut a 'flat' on the underside of the midrib of the leaf so that your 'cup' will not tend to rock about. If preferred, you may cut a slice across the lettuce heart, dress the slice of tomato on this and finish with a slice of hard-boiled egg. Whichever way you use, season the salad with a vinaigrette to which has been added a good sprinkling of chopped tarragon.

343.

Cut your hard-boiled eggs in halves through the 'waist', either in one cut or by using a small knife and making a series of small cuts give the halves a serrated or 'dog's tooth' outline. Take out the yolk and stuff the white cup with a salad of shrimps bound with mayonnaise.

344.

As above, stuff the cups of egg-white with a salad of vegetables, a macédoine or à la Russe with or without the addition of anchovy essence.

345.

Use sardine or similar butter and pipe it from a star tube into the hollow whites. Finish with a tiny sprig of parsley and stand the half-eggs on wee toasts the size of a shilling, thickly spread with the same butter.

346.

Make a 'butter' from the yolks and butter with a seasoning of essence of anchovies and a touch of cayenne pepper or Tabasco sauce.

Pipe this into your whites, stand them on toasts as before and wrap a strip of filleted anchovy round the egg where it 'sits' on the toast.

347.

As above, but cut the eggs into quarters or sixths lengthwise, pipe the 'butter' from a small plain pipe neatly to fill the place occupied by the yolk and finish with a thin strip of pimento along the top. Dress these sections of egg with some taste on your serving dish and sauce over the whole with a very thin mayonnaise.

348.

Oeufs Mollets, Salade à la Russe. Prepare a Salade à la Russe, and dress this in the required number of heaps on the service dish. Now prepare some oeufs mollets, use pullets' eggs for this on account of their smaller size, and place one, pointed end upwards, on each heap of salad. Sauce the egg with thinned mayonnaise at the moment of serving, and dust the top of each with a shake of paprika from a pepper caster. The border of the dish may be decorated with stars of beetroot or with sliced tomatoes.

349.

Oeufs Pochés à la Gelée. Have ready the required number of eggs poached, trimmed and cooled. Coat some moulds the shape of half an egg with aspic jelly—the ones to use are those in which chocolate eggs are cast, choose a size large enough—and place two leaves of tarragon crosswise in them. Now put in a poached egg and fill up with jelly. Allow to set and unmould on to the service dish, decorating this with chopped jelly piped from a cornet.

350.

Oeufs Pochés en Tomates. An effective dish of poached eggs may be prepared by cutting some tomatoes of the required size in half and scooping out the interior carefully so as not to break the 'walls'. Leave the skins on as this helps to keep them in shape in case they are on the ripe side. Poach the required number of eggs, allow them to cool, trim them and coat them with a mayonnaise sauce to which you have added a little half-set aspic jelly. Set them in your seasoned tomato halves and pipe a little chopped jelly in the hollow spaces. For decoration, which depends very much on the time you have to spare for it, you may choose from anchovy fillets, capers, pimento, tarragon leaves and the like; four chervil leaves with a round of pimento at the centre are easily applied and look well.

141

351.

Oeufs Brouillés en Tomates. One little dish of scrambled eggs is worth mentioning here as it is similar to the last. Cut the required number of tomatoes in halves and scoop them out with care. Now prepare some scrambled eggs, but only cook them to a light creamy stage as they are to be served cold. When they are cold, mix them with a little mayonnaise sauce to which you have added a small quantity of aspic and fill them into your tomato shells, which, by the way, you have seasoned with a few drops of vinaigrette dressing. Next sauce the tops of the filled tomatoes over completely with mayonnaise 'collée', decorate if desired and finish with a dab of aspic to give a gloss. Dress these on a seasoned salad of 'chicorée frisée' or a julienne of lettuce.

352.

Oeufs en Aspic avec Anchois Roulé. Take some ordinary dariole moulds (2 in. diameter at top, $1\frac{1}{2}$ in. at bottom and 2 in. deep), mask them with aspic in the usual way and place a leaf of chervil at the bottom. Set a little more aspic on this. Slice some hard-boiled eggs and spread on the yolk of each slice a thin smear of a paste made from paprika and aspic. Now put one of these prepared slices in the dariole mould, follow it with a little more jelly and when this has set, place a rolled fillet of anchovy in place. Continue until you have filled the mould to your satisfaction—I suggest two slices of egg with a rolled fillet of anchovy between them as sufficient, otherwise the thing becomes too big and clumsy and you must never forget that daintiness will very often tempt where mere size, however well made and neatly put together will be passed over. Unmould these little aspics on to a bed of 'chicorée frisée' (known quite wrongly as endive).

353.

Oeufs durs en 'barils'. Take some hard-boiled eggs, cut off a little of both ends and, by means of a column cutter, remove the bulk of the yolk. Fill the hollow with a salad of shrimps or a purée of smoked salmon or a tunny fish or other butter. Next prepare some very thin fillets of anchovy and use them to imitate the hoops on your barrels. You will find that they keep in place better if you make shallow V-shaped cuts round the egg at the places they will occupy. Dip them in a little aspic to fix them and use a caper for a bung. You may dress these on a croûton of jelly or on a salad or set them in jelly in a dariole mould of sufficient size, but whatever you decide upon do not lose sight of the fact that one of these eggs can form a meal and that unless you wish to satisfy your guests with hors-d'œuvre alone, it were better that you reserve this dish for an occasion when a single dish will be offered as a preliminary to the meal.

354.

Oeufs à la Tartare. An easy of preparation and effective egg dish is made by saucing over some poached eggs or oeufs mollets with Sauce Tartare to which has been added a little aspic jelly. Cut some oval croûtons of jelly with a crimped cutter and dress your eggs on these around a ready prepared vegetable salad. Decorate the eggs or not as you wish, personally I do not think in this case it is necessary; the speckled appearance of the sauced eggs being decorative enough. A proper finish to this dish may be given by placing a border of triangles of aspic around the edge of the dish, but this is not really needed.

355.

Oeufs en chaud-froid (I). Another eye-compelling dish is prepared by saucing over poached eggs with different chaud-froid sauces of contrasting colours. Sauce Cardinal and cream sauce, or sauce tomate and a sauce chaud-froid made green with a purée of spinach and fines herbes. Take care with this last combination, have your colours on the pale side or you will achieve a 'screaming success'.

356.

Oeufs en chaud-froid (II). By way of a variation you may sauce over your eggs half one colour and half the other. Season the different elements of a vegetable salad separately and dress 'en dome' in the centre of a dish. Now arrange your eggs round this, having first housed them on croûtons of jelly or in shallow tomato halves or in artichoke bottoms. The border of the dish may be finished by your piping a few scrolls of chopped jelly on it if desired.

EGG SALADS

357.

On your service dish place seasoned slices of tomato, and on them put slices of hard-boiled egg, one on each. Pipe a ball of anchovy or sardine butter on top, decorate with a slice of pimento-stuffed olive and sauce over with a mayonnaise sufficiently thin to show the colours through.

358.

Cut some hard-boiled eggs into quarters or sixths lengthwise and arrange them on the service dish. Pour over them a dressing of chopped ham, gherkin, and capers bound with mayonnaise. Finish with a thin strip of sweet pimento along the sharp edge of the egg.

359.

Thick slices of hard-boiled egg arranged on individual lettuce leaves are sauced over with mayonnaise dressing and sprinkled thickly with cooked lobster eggs or coral.

360.

Very often there are accumulations of ends and broken pieces of white of hard-boiled egg for which there does not seem to be a use. If you will cut these into a julienne this little salad will help in their disposal. Julienne of white of hard-boiled egg, julienne of cooked prune, of cooked potato and of hareng mariné mixed with peeled and de-pipped sections of orange, the whole bound with French mustard dressing. Dress in individual piles on lettuce leaves or on a bed of shredded lettuce.

361.

Or another, julienne of white of hard-boiled egg, of potato, pimento and celery with sections of orange and bound with mayonnaise. Dish as before.

362.

Or again, julienne of white of hard-boiled egg, of prune, pimento and agoursis. This time use vinaigrette as the dressing. Dish on rounds of nasturtium leaf.

363.

Sometimes there may be rings of hard-boiled white of egg to spare. Mount them on a slice of tomato, potato or other base and stuff them with cottage cheese mixed with chopped agoursis, place a round of hard-boiled white on top and sauce over with a mixture of piccalilli dressing and French mustard dressing with a dash of chopped fennel.

364.

As last, substituting cottage cheese mixed with chopped or crushed pickled walnut.

365.

A slice of skinned tomato has a slice of cold left-over liver mousse placed upon it with a blob of mayonnaise in between. Another blob of mayonnaise is placed on the mousse which is surmounted by a slice of hard-boiled egg. The centre of the egg slice, i.e. the yolk, is covered with a round of pimento. Sauce over with thinned French mustard dressing.

Egg Salads

366.

A nasturtium leaf with a slice of tomato and a spot of tartare sauce on it has a slice of hard-boiled egg placed thereon. This is surmounted by a neat ball of sardine butter with a slice of sweet pickled onion (American pickle) on top. The whole is masked with a thinned tartare sauce and decorated with a strip of pimento.

367.

On a slice of tomato surmounted by a slice of hard-boiled egg arrange a dome of chopped ham, beetroot and agoursis bound with piccalilli dressing let down with vinaigrette. Place a tiny tomato the size of a threepenny piece to decorate.

368.

A round of lettuce, a round of hard-boiled egg, a blob of cottage cheese, a stoned prune, a small ball of meat paste are assembled with a touch of stiff French mustard dressing and a round of pimento on top.

369.

Cook a sufficient quantity of asparagus tips. Season these with oil, vinegar, salt, and pepper, with a dusting of fines herbes, and dress them in porcelain cocottes. Cook some oeufs mollets and either mask them with jelly or 'chaufroiter' them, decorate and mask with jelly. Arrange the eggs in position and surround them with a little chopped or whipped jelly.

370.

A round of cooked cucumber, or an inch-thick slice of cooked cucumber hollowed out, filled with a mixture of cottage cheese and chopped débris of hard-boiled egg. Decorate with a slice of cold cooked sausage and a few capers. Sauce over with a mixture of French mustard dressing and mayonnaise let down with a few spots of Worcester sauce (or with the addition of a few specks of cayenne pepper and some vinegar).

371.

A slice of hard-boiled egg, a blob of mayonnaise, a round of cooked sausage; on this pile a julienne of cabbage pith seasoned with vinaigrette with a cerise au vinaigre on top to finish.

372.

Cut some cold curried tripe into small pieces. Drain it of most of the sauce and fortify it with chopped chutney. Mix it with boiled rice and dress it on slices of hard-boiled egg.

373.

Take a hard-boiled egg and cut it from the pointed end downwards nearly but not quite through, with three or four cuts. This, when opened out will give you a six or eight-petalled 'marguerite'. Remove the yolk and arrange a few thin slices of pickled beetroot covering the centre. On this pile one of the potato salads already mentioned and dust a little chopped parsley on top. This salad takes up rather a lot of room and is included here because it is ideal for individual presentation if dressed on a round egg dish. Use it to give a touch of colour to a corner of your display.

374.

Oeufs Pochés Froids à la Rachel. This is the one elaborate egg dish that I will permit myself to offer you. Use the ex-Easter egg half-moulds as recommended already and line them carefully with a thin coating of jelly. On this lining arrange the decoration which consists of squares or diamond-shaped pieces of truffle and hard-boiled white of egg in decreasing sizes. It saves much trouble if you separate some whites and cook them in a mould as you would a custard. Slices may then be cut from this more easily than from an egg. You may find that this occupies too much time and be forced to content yourself with a few fancifully cut pieces of truffle at the bottom of the mould. Fix the decoration in place with a little more jelly and place a small poached egg in position—again I recommend you to use pullets' eggs on account of their smaller size—and fill up with jelly. To dress: arrange a Salade Rachel in the centre of your dish and surround it with a border of cold boiled potato and truffle, both trimmed with a round cutter the size of a two-shilling piece. Now unmould and arrange the eggs neatly around this and finish by placing a border of crescents of jelly cut out with a crimped cutter from some aspic made more firm than usual, and fill any crevices with chopped jelly mixed with a spoonful of melted jelly and piped from a paper cornet.

375.

Salade Rachel consists of equal parts of julienne of celeriac (or failing that, of celery) which you must blanch for five minutes if there is any suspicion of toughness, julienne of truffle, slices of cold boiled artichoke bottom in neat slices and asparagus tips. Normally, this salad is dressed 'par bouquets', i.e. in neatly formed little heaps. But in this case you should mix the components together carefully, dress and then season 'in situ' with thinned mayonnaise sauce.

A simpler way to prepare this good-looking egg dish is to poach the eggs, 'chaufroiter' them with a cream sauce, decorate with a détail of truffle and finish with a covering of limpid aspic. Prepare a Salade Rachel more simply by adding a truffle cut into julienne, to a julienne of celeriac and seasoning with a vinaigrette to which, at the last moment, you have added a spoonful of thick cream. Dress this in a porcelain egg-dish and surmount it with the ready-prepared poached egg. Not so effective perhaps, but still an excellent dish.

PLOVERS' EGGS

More correctly it should be Lapwings' or Peewits' eggs. I do not feel it is out of place to mention this greatly esteemed delicacy. Plovers' and lapwings' eggs are slightly larger than a pigeon's egg, are darkish green in colour, liberally splashed with black, and were never cheap. The haphazard method of collection and the extremely fragile shell, which sometimes accounted for fifty per cent of casualties in a boiling, maintained the high price. There is nothing much to recommend them except novelty, and some people will go to any length for *that*. In the old days, many a swain had his pocket lightened when his inamorata could not resist the 'Oeufs de pluvier au nid' placed on the table by a cunning maître d'hôtel. If you have a liking for these eggs, keep your eyes about you on your next plough or grassland walk in the early spring, especially when you hear the cry of 'pee-wee-wit' and the unmistakable beat of the wings of the lapwing, remembering that these birds have nothing to learn in the art of camouflage. Remember also that the period of incubation of the eggs is only about twenty days or so, or you may get a surprise! It is safest, if you are lucky in finding any, to test them in a brine made from one part of cooking salt to seven parts of water. A fresh egg will sink to the bottom, others will occupy varying levels according to their age until we reach the one which floats half submerged and is to be discarded.

376.

To cook plovers' eggs. Having got your eggs, cook them gently (the shells being so brittle that fast-boiling water will crack them) for eight minutes and cool them.

377.

To dress plovers' eggs. Dress them pointed end upward, having taken the shell off for about half an inch at the top, on a bed of cress or in a nest made of moss and serve with them a plate of thinly cut brown bread and butter. There are many ways of preparing plovers' eggs in more or less fanciful guises as indicated for hens' eggs, but I do not think that any purpose will be served by occupying your attention with them now. In any case I do not think that plovers' eggs are quite so suitable as hens' eggs. The 'white' remains slightly translucent (as does that of a duck's egg) and the yolk never becomes really hard, even after long boiling. Two characteristics of a hard-boiled egg are therefore absent.

10. Cheese

COTTAGE CHEESE, CROWDIE, FROMAGE BLANC OR TWAROGUE
378.

All mean the same, the simplest form of cheese, soured milk.
To make cottage cheese. Collect all your soured milk over several days into a large bowl. When you have enough, stand the bowl on a cool part of the stove and allow the contents to heat slowly until the curd breaks, then put it away to cool. Next pour the curdled mixture into some sort of a cloth—an old pillow-slip, if without holes, is ideal for the job—and hang it up to drain. When the draining is completed, take the cottage cheese out of the bag and work salt into it. If you have a little cream to spare you may work that in too, and it will make an excellent cheese; but for use in hors-d'œuvre you may use it as drained.

379.
Cottage cheese, agoursis and fennel. Cottage cheese mixed with chopped agoursis and chopped fennel may be dressed on rounds of lettuce and decorated with a tiny sprig of fennel stuck in the top.

380.
Tomato, cottage cheese and pickled walnut with French mustard. Take small tomatoes and cut each into six from the flower end, but not quite through, so that the tomato still holds together. Open it out slightly and insert a ball of cottage cheese in the centre. Now re-form carefully and dish up, placing a slice of pickled walnut on the top and saucing over with French mustard dressing thinned slightly.

381.
Prunes, cottage cheese and paprika. Soak some prunes in cold water for twelve hours. Then make a cut in the side of each and remove the stone. Mix some cottage cheese with salt and sufficient paprika pepper to give it a pinkish tinge and use this to stuff the prunes.

382.
Chutney, cottage cheese and ham with French mustard. Mix some

Cheese

cottage cheese with chopped chutney and place a teaspoonful of the mixture on squares (2-in. sides) of thinly cut cooked York ham. Make these into little rolls and dress them on rounds of lettuce. Sauce them over with thinned French mustard dressing.

383.

Dominoes. Make rye biscuits, cut to the required size, into dominoes, by spreading on them a mixture of cottage cheese and crushed pickled walnut and using plain cottage cheese in dots to imitate the pips.

384.

Prunes, cottage cheese, pickled walnut and orange, vinaigrette. Use some of this same mixture of cottage cheese and pickled walnut to stuff cooked or well-soaked prunes. Place a carefully skinned section of peeled orange on top, and sauce over with vinaigrette dressing.

See also Grouse Cheese Paste and Kipper Cheese Paste (page 113) and Potted Stilton (page 114).

11. Fruit, Fresh, Canned, and Juice

More and more are we taking to a fruit diet, but those of us who wish for a complete one, may not, for a variety of reasons, achieve the full realization of our longings for many a year. We cannot grow all the fruit we should need for so desirable an end. If we had the space to grow them, I believe it would be possible to keep ourselves in various fruits; because for many years the plant breeder has been at his selective task and has succeeded in giving us apples, for example, all the year round except for two months. The mention of apples reminds one that nowhere does this fruit succeed so well as in this country; they are not, however, classed as a fruit hors-d'œuvre, and pride of place must be given to:

FRESH FRUIT

Melon (Canteloupe). This is squat in shape, has ribs and a warty exterior with a yellowish or greenish skin. The flesh of most is a pinky-orange and is very 'fondante', but this, I understand, depends upon the variety, hot sun and upbringing. One variety met with has green-tinged flesh but is not outstripped by its sister in flavour. The 'à point' or moment of perfect ripeness is exceedingly difficult to establish in a canteloupe. You can experiment if you wish by taking one in your hands and by using gentle pressure of your two thumbs on the area of the flower end, endeavour to discover a clue to it. I believe that in America use is made of the electronic cell in an inspection apparatus which can 'see' if a melon is ripe or indicate which day it will be at its best for eating. Of one point you must be certain, that your melon is served cold. The ideal way, in France, was to lower it in the bucket down the well and keep it there for an hour or two, but you will have to be content with chilling it in the refrigerator; but beware of freezing it.

385.

To serve melon. When ready to serve, cut it in half and remove the seeds with a silver spoon and continue cutting into slices of desired size: as a general rule you can use the ribs as a guide. Some guests like sugar with it, others ground ginger and sugar mixed, some pepper or salt, or both.

There is a smaller, rounder variety of melon which is grown in heat in this country. It is known as the **netted melon**, is green or yellow with greyish reticulations; the fact that the growing fruit is usually supported by a small net in the melon house has no bearing on its name. The flesh is pink, yellow, or green, and is slightly firmer than that of the canteloupe. The flavour is, however, held by many to be superior.

There is also the **sugar** or **honeydew melon**, similar to the last but darker green without markings and more of the shape of a Rugby football. The flesh is whiter, very sweet but the flavour is less pronounced. Lastly comes the **Pasteque** or **water melon**, whose only virtue apart from its thirst-quenching properties, lies in the excellence of the rind when made into a sweet pickle, q.v., yet how greedily and noisily we gulped them when we were young. As with caviar and oysters, so with melon, it is best to serve them all plainly, 'au naturel', but there are a few recipes for dealing with a melon more or less elaborately and you do not need to use a fine-flavoured canteloupe for the job.

386.

Melon en 'Trou Gascon'. Cut round the stalk, giving a good plug about two inches across, and with a spoon empty the interior of all seeds. Fill the melon with ripe raspberries or with wild strawberries or with a mixture of both, sprinkle a little sugar and add a glass of good Kirsch. Replace the plug and plunge the melon in cracked ice for about two or three hours, taking care that the melting ice does not invade the interior. Serve slices of melon and accompanying fruit together.

387.

Pastèque à la Provençale. Treat a water melon as above, but this time fill the interior with red wine. A good Tavel or an old genuine Châteauneuf du Pape would be used in the old days. Plug and chill in your refrigerator. (The old French method was to seal in the plug with wax, put the melon in the well-bucket and cool it at the bottom of the well.) When serving, strain the wine and offer a glassful with each slice of melon.

388.

Make a **melon basket** by pushing two skewers through a melon halfway down the side, keeping them about one inch apart. Use these as markers, then cut from the top vertically down to them and from the side horizontally to them. Remove the segments, also the melon flesh from under the strip of skin left in place. With a vegetable scoop make balls of all the melon pulp. These may be seasoned in a variety of ways: (*a*) with sugar, or syrup, and Maraschino; (*b*) with port wine and cream, and (*c*) with Kirsch, cream, sugar and ginger.

389.

Water melon in cubes. Peel a water melon very thickly (the peel may be preserved later), and cut in half. Remove the seeds, then cut the pulp into small cubes about half an inch square. Sprinkle with sugar and lemon juice, chill thoroughly and serve in coupes, the edges of which have been frosted with sugar and decorated with mint leaves.

390.

Any of the different seasoned melon balls can be dressed in **grapefruit or orange skins or baskets made from skins**. The best way to make a grapefruit or orange basket is first to empty it, having cut the fruit in half. Then cut a strip ¼ in. thick near the rim to a point not quite halfway across. Do this on both sides. You will now have two strips like loops still attached to the orange. Lift these up and tie them together in the middle with a bit of ribbon.

391.

Grapefruit can be emptied, seasoned, chilled and put back into the skins and decorated with a Maraschino or crème de menthe cherry. The skins may be notched round the edge, cut in a dog's tooth pattern or scalloped. Keep the skins in cold water whilst they are waiting for you to do things to the pulp removed from the inside.

392.

Certain **fruit cocktails** must be mentioned here. (*a*) Melon and grapefruit. Use the débris of melon made by cutting out the melon balls for the above recipes with either fresh or canned grapefruit.

393.

(*b*) Grapefruit and orange, made by cutting the skinned and de-pipped sections into smaller pieces. You may also give a little variety to these mixtures by adding a few green or black grapes or a few wild strawberries, either as an ingredient or as decoration. If you have a garden and can spare the room for a few alpine strawberry plants, you will not regret it. They bear fruit all summer until the first frosts, and a handful of these colourful little berries in a fruit salad adds a delicious flavour and air of distinction to it.

394.

There is a **Melon Confyt** or **Compote** which must be included here. Skin the melon and cut the de-seeded pulp into cubes or slices and

395.

cook it for about fifteen minutes in a **syrup**, i.e. two pounds of sugar and one and a quarter pints of water to which you have added a little root ginger. Drain the melon, reduce the flavoured syrup, pour over the fruit and chill.

396.

Orange and coco-nut salad. Peel an orange 'to the quick', that is, cut off the peel, removing at the same time the white pith. Slice the peeled orange across with a stainless knife and arrange the slices on a glass dish, then sprinkle liberally with coarsely grated coco-nut, and a little sugar.

397.

A **cherry** for a hors-d'œuvre! Test it for yourself, but select a hot day, gather it dead ripe from the tree, and choose the beautiful red, sweet, yet faintly acid variety, Empress Eugénie.

398.

Ripe figs are an excellent prelude to a meal. Chill thoroughly and dress them on a few green leaves, failing fig leaves, raspberry or vine may be used. At the same time, slices of raw smoked fillet of pork or raw ham or thin slices of saucisson should be served.

399.

A **pineapple** may be hollowed out; leave a wall of about three-eighths of an inch in thickness, having taken off the top slice with the leaves. Discard the core and break up the 'meat' and mix it with a variety of fresh fruit either sliced or cut into cubes. Macerate with a glass of either Kirsch or Maraschino (having sweetened with plain syrup) and chill. Fill this into the pineapple shell and keep in the refrigerator until required.

400.

Another pineapple hors-d'œuvre. Trim off the brown skin and remove the 'eyes', then slice the fruit. Put each slice on a fruit plate and arrange on it segments of pear, peach, orange or other fruit. These segments should radiate from the centre and be of several fresh fruits terminating with a cherry in the centre. Sprinkle with liqueur, chill and serve.

401.

Alligator or **Avocado Pear.** If you meet these do not allow novelty to put you off. Merely cut them in two, chill, remove stones, season with salt and sprinkle with lemon juice, or, having removed the stone, scoop out the flesh and mash it up, season with salad dressing, replace in the skins and serve on ice; the addition of a prawn or shrimp salad (with mayonnaise) to the pulped fruit is optional but desirable.

402.

Green olives. Remove them from the brine in which they are preserved and serve them on a ravier with a little ice, either crushed or in blocks. They must have liquid on them or they will discolour very quickly.

403.

Black olives. Ripe olives are served with a little of the liquor in which they are preserved or drained of it and a few drops of olive oil dribbed over them.

FRUIT JUICES

These are sometimes in demand before a meal and especially at breakfast time.

404.

Orange and grapefruit juices are the most popular, and are easily prepared by cutting the fruit in two and pressing out the juice in a fruit press.

405.

Pineapple juice comes from British Honduras in cans and has only to be chilled before serving.

406.

If **apple juice** is asked for, it is best to grate the apple, enclose the pulp in a piece of tammy or other cloth, squeeze in the juice press and chill. This method is also useful for preparing the juice of fresh grapes.

407.

Cocktail de raisins frais. Wash the grapes in several waters, remove them from the stalks and extract the juice as above. Allow this to stand until the sediment has fallen, then decant the clear juice. Now half fill a goblet with shaved ice, squeeze half an orange on to this, add a teaspoonful of honey and a little of the orange zest. Fill up with the grape juice, shake, strain and serve.

408.

Prune juice. Decant some of the juice or syrup made when stewing prunes (see below). If found to be too sweet, this can be rectified by the addition of lemon juice.

409.

Sauerkraut juice. This is sometimes asked for on account of its possessing a high vitamin value. It is a perfectly natural product and there is usually plenty of it at the bottom of the barrel; but check that there is not too much salt present. You can overcome this by the addition of sufficient weak lemon juice.

410.

Tomato juice, another popular favourite, is easily made in bulk when tomatoes are plentiful and fully ripe. Put the quantity you have to spare in a thick-bottomed pan on a cool part of the stove and allow them to come very slowly to the boil—it is not necessary to add any water, but the contents must be stirred occasionally in order to keep them from sticking to the bottom. When the tomatoes are cooked, pass them through the soup machine and season with salt and sugar. You may now bottle or can this juice and sterilize it for future use.

411.

To serve you simply chill it, but if you wish to spoil the natural flavour of the fruit with celery salt, Worcester sauce and the like— carry on!

STEWED AND BAKED FRUIT

Some varieties of baked or stewed fruit are served at breakfast time.

412.

Baked apple is the type of the former. Select apples of even size, of one kind, wipe them well, core them and with a sharp knife make a cut through the skin and no more round the region of the 'equator', or, if preferred, you can make six similar cuts from north to south as it were, on the lines of longitude, though some varieties of apple tend to open up too much if this method be adopted—if successful it certainly looks well. The first way is perhaps the better of the two as the top half of the skin can be lifted off the cooked apple. Whichever way is chosen, fill the hole left by the corer with sugar and top it up with a knob of butter. Bake in a moderate oven, preferably under cover and with a little water in the bottom of the pan.

413.

Stewed fruits to be served cold. Prunes and figs are best soaked in several changes of cold water, then cooked slowly in water with the addition of a little lemon peel and a short piece of stick cinnamon. Add sugar at the last. Prunes are cooked in the de luxe manner by using half red wine, half water.

414.

Canning of dried fruits for ready service. If you possess a home canning-machine, you will be able to save yourself much time in the stewing of dried apple rings, apricots, peaches and prunes. Pack these fruits into the cans, fill with boiling water and seal on the lids. Then sterilize for twenty minutes at fifteen pounds pressure, or, if you care to soak the fruits overnight, this time may be reduced to ten minutes. The great advantage of this process is that when you need the stewed dried fruit all you have to do is to open a can—there is no time wasted in soaking and cooking.

COMPOTES OF FRUIT
415.

The different **compotes of fruit** may be listed here, as they are in great demand for breakfast by Americans and others who wisely prefer to begin the day with fruit, either cooked or raw. **The syrup** I shall refer to is made by dissolving four pounds of sugar in five pints of water, i.e. bring slowly to the boil, skim and cool. Fruits to be stewed may be divided roughly into two categories: (*a*) those that are cooked in syrup in the oven and (*b*) the more tender kinds that are merely brought to the boil again after having been plunged into boiling syrup.

416.

Pears require slightly different treatment and after having been peeled are cooked in water acidulated with lemon juice. This preliminary cooking is necessary because of the wide difference in time taken to cook by pears of different varieties and at varying stages of ripeness. If small, leave them whole complete with stalk; if large, cut them in halves and remove the core with a vegetable scoop. When they are cooked allow them to cool under the cold water tap and immerse them in a syrup as indicated.

417.

Whole apples should be peeled and cored, brought to the boil in syrup and immediately put into a moderate oven with the lid on the pan to poach. Take great care that they do not 'fall' into mush; they will do so if you give them the slightest touch of overcooking.

418.

Peaches should be skinned; dip first into boiling water to facilitate this, then rub the 'fur' off with a towel. Cook them in syrup as above until tender. In some varieties the stone becomes loose when the fruit is sufficiently cooked, but this is not a reliable guide for all.

419.

Plums (red, golden, yellow, greengage, purple, including that best of all, the Mirabelle), **Apricots** and **Green Gooseberries**, into boiling syrup with them! Put them back on the stove until the first 'bouillon', then cover the pan (I hope you are using a flat one known as a 'plat sauté', so that you do not have more than one layer of fruit), then put the pan back in the oven to complete the cooking very gently.

420.

Cherries, Raspberries, Strawberries, Currants (red, white and black) should be put into boiling syrup and brought to the boil again. They are then ready.

A simple but extremely good way with raspberries is to have them fully ripe and piled in a bowl. Smother them with plenty of sugar, but do not mix. Leave for twenty-four hours or longer, then take off as much of the undissolved sugar as possible and serve the raspberries with the thick syrup which will have formed at the bottom of the bowl.

421.

Presentation of fruit compote. There is no reason why a fruit compote should not be served as a fruit hors-d'œuvre, and no more pleasing presentation of this can be devised than the following. Take paper doyleys of which the plain centre is roughly the same size as the coupe you are about to use for holding the salad. Dip the rim of the glass into white of egg or a thick syrup and then invert it on to a pile of doyleys. The top one will stick, so without disturbing it, place the decorated glass on one side for the fixative to harden. When you are ready to serve the compote, take a sharp knife and cut out the plain paper centre, leaving you with a lace border around the glass. Fil with whatever compote you have decided upon, but be wary of splashes of syrup on the border or you will spoil the effect. You can decorate with preserved cherries and angelica (or with other preserved fruits), crystallized rose petals, violets or mint leaves.

FRUIT SALADS

Fruit salads made from either fresh, canned or a mixture of both kinds of fruit may be served as a pleasing hors-d'œuvre. All fruits in season should be used, cut into pieces, not too small and certainly not in mush or grated. The exception to this being of course the case where a fruit such as raspberries, strawberries, or currants are pulped for use as a sauce or dressing, but the guest must at all times be able to identify what he is about to eat. Make your mixtures of every kind of fruit to hand, though I advise you to allow one kind to predominate in the mixture.

422.

You can, for example, prepare an **Apple salad** from raw apples cut into convenient-sized pieces together with discs of banana and sections of orange, peeled with pith and membranes removed, and if there are any débris of melon they may be added also, allowing the volume of apple to equal that of the other ingredients added together. This

423.

you can turn into an **Orange salad** by changing over the quantities of apple and orange, leaving the other ingredients as before.

SALADS OF OTHER FRUITS

Combinations of the following fruits will be left to yourself to devise: orange, tangerine orange, grapefruit, lemon, apple, pear, cherries, plums (all kinds), greengage, damsons, black, red or white currants, grapes, peaches, nectarines, apricots, raspberries, strawberries, loganberries, alpine strawberries, gooseberries, bananas, pineapples, fresh figs (these last are not very suitable as they ought to be peeled). Some of the cultivated sorts of blackberry may be included. Canned pineapple and canned grapefruit are very suitable for inclusion in this list and the juice of either is useful to 'season' the salad. Supplement this with a ladleful or two of simple syrup (above) and, if necessary, the expressed juice of several apples, sticks of rhubarb or other acid fruit.

MIXED SALADS CONTAINING FRUIT
424.

Red cabbage and apple salad. Take required amount of pickled red cabbage, drain and add one-quarter of its volume in julienne of sour apple. Season with a few drops of oil and very lightly with salt and pepper. Dress in one heap and grate a little horseradish on top.

425.

Prunes stuffed with apple, celery and agoursis. Stuff prunes with a salpicon (dice) of apple, celery, and agoursis bound with French mustard dressing.

426.

Chicken, celery, apple. Cut a julienne of chicken, celery and tart apple. Bind this with stiff mayonnaise and dress in tiny heaps on small even-sized nasturtium leaves.

427.

Diced tongue, potato, apple and red cabbage. Cut into dice cooked tongue and cold boiled potato, in equal parts, and add two parts of diced tart apple. Chop some pickled red cabbage slightly and add one part of this to the salad. Season this mixture with a vinaigrette containing an extra dose of chopped chives. Dress as usual in small heaps on tender cabbage leaves—rounds cut from the pale cream centre leaves. This salad is useful as it affords a means of using up the end (tip) of a tongue.

428.

Diced apple, potato, peas. Dice a raw apple, and take an equal quantity of diced potato and cooked peas. Bind this mixture with piccalilli dressing. Dress on rounds of lettuce leaves.

429.

Apple, sausage, potato. Take as the base of this salad a ring of raw apple; on this you heap a salad composed of dice of raw apple, cold cooked sausage and cold potato in equal parts. Bind with mayonnaise.

430.

Apple stuffed with chicken. Cut off a slice from the blossom end of medium-sized cooking apples and hollow out the core by means of a vegetable scoop. Stuff these apple shells with a mixture of minced chicken, highly seasoned, bound with Béchamel sauce. Cook these in the oven, allow them to cool and dress them on the service dishes.

431.

Apple rice. An excellent salad, but one of which the seasoning requires special care, is made by peeling a cooking apple, quartering and coring it, then slicing the quarters across into thin slices. Mix these with an equal quantity of rice. For the seasoning, place a small quantity of cream in a bowl, season with salt and a speck of cayenne pepper and acidulate very carefully with the pressed juice of another apple or failing that with lemon juice. A little sugar is necessary in this dressing. Arrange the salad in small heaps on a bed of shredded lettuce.

432.

Tomato, half-cooked apple, agoursis and sauerkraut, beetroot. Take a slice of tomato and on it place a $\frac{1}{4}$-in. thick slice of half-cooked cored apple. Fill the centre with a salad of chopped agoursis and sauerkraut. Decorate the top with a ball of beetroot.

433.

Apple, potato, new walnuts. Cut a short julienne of sour apples and an equal quantity of cold cooked potato also in julienne. Blend these in mayonnaise sauce and at the last moment stir in a few new walnuts, brown skin removed, which you have cut into thin slices.

434.

Apple, celery, beetroot, horseradish. Cut a coarse julienne of celery and of raw apples. Season these with a sour cream dressing, flavoured with a little grated horseradish. Dress this mixture on $\frac{1}{4}$-in. thick rounds of cooked beetroot.

435.

Lettuce, banana, beetroot and horseradish. A round of lettuce, cut out with a suitable cutter, on which place a round of banana. On this put a blob of stiff French mustard dressing, flavoured with grated horseradish and surmount it with a star of beetroot. Use for the cutting either a star or a crimped pastry cutter. Next place a smaller blob of the stiff F.M.D. on this and finish by placing a slice of black olive on top. If care is used, and the rings of colour kept reasonably concentric, you will have a very pleasing variety.

436.

Small melons stuffed with rice. Sometimes you have the chance of buying undersized melons not much bigger than a cricket ball. If so then choose them slightly under-ripe. Cut round the stalk, leaving a plug which you will need later. Through the hole thus made empty out all the seeds and strings. Then with a spoon remove all the soft interior pulp and cut this into dice. Season with salt and a pinch of ground ginger, add the same volume of cooked rice and keep in a cool place—the melon shells too should be in the refrigerator all this time. When the times comes for serving, dress with a mixture of cream, lemon juice and salt. Take care when adding lemon juice to your cream. Now fill the melons with the mixture, put back the plug and serve on crushed ice.

437.

Orange, sausage, potato. Peel some oranges 'to the quick' and separate the sections, which you cut into small pieces. Take some cold sausages, which you cut into dice, also some cold potato which you treat in a like manner. Equal parts of these three ingredients are bound with a piccalilli dressing. Serve as usual in individual piles on small bases of lettuce leaves.

438.

Pineapple, cottage cheese, mint. Make very thin slices of fresh pineapple into cornucopia and stuff them with cottage cheese thinned slightly with mayonnaise. Dress these points to centre on a large round white porcelain egg-dish or an oval fish-dish may answer the purpose, and sprinkle them with chopped mint.

439.

Pineapple and agoursis. Arrange alternate slices of fresh pineapple and agoursis on service dish. Cover these with a vinaigrette made with orange and lemon juice in place of vinegar and with chopped mint instead of fines herbes.

440.

Chicken, pimento, pineapple and endive. Make a julienne of cooked chicken and pimento. Mix this with slices of a small pineapple cut into radii and raw endive cut across the leaf. Season with mayonnaise let down with a few drops of lemon juice and enlivened with a 'pointe' of cayenne pepper or a few drops of Tabasco sauce. This salad may be dressed in one pile, the borders of the dish being decorated with 'eighths' of pineapple slice, points upwards.

Mixed Salads containing Fruit

441.

Carrot and pineapple. Grate equal parts of carrot and pineapple, season them with salt and mix together. Pile this mixture on rounds of lettuce leaf and cover with cream cheese dressing.

442.

Macaroni, tomato, pineapple, mint. Blanch some macaroni well enough to enable you to cut it easily into ¾-in. lengths. This do and return it to the pan to finish cooking, then cool it under the cold water tap. Add about half the volume of tomato flesh cut into small dice and an equal amount of fresh pineapple diced or grated on the medium shredder. Season with French mustard dressing let down, if necessary with a little of the pineapple juice and sprinkle with chopped mint.

443.

Pineapple, cheese, olives, capers, agoursis, pimento and almond. Make some fingers of pineapple, either by cutting them from a fresh pine or by dividing canned chunks into three lengthwise, and spread on them one of the following mixtures: (*a*) processed cheese pounded down with an equal amount of butter or margarine and thinned with cream to a soft consistency; (*b*) grated cheese mixed with cream, or (*c*) sour milk cheese mixed with a little cream. To any of these add chopped olives, capers, agoursis or gherkins, and for variety a pinch of paprika pepper, then spread on the fingers of pine giving a domed shape. Dress these on lettuce leaves and decorate tastefully with strips of green or red pimento, rings of stoned olive or roasted chopped almond.

444.

Orange and cheese. As above, using slices of orange 'peeled to the quick'.

445.

Poivrons, pimentos or piperoni make a delightful salad. Slit them and remove any seeds, then slice them (émincer) and add one-quarter of the volume in sliced onions and a few sliced tomatoes to help heighten the colour. Season with a plain French dressing. As piperoni are to be had in three colours, I leave it to you to make a decorative effect. If you care to use a large green, yellow or red piperoni as a base and fill with a salad of the three mixed, you will have a colour effect which will help your display.

446.

Chicken, peas, pimentos, rice. Take equal parts of débris of cooked

163

chicken cut into dice, cooked green peas, sweet peppers (or pimentos) and rice. Season with French mustard dressing with tarragon added. If you are using fresh sweet peppers, it will be necessary for you to remove the outside skin; this you do by holding them for a few moments in the gas flame. This chars the outside skin which you may then remove quite easily. Dress this salad in one pile.

447.

Potato, red cabbage, julienne of white of egg and Victoria plum. On a slice of cold cooked potato dress a little salad of red cabbage and julienne of white of egg seasoned with French mustard dressing. Top with an 'eighth' of uncooked Victoria plum laid skin side upward.

448.

Prunes, sausage and potato. Prunes stuffed with a $\frac{1}{4}$-in.-thick slice of skinned, left-over grilled sausage. Stand these on $\frac{1}{4}$-in. rounds of cold cooked potato and cover with tomato mayonnaise.

449.

Prunes, tomato, ham, gherkins. Arrange thin slices of even-sized tomatoes on the service dish, and on them stand stoned prunes which have been stuffed with a mixture of chopped ham and gherkin bound with mayonnaise. You may have to press the prunes slightly on a flat surface before placing them in position in order to stop them rocking about. Sauce with thinned mayonnaise.

12. Zakouska, Canapés, Toasts and Derivatives

If you were to ask me for a general definition of these, the most numerous and therefore very important class of hors-d'œuvre, I should reply that the term 'open sandwich' would cover all but a small number of them. A slice of some base, bread or other, which enables one to convey to one's mouth the 'interesting' part of the preparation. It used to be the fashion in Russia—it may still be —for a great variety of Zakouska or foretastes to be served in the ante-room whilst the guests assembled; each variety being, as it were, a sample of a dish to be offered at dinner. They were consumed with draughts of Wodka or other powerful spirits and from observation of the Russian in action, it seemed essential to down your glass in one draught, sip it and you were lost! There is one potent brew from the Caucasus called Arak, in comparison with which Wodka is a soft drink. I class along with these Russian spirits the following Czechoslovakian ones: Slivovice (plum brandy), Třešňovice (cherry brandy), and Zitna (corn brandy).

Canapés then are the basis of Hors-d'œuvre à la Russe, or à la Muscovite as they were once called; but do not confuse them with Piroschki which will be described later in their appropriate place (i.e. the section dealing with hot hors-d'œuvre). Canapés may be in different shapes and cut from different bases, spread with butters, cheese pastes or spreads and garnished on top with different elements. In some cases they are then masked with aspic jelly and all may receive a final decoration of a harmonizing coloured butter, piped as a border perhaps from a plain or star tube. In fact the work approaches most nearly that of the pastrycook. There cannot be even an attempt at a complete list of these preparations, but if I indicate how they are made, give you some examples and some hints and tips, the pleasure of making discoveries must be yours, for the field is limitless. Remember to preserve harmony in your decoration, avoid over-elaboration and thus uphold the principles of good taste.

165

BASES

450.

The simplest of these is **toast**. If you use ordinary white bread see that it is at least one day old; in this state it is more easily worked, for it is not easy to deal with a soft, pliable new loaf. If you require to toast the slices to be buttered, then in some cases it is preferable to butter them before toasting. You will thus obtain a 'beurre noisette' effect and flavour and also a moister toast, but be on your guard that you do not burn the butter. Remember also that toast so treated cannot be used indiscriminately.

For some of your canapés the bread may first be cut to a fancy shape, triangle, diamond, oval, pointed oval or boat-shaped, star, round or whatever you fancy and then be fried in butter or oil or a mixture of both; but by doing so you will sacrifice speed in working. In practice you will find that if you cover a large slice of toasted bread —cut lengthwise from a sandwich loaf—with a paste or spread and then proceed to make this into squares, rectangles, diamonds, triangles, or crescents, you will take minutes to complete the job as against hours if you deal with each little toast separately. Notice too that the shapes I have given you can all be cut with a minimum of waste. In general, round shapes are best left for varieties that can be piped on from a bag and tube, or to accommodate slices of tomato or egg. Having spread your slice and trimmed off the crusts, cut it lengthwise unto two equal bands. Next cut these bands across into fingers or wider into rectangular pieces. Similarly by cutting the slice into three bands of equal width, you may proceed to cut across, making squares, or by cutting at an angle with the line nearest you, make diamonds and if you cut the diamonds through the middle, you get triangles—small ones perhaps, but quite large enough for mounting a stuffed olive. To get crescents use a round cutter but make sure that it is of a diameter that does not exceed the width of the band you are using. All you have to do is to make a cut at one end of the band, and move the cutter along the size of the crescent you wish, cut again and so on.

451.

Pumpernickel (Westphalian black bread) is used for certain varieties, but it may be some time before we are able to get it freely; and, although I have come across excellent German black bread made in this country, we shall have to make do with a close-textured wholemeal or brown bread in its place. It is of no use your asking a baker to make a loaf or two for you, even supposing you can come by the requisite rye flour, for no less than a 'batch' or ovenful is possible. Rye has little, if any, gluten (the constituent of wheaten flour which enables your white loaf to become light in texture) and rye bread is not so much baked as dried out over a long period. This fact, together with the peculiar method of fermentation, accounts for the closeness and moistness of black bread.

452.

Continuing our survey of croûtons; in some cases the **bread** (white) is spread with a mixture which is cut into shapes, then baked and either served hot or allowed to cool.

453.

You may also make what are known as **Caisses,** by carving shapes out of the crumb of a stale white loaf. These may be round, square, oblong, oval or fancy and if you make an incision with a sharp knife about a quarter of an inch in from the top edge, you will be able to remove a lid when you have fried the caisse in deep fat, which lid you can replace when you have filled the emptied interior with whatever filling has been decided upon.

454.

An **alternative method** for making caisses is to cook rice, rice flour or semolina in seasoned stock to the consistency of porridge, bind it with yolks, tip it on to a greased plaque and spread it to a thickness of half an inch. Cover with a greased paper and allow it to cool. Then with a round cutter dipped occasionally in hot water, cut out your caisses. With another cutter slightly less in diameter than the first, make an incision in the top surface, leaving a border of about a quarter of an inch. Egg-and-breadcrumb these, fry them in deep fat, lift off the lids and empty the interiors to make room for the filling. These fried bases are suitable for the more 'sloppy' type of salad or salpicon, for on standing the dried exterior will absorb some of the moisture and make for better eating. Chicken, meat or fish salads in julienne or a salpicon, bound with mayonnaise are indicated here.

455.

Croûtes are chunks of stale bread carved out according to individual fancy and fried in deep fat.

Note. Croûte means a crust. Caisse a case or box and has a lid. Method of making distinguishes the two also, not perhaps to the layman.

456.

Small crackers may be used, but should be heated slightly in the

457.

oven and allowed to cool first. The large size **rye biscuits** may be cut into a more convenient size, but take great care or you will have far too many 'casualties'.

458.

There are also **Carolines**, which are small éclairs about two inches

459.

long (they may be curved as a C) and **Duchesses**—small choux no bigger than one and a half inches in diameter when baked—both of which are either slit and filled with a purée, butter, cheese or other filling from a palette knife or by forcing it into them from a bag fitted with a quarter-inch plain tube. The Carolines are then sauced with a chaud-froid sauce at about setting point, just as though they were sweet éclairs, and finished with a touch of aspic jelly to give them a sheen. Use white, pink or brown sauce according to the filling. Duchesses are finished by glazing them on the upper surface with a little aspic and perhaps a pinch of chopped Pistachio nut.

460.

I have found the best recipe for **Pâte à Choux** to be: $\frac{1}{2}$ pint of milk on to boil with 5 oz. margarine. When boiling fiercely with all the margarine melted, throw in 5 oz. flour and stir it in briskly. If you are handling a large quantity you must remove the pan from the fire, or you will get lumps. Allow the paste to cook for a few minutes, stirring the while, in order to gelatinize the flour, then cool slightly and beat in five eggs, one at a time. You may now pipe out your mixture as explained above from a half-inch plain tube on to a baking-sheet. Your choux will be lighter if you bake them under cover—the little éclairs should not be covered up however. Bake them in a fairly hot oven (380 deg. F.) and remember to dry them out well or they will fall flat on cooling.

461.

Another variety of Duchesses is made from a **Pommes Duchesse mixture**. You know this one—boiled potatoes passed through the sieve, mixed with a pat of butter, seasoned and then bound with a few yolks. The mixture is rolled into balls, egg-and-breadcrumbed and fried in deep fat. Cut off the top as a lid and empty the interior carefully but leave some of the mixture as a wall. These little cases should now be dried slightly.

462.

Croustades are simply made by lining different shapes of patty pan with short paste and baking them blind, i.e. with a filling of dried beans or small sea-shells which are emptied out after cooling, so that the cases retain their shapes. Croustades comprise **Barquettes** (boat-shapes), **Tartelettes** (a term which is self-explanatory), **Ovals** and other shapes, deep or shallow.

463.

Pâte à Croustades. Take 5 oz. flour, 1¾ oz. butter, 1 yolk, 1 dessert-spoonful of olive oil, a pinch of salt and a little water (add a spoonful of essence of anchovies if the filling of the croustades is to be of fish) and make into a clear dough.

464.

There are also **Coquilles** and **Cassolettes** in fireproof china, glass or metal; all useful for holding a salpicon or other mixture for either

465.

hot or cold hors-d'œuvre. **Cassolettes (Batter)** can also be made by heating a special iron mould in deep fat, dipping it in a frying batter and returning it to the deep fat until the coating on the outside has become crisp. This is then removed and the process repeated until a sufficient number have been made.

466.

Petits Pains of a very small size made from Brioche mixture are useful. A certain skill is required in handling fermented doughs, but if you wish to tackle the job, here is the best recipe I know.

467.

Pâte à Brioche. Dissolve ½ oz. of yeast in one-tenth of a pint of milk at blood heat and with it, 8 oz. of flour and 3 small eggs make an elastic dough which you toughen well by mixing and beating. Place this dough in a clean, warm bowl and cover loosely with a cloth. When the dough has doubled its bulk, mix in ½ oz. of sugar, 6 oz. of butter and a pinch of salt thoroughly, flapping the dough about with the hands on the table. Allow to rise again, 'knock back' once more and it is ready for use. Remember that yeast likes best a temperature of about blood heat, stops working if it is too cold or if in too con-centrated a solution of sugar, other food or salt, and that you kill it if you heat it too much. Divide the dough into pieces of the required size and roll them into small balls and form these into torpedo shapes. Allow to prove, covered as a protection from draughts, and when sufficiently risen, bake them off in a temperature of 400 deg. F., having first washed them over with milk or egg-wash. When baked and cooled, slit them down the side and fill them with a purée or mince of chicken, veal, fish or as required.

468.

From this mixture can be made small **'Brioches à Tête'**. These are baked in fluted bun moulds, and consist of a ball of dough with a smaller one on top as a Tête or head. To use, pull off the head, hollow out the interior a little, fill with whatever mixture is desired and replace the head.

469.

There are also **Bouchées**, which are of puff paste and may be made in two ways. Roll out your puff paste to one-eighth of an inch in thickness and cut out the required number of bottoms with either a plain or a crimped cutter, according to your fancy, and arrange them on a baking-tray that has been splashed with water. Now cut out the same number of pieces with the same cutter, but remove the centre with a small round cutter leaving a ring which you place carefully on the bottoms (these having been washed over with either water or egg-wash). Give the top surface a touch with the egg-wash brush and bake. Take care in both cases that the egg does not run down the sides or the bouchées will not 'spring' properly, also when you are about to bake them, they should lie for a quarter of an hour so that the paste will recover from the toughening it received when you rolled it out. If you omit this precaution you will get shapes that are anything but round. As to size, you must decide for yourself, keep them small but allow for a slight shrinkage in baking; about one and a half inches in diameter when finished is ideal. You will require lids; these are made from a sheet of paste thinner than for the bottoms and rings, and you proceed as follows: Cut out the required number, take a cutter one size less and cut out the same number, again one size less and repeat, finally from a band of paste or from assembled trimmings pinned out again cut the same number of diamond shapes. Give all these a touch of the wash brush and assemble them in decreasing sizes, that is to say, three rounds with a diamond of paste on the top. Give a final glaze with the brush, and, after allowing them to recover, bake them.

470.

For the **alternative method** mentioned above, roll out the paste a quarter of an inch in thickness, cut out the bouchées and with a round cutter slightly less in diameter, make incisions which, when the bouchées are baked, will give you lids. Do not press this cutter more than halfway through the paste. Baking completed, and the little bouchées cooled, you may either lift out the lids with the point of a knife or push them in and use separately made lids as already explained. This latter plan has certain advantages when a filling with a 'sloppy' consistency has to be used or when the bouchées have to be filled some time before use. The disadvantage is that by compressing the newly baked paste, you form a 'sad' layer of it in the centre of the bouchée.

471.

Cornets are made by assembling puff pastry trimmings and rolling them out into a sheet about one-eighth of an inch in thickness, cutting this into strips about three-quarters of an inch wide and rolling these on cream horn or cornucopia tins. Do not make them too large, and if you find that the paste is apt to slip when baking, try putting one prepared tin inside another one so that the paste is baked between two metal surfaces. Leave one without the extra cover as a check, but do not fail to give the covered ones a few minutes' extra baking to make up for the screening.

472.

Cheese Pastry is very useful and the recipe is: 4 oz. of plain flour, 4 oz. of grated cheese, a pinch of baking powder and water to make into a stiff dough. The fat in the cheese supplies all that is necessary but if you care to make a richer paste, you may add 1 oz. of margarine to the above.

473.

Other bases such as cooked artichoke bottoms, either whole or in slices, slices of hard-boiled egg, slices of tomato, agoursis or gherkin do not require special mention, and any others will be brought to your notice at the time of dealing with the variety or the dressing of it.

CANAPÉS

Now that we have our bases or 'montages', we will proceed to put something interesting on them, to fill in the picture as it were.

474.

Canapés d'Anchois. Take a slice of anchovy-buttered toast—any of those above mentioned—and cut it into three strips lengthwise. Cover these with anchovy fillets and run sufficient aspic jelly over them to glaze them completely. Cut across into diamond shapes as already shown, and from a paper cornet pipe a rope border of anchovy butter round each one.

475.

An **alternative method** of preparing Canapés d'Anchois is to spread the toasted bread with a good layer of anchovy butter and, using the prepared trimmed anchovy fillets, arrange these in the form of a grille across it. Now proceed to cut the toast into shapes and pipe a border of the butter round each from a bag and fine star tube. The merest touch of a brush dipped in aspic jelly on the little fillets is all that is required to brighten them; if you mask these canapés in the ordinary way, you will fill the spaces with aspic and spoil the effect. A tiny pinch of sieved yolk and chopped parsley mixed together and sprinkled in the centre of each is sufficient decoration, if needed.

476.

Canapés de Caviar. On some slices of buttered rye bread (failing which, toast) spread evenly a layer of caviar. Cut this bread or toast into fingers and if you feel you must decorate, dip the edges of the two long sides into chopped parsley and place a tiny section of a thin slice of lemon at each end.

477.

Cod roe toasts. This is a variety which does not please everyone—one either loves or loathes it—and can be made from cooked fresh cod's roe. For the cooking see under Cod Roe in the section on Fish. Slice a suitable diameter of this, not too thinly, and fry it on both sides. When cold arrange the slices on round toasts of the same size previously spread with mustard butter. Give them a dab of aspic to glaze them and sprinkle on top a fleck or so of parsley and lobster coral mixed together.

478.

Alternatively, the débris of the cooked cod's roe may be made into a spread with one-quarter of its volume in butter or margarine and a few drops of olive oil, seasoning with mustard, salt and a squeeze of lemon juice. This mixture should be spread thickly on the toasts and may be finished as before.

479.

Take some débris of cooked **Findon haddock** and pound them well with one-quarter of their volume in butter. Heighten the seasoning with cayenne pepper and a touch of anchovy essence. Spread this mixture on toasted bread in a thick layer and cut into the desired shapes. Give the tops a touch with your aspic jelly and before this sets sprinkle chopped parsley in the centre. You may, if you wish, make this variety into a sandwich by splitting some left-over toast and sandwiching it with the same mixture, the finishing touch may be the same as before.

480.

Gaffelbitar. Spread a slice of rye bread with herring butter (page 111) and cut it into lozenge shapes. On these place a piece of Gaffel-bitar—this is a variety of preserved herring, sweetish in taste, pre-pared from fat autumn-caught herring, and comes from Denmark, although the other Scandinavian countries have similar products—and garnish with a strip of pickled gherkin.

481.

Canapés de Harengs. Chop coarsely some left-over or débris of marinated, cooked or pickled herring. Bind this with mayonnaise mixed with a spoonful of French mustard dressing with a touch of jelly to make it set. Pile this mixture on rounds of toasted brown bread and on top place a fancifully cut slice of cooked beetroot. Give this a spot of jelly to glaze it.

482.

Canapés de Laitances. Cook a few soft herring roes by poaching them in a court bouillon (failing that in salted water with a spoonful of vinegar added) or in white wine. Spread some canapés with mus-tard butter and dress the cooled cooked roes on top. Sprinkle with chopped fines herbes.

483.

Canapés de Pinces de Homard. Sometimes there are left-over lobster claws. Of these you can make an unusual variety. With a meat saw, make a cut across the shell to the rear of the hinge which joins the two parts of the pincers. Do not cut more than halfway through. Then, holding the pincers up, with a stiff knife cut down to the other end of the upper part of the shell from both ends of the saw cut, thus removing a piece of the upper shell. I hope this explanation is quite clear. Now take out the lobster meat and with it prepare a lobster salad which you put back again into the empty claw shell. Sprinkle a pinch of sieved hard-boiled egg over the salad.

484.

Canapés de Homard. Another variety of lobster canapé is made in this way: spread some toast with lobster butter and cut it into the desired shapes. Before the butter sets dip the edges into a mixture of sieved white of hard-boiled egg and chopped parsley. Place an escalope of lobster meat in the centre and give this a touch of the brush.

485.

Canapé de Moules. Put a bed of tunny fish paste on a fried bread canapé. Equalize the sides and leave a shallow depression in the centre. In this place a cooked mussel from which you have removed the beard. Sauce over with a thinned rémoulade sauce and pipe a border of green butter round the edge of the canapé.

486.

Canapés de Sardines. Spread a strip of toast with sardine butter and cut into fingers of a size that will accommodate two fillets of skinned and boned sardines. Pipe a neat border of yellow butter round the edge, give the sardine a mere touch of the brush and put a tiny sprig of parsley or 'pluche' of chervil on top, or, dip the top edges only of the masked finger of toast into finely chopped parsley in place of the border of butter and finish as before, or mask the top with rémoulade sauce, or dispense with the fillets of sardine and pipe a scroll or 'S' of sardine butter from a fine-cut star tube on the masked finger of toast. No further decoration is needed.

487.

Canapé de Saumon Fumé. Take a long slice of brown bread, butter it and sprinkle on it a little finely grated horseradish. Next cover the prepared slices with thinly cut smoked salmon and sprinkle a few drops of lemon juice here and there. Press well to make the salmon adhere and cut into fingers. Do not mask with aspic jelly.

488.

(II.) Use some very thinly cut slices of smoked salmon to cover strips of toast, and arrange a line of caviar down the centre—very little is required. Use sufficient jelly to hold this in place and no more, then with a round cutter cut crescents from the strip in the manner already described.

489.

(III.) Slices of rye bread are spread with horseradish butter and then covered with narrow alternating bands of smoked salmon, caviar and fillets of smoked herring. These should be arranged diagonally. Cut into fingers or other shapes.

490.

Canapés de Crevettes. Cover a slice of toast with shrimp butter, and after cutting out the desired shapes arrange on them a bed of shelled shrimps. Pipe a border of the same butter and place a ring of pimento-stuffed olive in the centre of each canapé. Touch up with aspic.

491.

Tunny Paste and Walnut Toast. Mix some Tunny Fish Cheese Paste with pounded pickled walnuts, spread it on toast and cut it into diamonds. Place two very thin strips of fillets of anchovy down the middle with space between them for tiny pickled onions no bigger than peas. Cut this strip into crescents with a round pastry cutter of suitable size. This variety may be glazed with aspic if it has to be kept in a heated room for any length of time.

492.

White Fish Toast. Use herring butter for this one and spread a thin layer of it evenly on a slice of toast. Have ready some tiny pieces of cooked fish—firm-fleshed fish such as turbot—you will find it is better to cut them raw then poach them, rather than attempt to make cooked fish into small pieces or cubes. Put these little rectangles or lozenges of fish on the prepared toast which you have cut into the desired shapes. Decorate with a 'pluche' of chervil on top and surround the fish with a neatly piped border of tomato butter (page 111) and mask with a glaze of aspic. The above will give you some idea of what can be done with different kinds of fish in this interesting field of work. We will now consider a few of the meat ones.

493.

Canapés with Brains. Mask a canapé with horseradish butter fairly thickly and on it place an escalope of cooked brains—preferably sheep's as they are of smaller size and require less trimming—cover this with a spoonful of highly seasoned sauce rémoulade and arrange three overlapping slices of tomato—centre removed, making them into rings—over all.

494.

Tongue Toast. A variety using cold tongue is made by spreading a toasted slice of bread somewhat thickly with mustard butter and then covering it with slices of tongue—you will welcome here a chance of using up those tapering tips of tongue that are difficult to dispose of otherwise. When the butter has become firm use a sharp knife, dipped occasionally in hot water, to cut the slice into any desired shapes, or use a sharp pastry cutter, taking care not to make too many 'scraps'. I advise you to mask this variety with aspic jelly.

495.

Game, poultry or meat toasts. Fillets of grouse, duck, pheasant, venison, chicken, roast or boiled beef or even corned beef may be similarly treated.

496.

An alternative way. A good effect may be attained by spreading a slice of toasted bread with mustard butter as before, but this time grating the meat over it. Grouse done this way is especially good, and cold tongue or cold roast beef do not lag behind. Season with a pinch of salt and a dusting of cayenne pepper and cut into any shape.

497.

Canapé de Foie Gras. Cut a good escalope of foie gras about three-eighths of an inch in thickness, trim this to size and place it on a suitable base of toasted bread which has been spread with foie gras butter. Decorate the centre of this escalope with a slice of truffle, if the foie gras does not already have one, and touch the top surface with your aspic brush. The piece of truffle may be a diamond or other shaped piece.

498.

Canapé de Jambon. Slice very thinly some raw ham—Bayonne, Parma or Westphalian—and with it cover some strips of buttered toast. Cover with aspic jelly and cut the strips into squares and use green butter for the decoration of the border. Endeavour to get the fat and lean of the ham well intermingled on the slices of toast so that the finished canapés will have a little of each; by some people the fat of the ham is preferred to the lean.

499.

(II.) From a slice of rye bread cut out rounds about two inches in diameter. Do not toast these but on them arrange as a border some débris of raw ham which you have passed through the mincer. Leave a depression in the centre sufficiently deep to hold a raw yolk of egg from which you have taken all trace of white. On top place three or four very thin rings from a slice of raw onion.

500.

Canapé d'oeufs durs. Cut some hard-boiled eggs into six, remove the yolk and replace this by piping in some of the green butter. Place a strip of pimento along the top and stand the stuffed eggs on fingers of toast with a border piped from a star tube. Cover with aspic.

501.

(II.) With the yolks and any débris of white left over you may make another variety. Chop the egg finely and mix with it some chopped parsley. Pipe a border along each side of some strips of toast and sprinkle the egg mixture in the middle. Cover carefully with aspic jelly and when set cut into suitable pieces.

502.

Canapé d'Asperges. Make some small rounds of cheese pastry and spread them with cottage cheese, softened if necessary with a little cream. Place on these three asparagus tips and dust them with coralline or paprika pepper. Glaze.

503.

Canapés aux Beurres Composés. By using different coloured butters, pastes or spreads on long lengths of toasted bread, either by piping them alongside one another or by superimposing them, you obtain a great variety at relatively small cost of time or materials. When you have placed the butter on the toast, you should put this in the refrigerator for a few minutes to harden off before you cut it into pieces with a knife dipped now and again into a pan of hot water. You will also find that this slight chilling of the pieces helps when you mask them with aspic jelly which is the next and final job. I advise the use of a half-inch plain tube for the foregoing. If you pipe a line of tomato butter with a line of green butter alongside and touching and on top of these a line of sardine butter, you will have a pleasing combination easy of execution.

504.

(II.) As a variant of this idea, you can, by using a star tube, fill the strip of toast with blobs or a continuous star border and finish as above.

505.

(III.) Another variant is made by covering a strip with anchovy butter and stuffing a few stoned black olives with the same. Cut the strip into squares and on each square place four of the stuffed olives with a fifth one on top. Now put some green butter into a paper cornet and pipe a border round the edge and fill in the spaces with 'points' or 'leaves' or as your fancy prompts you. Touch the tops of the stuffed olives with the brush dipped in aspic.

506.

Canapé de Volaille Garnie de Cornichon et Betterave. Cover the toasted strip to be cut into canapés with chicken spread and garnish the top with thin strips of gherkin and beetroot. Glaze carefully with aspic.

507.

Canapé aux Olives farcies. Using the green butter, you may make another interesting variety. Stone some olives—there is a tool for this job—and stuff them with the butter from a bag and tube. Cut out a small round of pimento and place this on top. Next stand the stuffed olives on small rounds or triangles of toast which have been thickly spread with the same butter. If you think it necessary, and perhaps to help keep the olive upright, you may curl a fillet of anchovy round the base of the olive. Cover these canapés with aspic.

508.

Canapé mixte (Gruyère et Saucisson). Cut some thin slices of Gruyère cheese into rounds with a plain cutter. Do likewise with a few thin slices of salami, saucisson d'Arles or saucisson de Lyon. Now cut each round across into four segments, mask a fried slice of whole-meal bread with mushroom spread (page 114), and cut it also into rounds with the same cutter. Reassemble the rounds, using two each of the segments of Gruyère cheese and saucisson (four pieces in all), press slightly and mask with aspic.

509.

Other canapés mixtes. This idea may be exploited further by cutting out rounds of ham, tongue, smoked salmon, truffle, sweet pepper in addition to the various dried sausages and cheese already mentioned. These rounds may be cut into halves or quarters and a mixture of any two or four of them placed on toasts which have been spread with a suitable beurre composé, cheese paste or spread. A border of a similar or contrasting butter should be piped on to give a finishing touch and the completed canapé masked with a clear aspic jelly.

TARTELETTES, BARQUETTES AND CORNETS

I have already referred to the preparation and use of croustades such as tartelettes or barquettes and cornets as suitable bases for the type of hors d'œuvre now under consideration. I suggest that you keep barquettes for mixtures containing fish as the principal ingredient, cornets for creams or mousses and tartelettes for the remainder.

Barquettes

The filling of the first and last does not require any special mention, but that of the cornets is sometimes complicated by the fact that creams and mousses are apt to be in a semi-liquid state when introduced into them. Unless the cornets are stood upright until the filling has set, this tends to flow and become unsightly. In former times when it was customary to dress most dishes on socles or in croûtes, a croûte in pâte d'office or in fried bread would be made to accommodate the cornets in an upright position when dressed. This is no longer the fashion, dressing has been simplified, but this is not an excuse for slovenliness.

SALPICONS
510.

To prepare salpicons. Various kinds will be required to garnish these pastry cases. The term salpicon covers a wide field of preparations and may be either plain or mixed. The former consists of small regular dice of a single cooked element (three-sixteenths of an inch sides) bound with sauce, though some cooks cut the material for a salpicon into little batons.

Mixed salpicons are composed of two parts: (*a*) the principal element or elements, one of which may give its name to the salpicon, e.g. dice of chicken, ham and tongue; and (*b*) the subsidiary element(s), e.g. dice of truffle, mushroom, hard-boiled white of egg, gherkin, agoursis, or short lengths of cooked macaroni. The whole is bound in a suitable sauce. Sometimes the sauce or the type of mixture gives its name to whole, e.g. Chasseur or Tortue. Salpicons are generally served hot; our use for them at present is in a cold state and this fact will have some bearing on the choice of the sauce used to bind.

BARQUETTES
511.

Barquettes of caviar. Garnish halfway with pressed caviar and complete with a purée of, or fine escalopes of, smoked salmon. Place a trimmed fillet of anchovy at the junction of the two. The smoked salmon may be touched with aspic jelly but not the caviar.

512.

Barquettes of crab meat. Fill with crab meat made into a filling as for dressed crab. Place a slice of hard-boiled egg on top and a dusting of chopped parsley at each end. Touch the egg with aspic to prevent drying.

179

513.

Barquettes of crawfish and agoursis. Prepare a salpicon of crawfish and agoursis and bind with tomato mayonnaise. Fill the barquettes and sprinkle a little chopped truffle in the centre.

514.

Barquettes of crayfish tails. For this variety use cooked crayfish tails (écrevisses). Slice them into neat escalopes and arrange them in the pastry cases. Rub the creamy parts of the heads through the sieve and mix the resultant purée with sufficient mayonnaise sauce to coat the sliced tails and place a head shell at each end of the little boat.

515.

Barquettes of salpicon, crayfish tails, fish quenelles, mushrooms. Fill the boat-shaped pastries with a salpicon of crayfish tails, fish quenelles and cooked mushrooms bound with tomato mayonnaise.

516.

Barquettes of salads of fish. Various salads of fish may be used to fill these attractive little hors-d'œuvre and may be made very lively by decorating the top with sieved lobster coral, slices or details of truffle, anchovy fillets, strips of pimento, gherkin, egg-white or what you will.

517.

Barquettes of salpicon, lobster and truffle. A salpicon of lobster meat and truffle bound with a mixture of mayonnaise with one-quarter of its volume in whipped cream is used for the filling of this variety. Decorate by sprinkling a pinch of sieved lobster coral in the centre.

518.

Barquettes of shrimps. Filled with shelled shrimps bound with mayonnaise are used in this example.

519.

Barquettes of mousse of shrimps, shrimps as filling. Smear the insides of these boats with a mousse of shrimps, filling them with picked shrimps and covering with more mousse. Cook them gently at the mouth of the oven, and when they are cool give them a touch of aspic to brighten, with a tiny pinch of lobster coral in the centre.

520.

Barquettes of tunny fish cream, and fillets of anchovy. Another variety may be prepared by filling the empty cases with a cream of tunny fish (pound the tunny in the mortar, mix it with the cream, season, and 'loosen' if necessary with a few drops of olive oil. A lattice work of fillets of anchovy, or even a few laid diagonally across is all that is necessary to complete.

521.

Barquettes of soft herring roes and anchovy butter. Push one or two cooked soft herring roes through the sieve and mix the purée thus obtained with an equal amount of anchovy butter. Plaster this mixture on the inside of several barquettes, leaving a depression in the centre. Garnish this with a salpicon of gherkin and kipper, with a slice of gherkin on top.

CORNETS

522.

Cheese cream. Cornets made as already described are used for the next variety. Make a well-seasoned cheese cream—cottage cheese mixed with a little whipped fresh cream and a spoonful of aspic jelly —and pipe this mixture into the cornets from a bag and star tube. Maintain the cornets in an upright position until the filling has set, then give the top surface a mere touch of aspic and a pinch of chopped pistachio.

523.

Four variants. Variants of the above are made by adding to the cream, chopped green olive with or without chopped red poivron, or chopped agoursis and chopped fennel leaves, or chopped ham and a small amount of chopped mango chutney, or chopped lean cooked veal and chopped gherkins.

524.

Chicken mousse. Use a chicken mousse, i.e. pounded cooked chicken, half-whipped cream, jelly to set and seasoning passed through the sieve, for this variety.

525.

Ham mousse. This is similar to the above, using ham mousse in place of the chicken.

TARTELETTES

526.

Tartelettes Châtillon. This is a hot garnish, but it is so remarkably good when cold that I have included it here in the hope that you will sample it yourself and approve. A slight adjustment of the seasoning and sauce is necessary. Cook a few mushrooms in the usual way, i.e. in a little water, a squeeze of lemon juice, pepper and salt; give them three minutes' boiling only. Prepare a small quantity of sauce velouté (equal weights of butter and flour for the roux, a little bouillon and the cuisson of the mushrooms, then a liaison of one yolk and a spoonful of cream and seasoning). As I said above, keep this sauce on the thin side. Slice the mushrooms when they are cold and add them to the sauce. Next prepare a farce of chicken or, in default, of veal (pounding meat, adding a trace of egg-white, seasoning, passing through sieve and finishing with cream). Smear the insides of the ready-baked tartelettes with the farce, fill with the prepared mushrooms and spread more of the farce on top. Then place the tartelettes on a tray at the mouth of the oven to 'poach' the farce. When the tartelettes are cool, put a small slice of truffle on top and give them a gloss with aspic.

527.

Tartelettes with chicken and ham and salpicon. Make a chicken and ham spread (or mix about one-third of finely pounded lean ham into the required quantity of chicken spread). Plaster the insides of some tartelettes with this mixture, leaving a depression in the centre in which place a neat little pile of a salad made from a salpicon of gherkins and hard-boiled whites of eggs. *Note.* It is best to cook the whites in a charlotte or other plain mould as for a Royale. You will find it is much easier to cut into regular pieces when cooked in this way than if you have to use the white from a hard-boiled egg.

528.

Crème de foie gras. Make a cream of foie gras by pounding and mixing it in the mortar with sufficient fresh cream and use it to fill some tartelettes. Give them a domed effect and sprinkle a little chopped truffle on top or place a glazed slice of truffle in the centre.

529.

Salpicon of ham, tongue, chicken, etc. I have told you earlier of my preference for dishing salads in individual portions. Tartelettes give one an opportunity of carrying out this plan with ease and success. As an example, cut a salpicon of lean ham, tongue, cold boiled fowl, gherkins, beetroot, white of egg and truffle in about equal quantities. If you blend this salpicon with vinaigrette, the colours remain distinct, whereas if a mayonnaise is used, in addition to masking them, it tends itself to become tinted with the beetroot. Dress this salad in the small pastries and arrange them on the service dish. Other salads

Various

may be treated in a like manner and help to remove any appearance of stodginess from a platter holding only canapés; an effect which can also be attained by the use of two very delicate and light varieties of cold hors-d'œuvre, namely Moulded Creams and Royales.

530.

A **Salade Russe** or a **Macédoine** seasoned with a mustard-flavoured mayonnaise, with the addition of a spoonful of aspic, looks well in a pastry case and you have the additional satisfaction of knowing that the first portion served will not upset the looks of the whole dish.

VARIOUS

531.

Carolines. Carolines may be stuffed with a cream of fish made in the same way as the Tunny Fish Paste (see under Barquettes) mentioned above.

532.

Carolines with soft herring roe. An excellent Caroline may be made from cooked soft herring roes passed through the sieve and mixed with a spoonful of double cream and seasoned with salt and paprika.

533.

For the little **Duchesses (pâte à choux)**, a cream of cooked game—grouse or hare for preference—is ideal.

534.

The other variety of **Duchesses (potato)** may be utilized by filling into them a salpicon of game or fowl bound with mayonnaise and well seasoned.

535.

Petits Pains. Slit down the side and stuff with either a potted meat or potted fish. Any salpicon of fish, meat, fowl, or game with a suitable subsidiary and sauce may be used. For better eating it is advisable to make the petits pains from brioche dough, rolling them to the familiar torpedo shape. They may be smeared inside with mayonnaise before filling to make a softer eating.

536.

A **crusty roll** (flute) is useful for picnics or race meetings, and should have a plug removed from one end, which is replaced when the roll has been filled. Part of the crumb may be removed. The filling may be a spread made from débris of ham, cold meat, chicken or game pulped in the high-speed electric liquefier with the addition during the process of milk, cream, mayonnaise or tomato purée. Some cream cheese may be blended with the mixture to make it of a smoother consistency and seasoning should be rectified. A filling made on these lines is a useful standby.

537.

Brioches à tête. Pull off the head, hollow out the interior a little and fill with the selected stuffing or salpicon. Make a salpicon of prawn (or crayfish), hard-boiled whites (made into a mould as already described), agoursis or a few capers and truffle. Mix this with sauce rémoulade, use to fill the brioches and replace the head.

538.

Bouchées or croustades with poached eggs. Bouchées in puff pastry or croustades as previously described make very good 'montages' for cold poached eggs, and may be filled first with a salpicon, julienne or jardinière of whatever garnish may have been decided upon as an accompaniment.

The above croûtes, caisses, bouchées or croustades in addition to being used as receptacles for salads, may also hold meat or fish pastes or other fillings of whatever kind, shape or variety. This applies equally to the little cassolettes in fried batter and to the porcelain soufflé, coquille, cassolette and au plat dishes.

13. Hot Hors-d'œuvre

Hot hors-d'œuvre do not present any real difficulties to the trained cook, for in general they are neither more nor less than light entrées under another name but of slightly smaller dimensions. Many savouries too, may be adapted for service as leaders of the gastronomic attack.

ALLUMETTES

539.

To make allumettes. These have been adapted from pastries of the same name. Roll out some good puff pastry a quarter of an inch thick; do not incorporate any trimmings or scraps in this one please, or the allumettes will twist and deform on baking. Cut from this sheet of paste bands about three inches in width and on these spread the foundation stuffing. Then cut the bands into strips about three-quarters to one inch in width, place them upon a baking-sheet, allow them to lie for a quarter of an hour and bake them in a quick oven. Thereafter the treatment may vary; some are served as they come from the oven, others have a garnish bearing some resemblance to the stuffing, placed on them; some (only if to be served cold) are then touched with our old friend, the brush dipped in aspic jelly. All are kept small in size, for no one except an outsize in gourmands would expect to gorge himself with hors-d'œuvre, be they never so tempting, and lastly they are served 'roasting' hot.

540.

Allumettes aux Anchois. Make a fish farce mixed with anchovy butter and use this for spreading the bands. Garnish the strips on withdrawing them from the oven with trimmed fillets of anchovy.

541.

An alternative method is to bind some chopped fillets of anchovy and chopped hard-boiled egg in equal proportions with a well-reduced Béchamel sauce and use this for spreading on the bands. Garnish as before.

185

542.

Allumettes au Fromage. Use grated cheese when giving the last two folds to your puff paste (this means cutting off the required amount of paste at the fourth fold and completing it separately). Cut into fingers as before and dust each with grated cheese or give the baked allumettes a touch with the glaze brush and dip them into grated cheese at once.

543.

Chicken farce with onions, ham and paprika. Allow some chopped onions to fall in butter and add the same volume of lean ham cut into dice. Season this mixture highly with paprika and add it to an equal amount of chicken farce, also seasoned with paprika. Spread this mixture on the bands of paste and continue as before.

544.

Chicken farce with salpicon of mushrooms, truffle, chicken. As an alternative to the above, use a chicken farce without paprika but add to it a salpicon of cooked mushroom, truffle and white chicken meat.

545.

Purée Findon Haddock and Béchamel. For the spread use a purée of cooked Findon haddock bound with a well-reduced Béchamel sauce.

546.

Liver paste, Béchamel, Truffle. Take sufficient of the liver paste (page 81), mix it with a little Béchamel sauce and some chopped truffles. Use this to mask the puff paste and proceed as above.

547.

Fish farce and shrimp. For this use a fish farce, incorporating some shrimp butter. On removing from the oven, place a neat row of shelled shrimps on each.

548.

Spinach purée, cheese. Take some spinach purée, bound with Béchamel, and mix with it some grated cheese. Spread this on the paste and just before baking, sprinkle thickly with grated Parmesan cheese.

549.

Veal farce and salpicon of tongue. For this variety use a veal farce mixed with a salpicon of cooked ox tongue.

ANCHOIADE

550.

Anchoiade à la Nicoise. Fry some slices of stale bread in olive oil until golden brown, and on them spread a mixture of purée of anchovy thinned slightly with oil. Add chopped shallot and parsley. Sprinkle with a mixture of breadcrumbs, chopped parsley and garlic. Dribble a few drops of olive oil over and gratinate, then cut into rectangular pieces.

551.

Anchoiade à la Provençale. Similar to the above, but this time a few drops of vinegar are added to the purée of anchovies mixed with oil. Chopped onion and hard-boiled eggs are used to cover the layer of anchovy purée on the toast or fried bread, a dribble of oil is then run on this and the slices are gratinated in the hot oven. Cut into convenient-sized pieces.

ATTEREAUX

552.

To prepare attereaux. These consist of small squares (1-in. sides) or rounds of any delicate meat or fish that can be grilled or fried. These small pieces are threaded on skewers alternating with complementary substances such as small mushrooms (or sliced), bacon or petit salé, tongue or truffle. Two points distinguish attereaux from brochettes. First, when they are assembled on the skewers, they are smeared with a well-reduced sauce Duxelles or a sauce Villeroy and this is allowed to set. Second, they are egg-and-breadcrumbed and fried in deep fat at the moment required for service. It used to be the practice to prepare the attereaux on little wooden skewers, changing these for silver ones before sending them to table, but in order to save handling, time and loss by breakage I suggest you use stainless steel skewers, which although they may not look so well as the silver ones, do not have to be changed. For service of these useful little hors-d'œuvre prepare a tampon of fried bread into which you can stab the skewers and place a bouquet of fried parsley in the centre. It is as well to stick the tampon to the service dish with flour and water paste in case of accident.

553.

Attereaux de cervelle d'agneau à la Villeroy. Use lambs' brains which have been poached in salted water acidulated with vinegar in the customary manner. Alternate the escalopes with small slices of tongue, season with a few drops of lemon juice and a dusting of parsley and coat with sauce Villeroy. When this is quite cold and set, egg-and-breadcrumb the attereaux and fry them in hot fat. Dress as suggested on a fried bread tampon. Convenient-sized escalopes of calves' brains may be treated in a like manner.

554.

Attereaux de ris d'agneau ou de veau. As above, using cooked ris 'dagneau. Begin and end each skewer with a cooked button mushroom. Calves' sweetbreads may be substituted for the lambs' breads.

555.

Grouse or other game. Pieces of cold cooked grouse or other game may be skewered alternately with pieces of cooked ham and rounds of cooked mushroom. The attereaux should be well covered with Duxelles sauce and allowed to set before being egg-and-breadcrumbed.

556.

Chicken, ham and artichoke bottoms. Pieces of cooked chicken or of boiled fowl may be used along with escalopes of cooked artichoke bottoms and small slices of cooked ham. Deal with this variety as with the last one.

557.

Foie gras, ham and tongue. Small pieces of foie gras alternating with slices of ham or tongue of the same size make a good variety. Dip the filled skewers into sauce Villeroy and pass twice through egg and breadcrumbs. Fry in deep fat as before.

558.

Mussels, fish farce, mushrooms. Fill the skewers with large mussels, beards removed, stuffed with a fish farce and alternate them with rounds of cooked mushrooms. Mask them with sauce Villeroy which has been reduced with some fish stock and finish the skewers as before.

559.

Attereaux au Parmesan. Cook two ounces of semolina in half a pint of consommé. It will become like porridge, season with cayenne and a little salt, and stir in one and a half ounces of grated Parmesan cheese and one ounce of butter. Then turn this mixture on to an oiled dish and spread it to a thickness of half an inch. Cover with an oiled paper and allow to cool, then cut into small squares or rounds. Cut also similar pieces from Gruyère or other cheese and skewer these two elements alternately. Do not dip them in an enrobing sauce, egg-and-breadcrumb then fry in hot deep fat as usual.

560.

Chicken livers and bacon. Escalopes of cooked chicken livers with

188

square pieces of bacon make a good variety. Mask the filled skewers with sauce Duxelles and complete as above.

561.

Attereaux à la Niçoise. Select some large ripe olives, stone them and stuff them with a purée of anchovies. Fill the skewers with alternate olives, small slices of cooked mushrooms or cèpes à l'huile and pieces of tunny fish (thon mariné). Mask the skewers with Duxelles tinged with more than a suspicion of garlic and holding sufficient coarsely chopped tarragon to give it a flavour. Finish in the usual way.

562.

Attereaux de Homard. Small escalopes of cooked lobster, slices of truffle and of cooked mushrooms arranged on the skewers are masked with a sauce Villeroy in which some lobster butter has been incorporated. Complete the crumbing and frying as before.

563.

Vegetables. Certain vegetables may be made into attereaux. They must be cooked either by boiling in the ordinary way, or by 'sweating' in butter under cover. It is advisable to cut the vegetables in quarter-inch slices and preferable to mix different kinds rather than use only one. Artichoke bottoms, new carrots, celeriac, turnip-rooted cabbage, salsify, small marrows or courgettes, beetroot and many others all lend themselves to treatment in this manner. The skewers when filled should be masked with sauce Villeroy. Ham, tongue, bacon and mushroom slices may all or any of them be used in conjunction with an assortment of vegetables and the combination is dealt with in the usual way.

564.

Saucisson and potatoes. Cut rounds from quarter-inch-thick slices of Saucisson de Lyon by means of a suitable column cutter and from similar slices of cooked potato. Pierce these with the skewers, mask them with Duxelles, egg-and-crumb them and fry in the usual way.

It should be your aim to give a neat appearance to the attereaux, and you should endeavour to make them either into cylinders or square prisms, rolling them (when breadcrumbed) for the first and shaping them with the aid of the flat of a knife for the second.

DISHES OF AUBERGINES

565.

Acrats de Bélangères (French W. Indies). Peel four aubergines and cut them into half-inch slices. Boil these in salted water until they are tender enough to be rubbed through a sieve. To this purée add two tablespoonsful of flour and a well-beaten egg. Beat thoroughly, add salt, pepper, and ground chillies and drop spoonsful of the mixture into the deep fat. Fry to a golden colour and serve quickly.

566.

Aubergines aux Anchois. Cut the aubergines in two lengthwise, run the knife round the interior near the skin and cook them, cut side down, slowly in oil until the pulp can be removed. Chop this roughly and mix it with chopped fillets of anchovy at the rate of two or three for each half-aubergine. Meantime make a bread panade by soaking a small amount of stale bread in milk, then squeezing out the surplus moisture and passing the softened crumb through the sieve. Add to this a clove of garlic, chopped and cooked in oil and the necessary seasoning. Mix together, then stuff the half-aubergine skins, place them on a fireproof dish, sprinkle with browned breadcrumbs and heat them thoroughly in the oven.

567.

Aubergines à l'Egyptienne. Cut them in two lengthwise and make a small cut near the skin all the way round the cut surface, so that the interior pulp may be easily removed later. Fry the halves in oil and take out the pulp, leaving the skins whole. Have ready some onion chopped with a little garlic and fried together in oil. Mix with this the coarsely chopped aubergine pulp, season and fill into the skins which have been arranged on fireproof dishes. Heat the stuffed aubergines in the oven, and when serving place on each half-aubergine four slices of small tomato which have been seasoned, dipped in flour and sauté in hot oil.

568.

Aubergines au Gratin. Treat the aubergines as above up to the point of the removal of the pulp. Chop this and add to it an equal quantity of Duxelles and a good sprinkling of chopped parsley. Arrange the skins on a greased gratin dish, fill them with the mixture, sprinkle with fine breadcrumbs and with a few drops of oil and gratinate. A spoonful of demi-glace sauce should be run on the bottom of the dish at the moment of serving.

Six Variations of Aubergines au Gratin
569.

As above, and filled with the chopped pulp mixed with chopped hard-boiled egg, onion chopped and allowed to 'fall' in oil, fine bread-crumbs, garlic and parsley chopped together. Complete as before.

570.

As above, substituting a risotto for the hard-boiled egg and bread-crumbs.

571.

As above, adding sausage meat to the chopped pulp, garlic and parsley and omitting the risotto.

572.

As above, adding the same volume of tomatoes cooked in oil with half their volume of chopped onions to the aubergine pulp with the usual seasoning of parsley and garlic.

573.

As before, adding a salpicon of cooked chicken meat bound with a spoonful or so of well-reduced velouté to the aubergine pulp. This time the garlic may be omitted, but the dish is completed as before. Use a spoonful of chicken velouté to sauce bottom of the dish.

574.

As before, adding to the pulp half its volume in dice of braised mutton and half in boiled rice. To this stuffing add the garlic and parsley seasoning chopped finely together, and a pinch of cayenne pepper. Gratinate as before and run a cordon of tomato sauce round the dish.

575.

Imam Bayeldi, a Turkish dish, is composed of aubergines which have been very deeply scored, almost cut through, in three places for their entire length. These deep longitudinal cuts are then stuffed with a mixture of onions with a small proportion of garlic allowed to fall, and take colour slightly, in oil, and tomatoes skinned, de-pipped and chopped. The whole mass is allowed to cook together for a few minutes, being stirred the while, and is seasoned with salt and pepper. The stuffed aubergines are now placed in a shallow pan and sufficient water is added to cover them, almost. They are then allowed to boil until the liquid has completely disappeared. This dish may be served either hot or cold.

576.

Aubergines soufflées. Prepare the aubergines as before to remove the pulp and pass this through the sieve. Mix this purée with an equal amount of stiff Béchamel sauce, bind with yolks of egg, season with salt and pepper and at the last moment incorporate the stiffly whisked whites. With this composition, fill the aubergine shells, place them on a baking-sheet and bake them in a moderate oven as ordinary soufflés. Serve immediately they are withdrawn from the oven.

577.

La Ratatouille de Nice. This delectable dish consists of sliced onions with a proportion of garlic, sliced de-seeded poivrons, sliced skinned aubergines and tomatoes in roughly equal proportions. All are sauté in oil and are added to the mixture in the order given. Season with salt and pepper.

578.

Rougail d'Aubergine. Boiled or grilled aubergines are peeled and pounded in the mortar with chilli peppers to taste, salt, lemon juice and oil. Rub this mixture to a smooth paste. There are several varieties of rougail made in the French West Indies—Rougail de Crevettes, an excellent one made from shelled prawns, Rougail de Morue made from salt cod, Rougail de Tomates—all in almost identical ways. They are eaten as hors-d'œuvre or remain on the table as condiments throughout the meal, and though usually served cold may be eaten hot, spread on bread.

BARQUETTES

Barquettes to be served as hot hors-d'œuvre should be reserved for garnishes of fish; it simplifies the guest's selections if he is aware of this as some do not like fish dishes. The fillings may be picked from a salpicon bound with a suitable sauce, a little stew containing fish, a fish purée or soufflé mixture which can be cooked at the moment of service.

579.

Barquettes aux Anchois. Make a little salpicon composed of dice of anchovy fillets and of cooked mushrooms. Add to this a spoonful of chopped onions which have been allowed to 'fall' in oil. Bind the mixture with sauce Béchamel and use it to fill small barquettes, sprinkle them with polonaise, i.e. breadcrumbs browned in butter, and heat them in the oven.

580.

Barquettes de Crevettes. Toss a few picked shrimps in butter and allow them to cook for a few minutes in a fish velouté. Use them to fill some barquettes, sauce them over with sauce Mornay, sprinkle with grated cheese and gratinate carefully.

581.

Lobster or Langouste. Any left-over lobster or langouste à l'Américaine may be cut into dice, reheated in its own sauce, filled into barquettes, sprinkled with polonaise and kept hot at the mouth of the oven.

582.

Two Barquettes de Moules. Garnish the baked pastry cases with Moules à la Poulette, sprinkle them with polonaise and heat them thoroughly in the oven or fill the cases with Mouclade—a fine stew of mussels in cream, a regional dish met with in and around La Rochelle and the Pays d'Aunis generally.

583.

Barquettes de Laitances Florentine. Poach the soft roes in salted water acidulated slightly with vinegar. Have ready some boiled leaf spinach coarsely chopped and tossed in butter. With this line the bottoms of the barquettes, arrange pieces of the roe on top, cover with sauce Mornay, sprinkle with cheese and gratinate.

584.

Barquettes Soufflés à la Dieppoise. Prepare a salpicon of shelled shrimps, mussels and mushrooms bound with a fish velouté and with it cover the bottoms of the small barquettes. Have ready a fish soufflé mixture and pipe this over the top from a half-inch plain tube. Bake these little soufflés in a moderate oven when required for service.

BEIGNETS

Beignets may be divided into two groups: (*a*) those made with pâte à choux as a base, and (*b*) those dipped into frying batter. Both kinds are fried in deep fat. The latter are further subdivided into: (i) slices or escalopes of pre-cooked fish, meat, fowl, or game which have been marinated in oil, lemon juice, salt and pepper with chopped parsley (left-overs may be used), or (ii) minces, purées, salpicons, etc., bound with a suitable well-reduced sauce, rolled in flour into shapes.

585.

Beignets au Fromage or **au Parmesan.** Make a pâte à choux and add grated cheese equal to half the weight of flour used in the mixture.

Season with a pinch of cayenne, and put teaspoonsful of the mixture into the deep fat which is not too hot. I use the word 'put' with a reason; if you drop the mixture in you may splash yourself with hot fat. Do not attempt to fry too many at once and they will turn themselves over when cooked on one side. The reason for not having the fat too hot is that the beignets require to be well cooked. When they are ready take them out with a 'spider' and drain well. As an extra refinement the finished fritters may be rolled in grated cheese before being served.

586.

Beignets à la Mathurine. Add to the pâte à choux one quarter of its weight in a mixture of sardines à l'huile in small pieces and fillets of anchovies or filets de hareng in small dice. Mix this garniture well throughout the pâte à choux and season with a pinch of cayenne pepper. Fry in deep fat as before. An alternative is to use flaked cooked salmon (left over) and dice of filets de hareng, completing as before.

587.

Beignets Pignatelli. Take the required amount of pâte à choux and mix with it a small quantity of lean ham cut into small dice together with a handful of filleted (strip) almonds or preferably of pine kernels (pignons). Fry small lumps of this mixture about the size of filberts in the deep fat as before and when thoroughly cooked dish on a lace paper in a neat pile.

588.

Beignets d'Anchois. Use salt anchovies for this variety. Soak in water to rid them of as much salt as possible, wipe to remove scales and to dry them, fillet them, dip the fillets in a frying batter and drop them into the deep fat. They cook quickly.

589.

Beignets de Foies de Poulets. Make a salpicon of cooked chicken livers and cooked mushrooms bound in sauce demi-glace. Allow this to set then roll it into small balls, dip into frying batter and fry in hot fat.

590.

Beignets of all kinds of **left-over cold meats** may be made such as: beef, chicken, game, ham, lamb, mutton, pork, veal. Cut the meat into a salpicon, add mushroom or truffle also in dice and bind with a suitable sauce either white or brown. Allow to cool spread out on a dish, then form into shapes on a floured table, keeping them small. Dip into frying batter and fry as before.

591.

As an alternative to the above, left-over ham, tongue, chicken, in fact any cold meat may be cut thinly into neat pieces, round or square or in small escalopes, allowed to marinate in a mixture of oil, lemon juice, salt and pepper, then drained, dipped in a light frying batter and browned in the deep fat. Or thin slices of even shape may be sandwiched together with a complementary sauce or purée and then treated as above.

592.

Beignets of **left-over fish** are best treated in a pâte à choux as indicated above.

593.

Beignets of Gruyère cheese. Add to some well-reduced Béchamel of good flavour a brunoise of lean cooked ham. Cut slices of Gruyère or other cheese into squares or rounds and sandwich these with the Béchamel-ham mixture. Dip into light frying batter and treat as before.

594.

Beignets à la Niçoise. Cut from a suitable piece of preserved tunny fish (thon à l'huile) slices about the size of a penny and half an inch in thickness. Wrap a fillet of anchovy round the circumference, dip into frying batter and fry in hot fat.

595.

Beignets à la Perigourdine or **Beignets Lucullus.** Prepare a purée of foies gras and with it sandwich together two fairly thick slices of truffle. Cover these with light frying batter and fry as usual.

596.

Beignets of vegetables. Beignets may also be made from vegetables in slices, buds, or in small pieces. Those which lend themselves best for this are: artichoke bottoms in slices (cooked), the cooked tips of the white variety of asparagus, aubergines in slices (peeled) marinated as above and drained well, cooked beet in slices and marinated, young carrots of the round variety whole, cooked marinated celery in suitable lengths, cooked marinated cauliflower in smallish buds, cooked marinated endives cut into pieces, cooked marinated kohlrabi cut into slices, young marrows peeled, cut into slices, blanched and marinated salsify cut into lengths and marinated,

Brussels sprouts cooked and marinated, and tomatoes cut into sixths or eighths and marinated. All these are dipped into a light frying batter piece by piece and fried in hot fat.

BEURRECKS

597.

Beurrecks à la Turque. Cut some Gruyère cheese into small dice and add sufficient stiff Béchamel sauce to bind it; on no account make it sloppy. Allow the mixture to become quite cold then form it into small torpedo shapes. Have ready some pâte à nouilles rolled into a sheet as thin as paper. Take ovals of this and envelop the cigar shapes of cheese mixture, sealing the edges with beaten egg. Egg-and-crumb with fine breadcrumbs and fry in the deep fat at the last moment.

BOUCHÉES

Bouchées for hors-d'œuvre must be small, they are, as the name implies, a mouthful and no more. You have the choice of making them round, oval, square, lozenge-shaped, rectangular or triangular and either plain or crimped. It is customary to dispense with a cover of pastry and to use a slice of truffle, a trimmed slice of ham or tongue, a small turned mushroom, a slice of gherkin or of cooked vegetable for this purpose. Full details on the making of bouchées are given under the heading 'Bases', q.v. In Britain we have three preparations known as Chicken, Game and Lobster Patties, which are almost identical with their French counterparts and only require to be made smaller to act as hot hors-d'œuvre.

598.

Bouchées à la Reine (or **Chicken patties**). Cut out the puff pastry with a round crimped cutter 1¾ in. in diameter and make small lids for them in the same paste. Garnish when baked with a salpicon of white chicken meat, mushroom and truffle bound with a rich velouté of chicken.

599.

Bouchées de Homard (or **Lobster patties**). As above, garnish with a salpicon of lobster bound with Béchamel sauce finished with lobster butter.

600.

Bouchées aux Crevettes or **Bouchées à la Langouste** are made in the same way.

Bouchées

601.

Bouchées à la Saint-Hubert (or **Game patties**). As above, but oval in shape, garnish with either a game purée or a salpicon of game bound with a sauce salmis made from the same game. Use a turned mushroom as cover.

602.

Bouchées with spring vegetables. Make a brunoise of new spring vegetables as assorted as possible and bind it with a Béchamel sauce containing cream. Garnish some lozenge-shaped bouchées with this preparation and use a lozenge-shaped slice of cooked carrot as cover.

603.

Bouchées with asparagus tips. Fill rectangular-shaped bouchées with asparagus tips bound with a sauce mousseline and use a trimmed slice of truffle as cover.

604.

Bouchées à la Clamart. Make a purée of fresh green peas with cream and with it fill some triangular bouchées. Use a slice of cooked carrot cut out with a small crimped cutter as lid.

605.

Bouchées à la Crécy. Similar to the above. Prepare a purée of new carrots and pipe it from a star tube into the little triangular bouchées. Put a row of tiny new peas where purée and pastry meet.

606.

Bouchées with salpicon of tongue, chicken and foie gras. Make a salpicon of tongue and white chicken meat bound with a sauce Béchamel to which has been added a little foie gras purée. Fill crimped square bouchées with this and use a square slice of truffle for the lid.

607.

Bouchées Nantua. Prepare a salpicon of cooked crayfish tails and truffles bound with sauce Nantua. With this, garnish crimped lozenge-shaped bouchées and surmount each with a small head shell of crayfish stuffed with fish farce and cooked at the mouth of the oven.

608.

Bouchées with salpicon of foie gras, tongue, mushrooms and truffle.
Make some square crimped bouchées with sides 1¾in. Fill these with a salpicon of foie gras, tongue, mushroom and truffle bound with sauce Madère. Use a square slice of gherkin or agoursis as cover.

609.

Bouchées with soft roes. Prepare a purée of soft roes mixed with a little chopped truffle. Fill this into some crimped lozenge-shaped bouchées and use a lozenge of truffle as a lid.

610.

Bouchées are sometimes made from small **brioches à tête** (page 170). The têtes are pulled off, reserved as covers, and the interior hollowed out slightly. They are then dried a little at the mouth of the oven, filled with a salpicon of game or of foie gras and truffles bound with a suitable sauce and the heads replaced. Any of the garnishes given above for bouchées may be used.

BROCHETTES

611.

To make brochettes. Brochettes differ from attereaux in that the different elements are generally partly pre-cooked before assembly on the skewers and are dipped in melted butter and then in fine bread-crumbs before being grilled. The skewers are garnished very simply, the principal elements being small pieces of fish, cooked turbot or sole otherwise small fish such as smelts, escalopes of kidney sauté but not completely cooked, escalopes or pieces of liver, calves, chicken, deer, sheep, or pigs, escalopes of various poultry or meat, chicken, fillet of beef, of mutton or veal, escalopes of cooked calves' sweetbread or lambs' bread. When pieces of fish are used, slices of onion and pieces of bay leaf may be threaded alternately with them in place of the usual piece of bacon or blanched belly pork. Slices of cooked mushroom are also used as a complementary ingredient. If smelts are made into

612.

Brochettes d'Eperlans, the skewers should be passed through their heads. The fish are then dipped in milk and next into flour. Fry the brochettes in hot deep fat, drain them and dish up on lace papers with a garnish of fried parsley, and quarters of lemon.

PETITES CAISSES OR CAISSETTES

613.

To prepare. Small fireproof china, oven glassware or even metal round or oval moulds are used for these. They are filled with a ragoût of, for example, lambs' breads, with a salpicon as already indicated for barquettes, bouchées, tartelettes, etc., with a purée or may be used for small soufflés. They may be finished by a sprinkling of cheese or bread raspings and gratinated or a little polonaise may be lightly sprinkled over them and they are passed in the oven to reheat, or if these finishes are not desirable they may be decorated with a turned mushroom or cut pieces of truffle, ham or tongue. For other caisses see 'Bases'.

CANAPÉS CHAUDS OR TOASTS GARNIS

These are quite different from the cold canapés which have been listed above. Usually they are toasts, spread with a savoury butter and garnished with a salpicon, to be gratinated or sprinkled with polonaise.

614.

Canapés au fromage. For these you may use either a Welsh rarebit mixture or a Béchamel sauce in which you have incorporated some grated Gruyère cheese. In the latter case, once the toasts have been garnished with the mix, some small cubes of the same cheese should be sprinkled over prior to gratinating.

615.

Canapés au jambon. Garnish the toasts with a salpicon of lean ham bound with sauce demi-glace. Place a lozenge-shaped piece of ham on the top and sprinkle with polonaise. Reheat at the mouth of the oven.

616.

Canapés with kipper cheese spread. Spread slices of toast cut from a sandwich loaf with kipper cheese spread. Sprinkle with grated cheese and gratinate.

617.

Canapés with lobster or langouste, mushrooms and truffle. Prepare a salpicon of cooked lobster or langouste, cooked mushroom and truffle and bind it with a well-reduced Béchamel to which some lobster butter has been added. With this preparation spread the toasts, cut them into even-sized canapés, sprinkle with polonaise and heat for a few seconds in the oven.

618.

Canapés aux oeufs brouillés. Prepare some scrambled eggs and with them spread the toasts, cut them to the desired shape and size, sprinkle them with cheese and gratinate.

619.

Canapés aux oeufs durs. Dice a few hard-boiled eggs and bind them with sauce Béchamel. Spread this mixture on the toasts, cut these into rectangular pieces and garnish the top with a slice of egg. Sprinkle with polonaise and re-heat thoroughly.

620.

Canapés aux sardines. Skin and bone some sardines and with them cover some slices of buttered toast. Cut these into square or rectangular pieces, trim the corners, sprinkle lightly with grated cheese and re-heat but do not gratinate. Sprats may be used in place of sardines and all the foregoing canapés should be seasoned with a pinch of cayenne pepper.

621.

Canapés Windsor. Reduce some scraps of ham to a paste, season this well and spread it on some toast buttered with mustard butter. Cut the toast into convenient-sized pieces and cover with sliced cooked mushrooms. Heat thoroughly.

CANNELONS

622.

Methods of making cannelons. There are several ways of making these. (*a*) Roll out some puff pastry about one-eighth of an inch in thickness and cut from it rectangular pieces four inches long and one and a half wide. On half of these pipe the selected filling, which must be a purée of some kind, dampen the exposed edges of the paste and cover with the remaining pieces of the paste. Egg-wash the tops

623.

and bake as usual. (*b*) Have some round sticks made fourteen inches long by three-quarters diameter. Roll out some puff pastry as before and cut it into bands four inches in width. Arrange three of these on the table with half an inch between each. Place a greased stick on the paste and roll on three pieces. Give a touch of the wetted brush to fasten the paste together and cut off. Continue with more sticks until you have the required number of cannelons. Place the sticks carefully on the baking-sheet, closing down, and handle so that they do not roll when you put them into the oven. After baking these should be removed from the sticks and filled with either a salpicon or a purée

624.

of meat, fish or shellfish of stiff consistency. (*c*) If you do not have the sticks, prepare the bands as above and spread them with the filling. Roll them in the manner of small Swiss rolls and bake them as before.

CANNELLONI

625.

The Italian variety is Cannelloni. **To make,** use six ounces of flour, one egg, one yolk and a pinch of salt and make into a stiff paste. Allow this to lie on the table with a wet cloth over it for half an hour, then roll it out very thinly and cut into squares four inches by four.

626.

Cannelloni ripieni alla toscana. Cook the squares of paste in plenty of boiling water for a few minutes—they should have a 'bone' in them when you take them off to drain. Prepare a filling from Parmesan cheese, chopped cooked chicken livers, chopped cooked meat and truffles bound with beaten egg. Put a little of this filling on each square and roll them into tubes. Arrange them in a flat pan (plat sauté), pour over them a rich stock containing tomato pulp and heat through. Sprinkle with Parmesan cheese before serving.

CASSOLETTES (PORCELAIN)

The little porcelain, glass or metal shapes may be used as a simple receptacle, have a border in duchesse potato or puff paste, or carry a lid of either of these like tiny dish pies. A further variety is made by completing the filling with a soufflé mixture and baking them so that they are ready at the moment of service.

627.

Cassolettes with chicken, foie gras, truffle and cheese soufflé. Place a border of puff paste round the edge of some oval cassolettes, half-fill with a salpicon of chicken, foie gras and truffle bound with sauce demi-glace and complete the filling with a cheese soufflé mixture piped in from a plain tube. Bake.

628.

Cassolettes with chicken livers. Place a border of duchesse potato on the rim of some small cassolettes and fill three-quarters with chicken livers sauté and finished in sauce madère. Cut a lid with a crimped cutter from a sheet of duchesse potato, place this on the rim, gild it with beaten egg yolk and colour in a hot oven.

629.

Cassolettes with salpicon of lobster. Three-quarters fill the cassolettes as before with a salpicon of lobster or other shellfish, finished
in cream flavoured with lobster butter. Cover with a lid of duchesse
potato and finish as above.

630.

Cassolettes with shrimps, truffle, mushroom. As a variant of the last,
use shelled shrimps with a salpicon of truffles and mushrooms bound
with a fish velouté. Make the lid from puff pastry and treat the cassolettes as though they were little pies.

631.

Cassolettes with salpicon of sweetbreads, truffle and mushroom. Make
a salpicon of sweetbreads, add truffles and mushrooms if desired and
bind with a velouté or a sauce suprême. Fill the cassolettes with this
mixture and dredge lightly with polonaise. Heat in the oven before
sending to table.

CASSOLETTES (BATTER)

Cassolettes may also be made from batter as explained in the notes
on bases (page 169). I recommend you to reserve these for fillings
composed wholly or in part of vegetables.

632.

Cassolettes Bouquetière. Make some batter cups and fill them with
a macédoine of new vegetables finished in cream. As a cover use a
tiny bouquet of asparagus tips, a small bud of cauliflower or a slice
of cooked carrot trimmed with a crimped cutter.

633.

Cassolettes à la Florentine. Use the batter cups as above and three
parts fill them with leaf spinach (épinards en branches) tossed in
butter. For a lid, use a spoonful of salpicon of chicken bound with
velouté and sprinkle lightly with polonaise.

CAROLINES

Carolines are very small C-shaped éclairs and are usually filled
with a purée or cream of fish, game or meat.

634.

Carolines au fromage or **au Parmesan.** A cheese cream or a mixture of a cream cheese softened with cream with an addition of grated Parmesan may be piped into the carolines from a bag and quarter-inch plain tube. The carolines may either be split with a knife down the side or the tube can be forced into one end and the interior filled by a slight pressure on the bag.

635.

Carolines à la Saint-Hubert. A purée of game (left-over) may be used to fill these. Re-heat them in the oven before serving.

636.

Carolines à la Strasbourgeoise. Slit the carolines and fill them with a salpicon of foie gras and truffles bound with sauce demi-glace.

637.

Carolines au Vert-pré. Fill the carolines with a purée of green peas, haricots verts and asparagus tips bound with cream.

CHACHOUKA

Chachouka is a North African dish.

638.

To make. Slice equal quantities of onion, tomato and sweet pepper (poivron). Allow the onion to 'fall' in oil, then add the tomatoes and finally the poivrons. This mixture should be cooked together for a time in order to blend the various ingredients. Season with salt and cayenne, then arrange it on eared egg dishes or other ovenware, leaving a depression in the centre in which you drop one egg per person. Put the dish in the oven to set the eggs—take care not to over-cook. Alternatively, the eggs may be stirred into the onion, tomato, poivron mixture and cooked as though for scrambled eggs. The effect of this is not so good as that of the first method but it is quite admissible.

COLOMBINES

639.

Method. Make a mixture of cooked semolina and Parmesan cheese as indicated for Attereaux au Parmesan, but in this case bind with a yolk of egg. Spread some of this mixture in tartlet moulds, fill the interior with a mince, purée or salpicon—any preparation usually employed for barquettes, bouchées and suchlike hors-d'œuvre is suitable. Cover this with a layer of the semolina mixture, sealing the edges well. Unmould the tartlets—you may have to dip them in hot water to do this, egg-and-breadcrumb them and fry them in deep fat at the last moment. Dish on a lace paper with a bouquet of fried parsley.

COQUILLES

Save all the rounded scallop shells you can collect, coquilles Saint-Jacques. The flat half-shell is of no use for this dish. Scallop shells are not so fragile as porcelain ones and will last years. It is a matter of satisfaction these days to get something for nothing!

640.

To prepare the shells. There are many ways of preparing the shells prior to filling them with the selected garnish. The most common is to pipe a border of duchesse potato round the edge, either a plain or a star tube being used. Slices of cooked potato may also be used, or a piped border of chicken, fish or veal farce. Other vegetables in the form of a purée, finely cut brunoise or julienne give a variety and cooked rice a change. In general the procedure is to arrange the border, place a spoonful of sauce at the bottom of the coquille, then the garnish, finally more sauce with a sprinkling of either cheese or polonaise. The dish is then gratinated. In cases where it is not, the potato border must be browned first.

641.

Coquilles with brains. Prepare the shells with a border of duchesse potato. Arrange some escalopes of cooked brains in the centre and cover with sauce Duxelles. Sprinkle with bread raspings and a few drops of lemon juice and gratinate.

642.

Coquilles with left-over chicken. Chicken left-overs may be treated in a like manner on shells with a border of duchesse potato, using sauce suprême. Gratinate under the salamander.

643.

Coquilles de Crevettes. Pipe a border round the rim of the shells as before, place shrimps bound with fish velouté in the hollow, sprinkle with grated cheese and gratinate.

644.

Coquilles with left-over white fish. Left-over white fish may be accommodated in the same way. Use sauce Mornay to cover, with grated cheese, and gratinate.

645.

Coquilles with hard-boiled eggs. Hard-boiled eggs may have similar treatment. Cut them into medium-sized dice and again use sauce Mornay with a sprinkling of cheese and gratinate as above.

646.

Coquille de Laitances à la Florentine. Line the shells, bordered with duchesse potato, with leaf spinach cooked and tossed in butter, and on this base arrange some cooked soft herring roes. Cover with sauce Mornay, dust with grated cheese and gratinate.

647.

Coquilles with boiled beef. The boiled beef from the marmite may be chopped roughly, seasoned highly and bound with tomato sauce, with the addition of a spoonful of demi-glace sauce. Put this on shells bordered with sliced cooked potato, sprinkle with raspings and gratinate.

648.

Coquilles Saint-Jacques. For these select the smallest scallops, open them by putting them on a warm part of the stove, remove and reserve the coral and the fleshy muscle. Finish cooking these in a good fish stock and cut them into escalopes or dice. Put a border of duchesse potato on the rim of the washed and cleaned deep shells and fill with the cooked scallop flesh, having put a spoonful of Duxelles sauce in the empty shell. Cover with the same sauce, sprinkle with raspings and gratinate.

649.

Coquilles de Volaille à l'Écarlate. Pipe a border of chicken farce from a rose tube around the edge of the shells and allow it to cook gently at the mouth of the oven. When the farce is set, a touch with a brush dipped into beaten yolk will enable you to colour the top. Put a spoonful of rich velouté sauce in the bottoms of the shells and on this arrange the escalopes of white chicken meat and tongue. Cover with the sauce and sprinkle chopped tongue on the top. Do not gratinate.

CHAUSSONS

650.

To make. Chaussons are what we know as turnovers. They consist of a round of puff pastry trimmings rolled out to one-eighth of an inch in thickness, garnished in the centre with the filling which must be cold, folded in half and the semicircular edge turned over and sealed with a pinched border. They are then egg-washed and baked as any article made from puff paste. For hors-d'œuvre, chaussons should be kept on the small side.

651.

Chaussons with chicken purée, mushroom and truffle. Use a chicken cream purée mixed with dice of mushrooms and chopped truffle. Finish as before.

652.

Chaussons with fish farce, anchovy and truffle. Fill the centre of the chaussons with a fish farce in which dice of anchovy and a little chopped truffle peelings have been incorporated. Fold and finish in the usual way.

653.

Shellfish may be cut into dice, bound with a fish velouté or a Béchamel to which some lobster butter has been added and used as a filling.

654.

Chaussons de Sardines. These differ slightly from the above. Roll out a band of short paste twice as wide as a sardine is long. Now arrange the sardines in a line heads to tails along the edge nearest to you, leaving a gap of about half an inch between the back of one sardine and the belly of the next. Dribble a few drops of anchovy essence and a dusting of cayenne pepper over each sardine. Egg-wash the other half of the paste and lift it gently over the laid-out little fish and, with the back of a knife handle or the handle of a wooden spoon, press down well between each. Next using a pastry wheel, cut off the chaussons each from its neighbour. Arrange them on a baking-sheet, egg-wash the top surface, stab with a knife and bake in a fairly hot oven.

CLAMS

Clams are important as hot hors-d'œuvre, and I would promote them from the lowly position they seem to occupy to a more important one in the 'attaque gastronomique'. No one but an addict would expect to dine exclusively off clams, be they never so cunningly prepared or cooked; a well-executed dish of them will, however, add piquancy and interest to an otherwise poor meal.

655.

Clam Chowder. If you are using fresh clams, remove the hard parts and chop them finely. Cut some salt pork into small pieces and fry these in a thick-bottomed pan, then add a sliced onion and continue frying, but do not brown. Parboil some half-inch cubes of potato (or use sliced potatoes) and place these on the pork and onions. Add the chopped hard parts of the clams and dredge with flour. Season with pepper and salt, add more potatoes and pour over boiling water. Simmer until the potatoes are cooked, then add the soft parts of the clams and crackers (cheese or water biscuits) which have been soaked in milk. Next bring the clam juice—reserved in the beginning—to the boil, strain it and thicken it with a beurre manié, i.e. equal parts of butter and flour melted together. Add this to the chowder last or it may curdle the milk. If you are using canned clams, strain off the liquor and reserve, then chop the clams and proceed as above, using the clam liquor mixed with water for the cooking.

656.

Manhattan Clam Chowder is similar to the above but has the addition of stewed tomatoes, strained or not, and the omission of the crackers and milk.

657.

Rhode Island Chowder is, as would be expected, a richer variety of the above. The milk and crackers reappear, with the addition of cream and a tiny spot of soda to neutralize the acid of the tomatoes.

658.

Fried clams. Open some well-cleaned clams by 'springing' them, i.e. placing them on the hot stove until they spring open. Remove them from the shell at once, dip them into frying batter and fry in deep fat. Drain well, dish and serve. They may be dished on canapés spread with cream sauce.

659.

Clam fritters. Make a fritter batter, i.e. a stiff one with about one-fifth the amount of milk you would use for a thin pancake batter. Clean the clams, drain them and chop them roughly. Season them with cayenne pepper and salt and mix them with the batter. Drop spoonsful of this mixture into a hot, well-greased frying-pan, and when the fritters are brown turn them over with a palette knife. You may use, as an improved method, small muffin rings measuring two inches in diameter by half an inch in depth in the frying-pan, placing the batter inside and turning to finish the cooking. The little hoops should be greased with a piece of raw mutton fat.

660.

Clams on skewers. Cut some salt belly pork (petit salé) into slices and then into square or about an inch and a half sides. Blanch these and thread them on skewers alternately with soft clams, beginning and ending with salt pork. Dip the garnished skewers into melted butter and then into soft breadcrumbs. Place them under the griller and allow them to cook gently, turning them so that they are browned evenly. Send to table with either a sauce-boat of Sauce Robert, Sauce aux Fines Herbes or smear the skewers over with maître-d'hôtel butter.

CROMESQUIS

661.

Method. These consist of a salpicon of the principal ingredient or ingredients together with the complementary ingredient(s) bound with a well-reduced sauce and egg yolks. This preparation is then spread on a dish or 'plaque', allowed to cool, then cut, or preferably, shaped to the size required. They are then wrapped in thin pancakes (crépine or toilette of pork, i.e. pig's caul, is sometimes used) dipped in a light frying batter and fried in deep fat. Serve on a folded serviette or a lace paper with a bunch of curled parsley in the centre or at one end of the dish. The principal ingredients may be selected from chicken, game, fish or shellfish with half the bulk in dice of mushrooms, one-quarter the bulk in dice of ham or tongue and one-eighth the bulk in small dice of truffle. I advise you to make cromesquis of a flat rectangular shape to distinguish them from similar preparations. Cromesquis are very useful for dealing with a 'sloppy' mixing. If very much so, spread the pancakes with the mixture and roll them like small Swiss rolls. They may be cut into cork-like pieces which are easy to coat with batter.

CROQUETTES

662.

To make croquettes. Croquettes are made from similar preparations to the above, but are fashioned into cork shapes (bouchons) or flat rounds (galettes). They differ from cromesquis in that they are egg-and-breadcrumbed, fried in deep fat and served with a sauce separately. They are dressed on a folded serviette with a bouquet of fried parsley. A salpicon of chicken, game, lamb, veal, or of fish, maize, or rice alone, or in suitable combination with complementary ingredients of mushroom (and under this head are classed other fungi such as cèpes, chanterelles, morilles, mousserons) together with truffles and hard-boiled white of egg, all in dice, are indicated as the basis of this preparation.

663.

Croquettes de boeuf. For these use boiled beef from the stock-pot. Chop it well, add a little chives minced very finely with four times its volume in parsley, half the amount of beef in dice of cooked potato, a beaten egg or two to bind the whole and season highly. Shape the mix into any desired shape, roll in flour and egg-and-breadcrumb. Fry the croquettes in deep fat and send to the table with a sauce-boat of tomato sauce.

664.

(II.) Add slightly less than half the amount of pilaff rice (left-over) to beef as a substitute for the potato in the above recipe and complete as before. The accompanying sauce should be tomato.

665.

(III.) Alternatively, cut the beef into small dice and add an equal volume of dice of ham. Bind this mixture with a well-reduced Béchamel sauce, shape and coat with egg and breadcrumbs as before. Fry in deep fat and serve with a boat of tomato sauce.

666.

(IV.) As a variant, dice of mushrooms may be added to the mix, which may also be bound with sauce demi-glace and after frying as usual, served with sauce piquante.

667.

Croquettes with corned beef. A type of meat 'cake' may be made with corned beef, which is not quite a croquette. Prepare some 'hashed brown' potatoes, seasoning with an onion chopped and allowed to 'fall' in fat and a pinch of rubbed thyme. Add to this twice the amount of chopped corned beef and mix well. Shape on a floured table into round flat cakes and fry in shallow fat. Turn them over when well browned on one side and continue frying, and serve with tomato sauce.

668.

Croquettes with cooked brains and mushrooms. Make a salpicon of cooked brains and mushrooms bound in suprême sauce. When cool, form into any desired shape and finish as usual. Sauce tomate.

669.

Croquettes de Foie Gras à la Pèrigueux. Cut dice of foie gras and truffle and bind with well-reduced sauce madère. Terminate in the usual way and serve with sauce Périgueux.

670.

Croquettes de Foie Gras à la Reine. Make a salpicon of foie gras and bind it with reduced sauce Parisienne. When cold form into rings, egg-and-crumb carefully and fry. Serve with sauce suprême with the addition of chopped truffles.

671.

Left-over fish may be made into a useful croquette. If firm fleshed such as turbot merely cut into dice, bind with sauce Béchamel, adding mushrooms and proceed as above, but if of the softer varieties add a proportion of duchesse potato and a good sprinkling of chopped parsley. These last are similar to the well-known fish cakes. A good fish sauce can be served with the former and tomato sauce with the latter.

672.

A salpicon of game, either one variety or several mixed together, and mushrooms, with or without truffles may be bound with a well-reduced sauce salmis and dealt with as usual. Thin some of the sauce as an accompaniment.

673.

Lobster (or other shellfish) cut into dice with optional addition of mushroom and truffle, bound with Béchamel sauce with lobster butter added, made into croquettes in the usual way is served with either lobster or fish sauce. Pilaff rice or duchesse potato may be used to increase the bulk when there is not sufficient left-over shellfish.

674.

Croquettes with lamb, veal or chicken. Croquettes may also be made with either left-over lamb, veal or chicken. Proceed in the usual way and serve with tomato or other suitable sauce.

CROQUE-MONSIEUR

675.

Croque-Monsieur. Butter some slices of bread and place on them thin slices of Gruyère cheese. Now cut lean cooked ham into very thin slices and place between the prepared bread when assembling the sandwich so that you have bread, cheese, ham, cheese and bread. Press the slices well together and cut into pieces about two inches square, then fry them on both sides in butter.

Croustades

676, 677.

Two ways of making croustades. Croustades are divided into two groups. The first consists of pastry shells baked in croustade moulds, round or oval. These are deeper than ordinary tartelette or patty pans. Having lined the moulds with pâte à croustade, place a piece of paper at the bottom and fill with the usual beans or small sea shells prior to baking. The second group includes all those shapes made from duchesse potato, nouilles (allowed to set in a mass about one inch thick before being cut to shape), rice and semolina. In each case these are cut to shape, egg-and-crumbed twice for safety, the position of the lid marked with a cutter slightly less in size on the top surface before being fried in deep fat. The lid is then lifted off and the interior hollowed out.

678.

Croustades à l'Alsacienne. Prepare some croustades in duchesse potato and fill them with braised sauerkraut. Surmount this with a thin slice of ham cut with a round cutter and place a slice of cooked Strasbourg Sausage on top.

679.

Croustades à la Bretonne. Duchesse potato croustades garnished with a purée made from haricots flageolets bound with sauce Bretonne.

680.

Croustades aux Champignons à la Crême. Make the croustades in pastry, garnish them with mushroom purée bound with cream and surmount them with a small turned mushroom.

681.

Croustades de Crevettes. Croustades in rice are used for this variety. Garnish with a salpicon of shrimps, mushrooms and truffles bound with sauce Joinville.

682.

Croustades à la Marinière. Prepare some mussels 'marinière' style and with them garnish some croustades made in pâte à croustades.

683.

Croustades en Pâte à Nouilles. These may be garnished with any of the salpicons already listed for bouchées, etc.

684.

Croustades a l'Orientale. Make the croustades in rice and garnish them with a fondue de tomates à l'orientale, i.e. allow four ounces of chopped onion to 'fall' in oil, add one pound of tomatoes skinned, de-pipped and roughly chopped, a chopped clove of garlic and the necessary seasoning of salt and pepper. Cook this mixture together until most of the liquid has evaporated, then stir in a good pinch of saffron. When the croustades are garnished surmount them with three onion rings which have been dipped in frying batter and fried in deep fat.

685.

Croustades Vert-pré. Fill some croustades made from duchesse potato with a mixture of equal parts of diced haricots verts and new peas tossed in butter and place a small bouquet of asparagus tips on top.

686.

Croustades Vichy. Prepare croustades in rice and fill with carrots cooked à la Vichy.

Croûtes

This word means crusts, such as are served with soup, e.g. Croûte au pot, but croûtes of larger size are used as bases for hors-d'œuvre, and it is this type which interests us.

687.

To prepare. There are two varieties, both cut from a stale loaf. Round ones are cut with a pastry cutter from an inch-thick slice of bread, a shallow cut made with a smaller cutter on top to form a lid which is lifted off when the croûte has been fried in deep fat. Others are carved from a similar slice of bread in the form of a six or eight-petalled flower with a depression in the middle to hold the garnish. These are usually buttered with oiled butter by means of a brush, and browned either in a hot oven or under the salamander.

688.

Croûtes Brillat-Savarin. Prepare a salpicon of hard-boiled eggs, mushrooms and truffles bound with sauce Béchamel. With this garnish some of the second variety of croûtes above mentioned, and on top arrange a lattice of trimmed anchovy fillets. Sprinkle with polonaise and gratinate.

689.

Croûtes à la Diable. A salpicon of ham and mushrooms bound in sauce demi-glace is required for this. Add a pinch of cayenne pepper to the seasoning. Dress the salpicon in the first variety of croûtes, sprinkle with polonaise and gratinate.

690.

Croûtes Dubarry. Cook a cauliflower in the ordinary way and cool it under the cold tap. Take the buds, and, using a kitchen rubber, squeeze them into small even-sized balls. Place one of these on each croûte, cover with sauce Mornay, sprinkle with grated cheese and gratinate.

691.

Croûtes aux Laitances. Poach some soft herring roes in the ordinary way and garnish the croûtes with them. Give them a squeeze of lemon, a sprinkle of polonaise and re-heat them in the oven. Dredge with parsley.

692.

Croûtes à la Moelle, or as we term it, **Marrow on toast.** Crack the marrow bones and extract the marrow. Cut the best pieces into slices and the rest into dice. Poach all in salted water, drain and reserve the best slices. Bind the rest with sauce demi-glace. Cut some croûtes from a stale loaf, rectangular in shape with the centre hollowed out and fry these in butter. Garnish them with the dice of marrow and surmount with the slices. Touch them with the glaze brush before sending to table.

693.

Croûtes à la Paysanne. Take the vegetables of the marmite, chop them, season and mix them with grated cheese. Garnish the croûtes with this mix, sprinkle with grated cheese and gratinate.

694.

Croûtes with duck liver farce and mushrooms. Garnish the croûtes with farce à gratin made from duck livers. Spread this thickly and place a cooked mushroom, cup upwards, firmly on top, and fill with well-reduced sauce bordelaise at the moment of serving.

695.

Croûtes à la Zingara. Prepare a julienne of ham, tongue and truffle bound with sauce demi-glace tomatée and garnish the croûtes. Place on this a round of ham surmounted by a grilled mushroom.

Hot Hors-d'œuvre

696.

Csipetke. Roll out some nouilles paste into a thin sheet and from this cut strips about one and a half inches wide. Tear off pieces with the thumb and forefinger about the size of a penny and you will make Csipetke, a Hungarian variety. Allow them to dry slightly, then cook them in boiling salted water. When they rise to the surface, skim them off and cool in cold water. To use, drain and heat them in hot lard, blend with dry, crumbly cottage cheese and dish. Pour over them a liberal helping of sour cream which has been heated slightly and sprinkle with a few cubes of salt belly pork fried very crisp and brown in the fat they render when cooked.

697.

Topfen-Haluska is a variant of this national Hungarian dish. The first word means cream cheese and the second the pieces. For this dish, the paste, cooked as before, is heated in the cream and stewed until some of it has been absorbed. It is dressed in a timbale or a fireproof dish with a layer of the pieces at the bottom followed by one of the crumbly cream cheese and one of the fried dice of pork. Continue thus until the mould is full, finishing with a layer of haluska sprinkled with cream cheese. Re-heat the now prepared dish thoroughly in a moderate oven in a bath of hot water.

Csipetke may also be cooked or re-heated in a sauce (or soup) Gulyás. Let us be quite sure that we are agreed on what is meant by a Gulyás. Chopped onions lightly fried in lard without colour and small cubes cut from neck of beef or other cheap parts are simmered with water, salt and paprika. When the meat is nearly cooked, cubes of potato and more water are added and the simmering allowed to continue until the meat is quite cooked. At the last a sliced tomato is added, the seasoning rectified and the Csipetke thrown in. When the latter are cooked the Gulyás is ready to serve. Now I suggest to you that here is a very palatable little hot hors-d'œuvre.

698.

To make Csipetkegulyas. Take out the required amount of cooked Csipetke from the Gulyás, add a small quantity of well-drained sour milk cheese and dress the result in a fireproof dish. Strew the surface with well-browned pork cubes as before then re-heat in the oven and serve.

DARTOIS
699.

To make dartois. Roll out a sheet of puff pastry and from it cut two bands four inches in width. Place one of these on a wetted baking-sheet and garnish it with the selected filling, leaving a border on each side so that the covering sheet of pastry may be joined to it properly. When this is in place seal it well and notch it with the back of a knife. Egg-wash the top, allow the prepared band of dartois to lie for a quarter of an hour then bake it in a hot oven. On coming from the oven the band is cut into strips about an inch and a half wide, dished on a paper doyley and sent to table.

700.

Dartois aux Anchois. Spread a layer of fish farce finished with anchovy butter on the bottom band of paste, not forgetting to leave three-quarters of an inch of paste on each side clear to receive the top band. Garnish the fish farce with thinly cut anchovy fillets, place the top band in position, seal the borders and complete as instructed above.

701.

Dartois aux Sardines. Proceed as above, substituting fillets of skinned and boned sardines for the anchovies.

702.

Dartois au Thon. Use thin slices of preserved tunny fish in place of anchovies.

703.

Dartois may also be filled with a selected salpicon from those given for garnishing barquettes, bouchées, cassolettes and the like. The fish farce will be omitted from all but those containing fish as the principal ingredient.

DUCHESSES

The small choux may be filled in the case of a salpicon by having a slit cut in the side, or, in the case of a cream or a purée by using a bag and quarter-inch plain tube and pushing the end of the tube into the bottom of the choux. The requisite amount of filling can then be squeezed in. This last method is most speedy.

704.

Duchesses au Fromage. Whatever kind of cheese is used, it should be made into a cream and piped in as suggested above.

705.

Duchesses à la Jardinière. Prepare a salpicon of vegetables, the more mixed the better, and bind it with sauce Béchamel. Stuff the duchesses with this.

706.

Duchesses à la Purée de Crevettes. Make a purée of shrimps or prawns, binding it with sauce Béchamel and cream, seasoning it highly and adding a final flavour of shrimp butter. Pipe this purée into the duchesses as before. Lobster or other shellfish may also be used and the Waring Blendor is an excellent machine for dealing with all these rather tough fibrous 'meats'—with its aid they become creams or purées of smooth texture.

Other salpicons or creams already given may quite well be used to garnish these little choux.

ÉCLAIRS KAROLY

707.

To prepare Éclairs Karoly. Make some small éclairs from unsweetened choux paste not more than two and a half inches in length. Make also a purée from the entrails of a woodcock similar to that usually prepared for bécasse flambée (in practice the parts adhering to the backbone of any game bird may be used). Fill the small éclairs with this mixture and glaze the top with a brown sauce or grease the surface with melted butter and dip them in finely grated cheese.

FONDANTS

708.

Method of making fondants. These are very small croquettes usually made in the shape of a small ball, egg or pear. They consist of purées generally of liver or game, bound with a suitable sauce, but various cheeses and fish may also be used. The mixture is first chilled, then after being shaped, egg-and-breadcrumbed, is fried in deep fat. 'Fondant' signifies melting, be sure that the interior of your tiny croquettes lives up to its name.

709.

Fondants of purée of foies gras bound with a well-reduced sauce Madère.

710.

Fondants of purée of foies gras with chicken purée. Mixture of purée of cooked chicken and purée of foie gras bound with sauce Parisienne.

711.

Fondants of purée of cooked chicken livers with sauce Madère.

712.

Fondants of purée of game, other cold meats or ham bound with suitable sauce. In the second class creams of cheeses, purées of white or shellfish, or of vegetables are used.

FRITELLI DI SPINACHI
713.

Fritelli di Spinachi. Boil some leaf spinach, drain it well, leave it 'en branche', sauté it in a little oil, season and add a few sultanas which you have soaked in hot water and drained or add a few pignons (pine kernels). Chop or grate an onion finely and squeeze the juice into the mixture. Then break four eggs into a basin, whisk them slightly and stir into the spinach. Have ready a pan on the stove containing hot oil and fry spoonsful of this preparation in it, turning them over when they are cooked brown on one side. You will have a number of more or less round cakes which should be dressed overlapping around the edge of a salver, leaving the centre free.

FRITOTS
714.

Method. Escalopes (or pieces) of cooked chicken, brains, calves' head or feet, pigs' feet, sheep's trotters are marinated with lemon juice and chopped fines herbes for a few hours then drained, dipped in a light frying batter and fried in deep fat. Send to the table with a bouquet of fried parsley on the dish and accompanied by a boat of tomato sauce.

GNOCCHI
715.

Gnocchi au gratin. For the best results I recommend you to make them à la Parisienne. The mixture, a pâte à choux with an admixture of grated cheese, is: half a pint of milk and five ounces of margarine on to boil. When the fat is melted and the liquid in a rolling boil add five ounces of flour, stirring it in rapidly away from the fire. Allow the resultant mass to cook for a few minutes on the full heat to gelatinize the flour, then remove the pan from the stove and when the contents have cooled slightly, add five eggs, one at a time, beating well between the additions. There is your pâte à choux; now add two to two and a half ounces of grated cheese and a pinch of cayenne pepper (there is sufficient salt in the cheese). Have ready a pan of salted water at near boiling point, fill your paste into a savoy bag fitted with a three-quarter-inch plain tube and pipe it out over the water, cutting it off in half-inch lengths by means of a wetted knife. After a little practice you will be able to do this at speed. Allow the gnocchi to poach for a few minutes, then take them out with a skimmer and put them in a soufflé dish, sprinkling grated cheese on each layer. Put a spoonful of melted butter or margarine on top, followed by a sprinkling of grated cheese and gratinate in a very hot oven.

716.

Gnocchi alla Toscana. As above, but this time put a spoonful of tomato sauce over all before adding the final sprinkling of cheese. Bake in a hot oven as before—you will find that this variety does not tend to soufflé as does the gnocchi au gratin.

717.

Gnocchi verdi alla Bolognese. Same mixture, but this time add a few spoonsful of well-reduced spinach purée to the gnocchi mixture. Pipe out as before and place in the soufflé dishes—this time adding a few spoonsful of 'jus de veau lié'.

There are other kinds of gnocchi made from semolina or mashed potato, but from the standpoint of quality, I do not think you can beat the gnocchi à la Parisienne as given to you above. If you wish to make a trial of gnocchi from a semolina base, here is the recipe:

718.

Gnocchi di semolino alla romana. Put three-quarters of a pint of milk on to boil, and whilst it is doing so let three ounces of fine semolina fall into it in a shower. You must whisk vigorously all the time, season with a pinch of salt, cook for about ten minutes, then remove from the fire. Bind the mixture with two eggs and two ounces of grated cheese and add a pat of butter. Spread this mix about half an inch thick on an oiled dish and allow to cool. Next, with a crimped cutter cut crescent-shaped pieces from this sheet of semolina, arrange these in a fireproof dish, sprinkling grated cheese between layers, pour melted butter over and gratinate. If you consider that crescents necessitate too much waste, you may cut the semolina into squares or rectangles with a knife, but the effect is not so good.

719.

If you wish a potato gnocchi mix, here is one. **Gnocchi alla genovese.**

Hot Dishes of Liver

Weigh the required amount of potatoes, boil and mash them, then mix in one-third of their weight in flour, and season with salt. Shape them on a floured board into small cork-like pieces and poach them for about ten minutes in boiling salted water. The appropriate sauce for this is one made by pounding garlic with herbs (usually basil, savory or marjoram) adding grated Parmesan cheese and finally making into a sauce, after the manner of a mayonnaise, with olive oil. You may need to stir in a spoonful of the liquor in which the gnocchi were cooked if the sauce requires to be thinned. Sprinkle the dressed gnocchi with grated cheese when sending to table.

HARENGS À L'ESTHONIENNE

720.

To prepare Harengs à l'Esthonienne. Pass several herrings through the sieve and collect the resultant purée in a basin. To this add one or two whites of egg and mix well. Season with salt, pepper and a trace of nutmeg. You will find that the purée stiffens when you add the salt, so thin it down with sour cream. This is now ready for making the dish as it is served in Esthonia. There, small pancakes are made of the preparation, but if you will take my advice you will add sufficient dry breadcrumbs to the mixture in order to give it the necessary consistency so that you can form it into pointed oval cakes about four inches long by half an inch thick. Fry these on both sides in hot lard (shallow), dress them in a circle on a hot dish and serve. Twelve herrings will make sufficient for thirty-six portions.

HOT DISHES OF LIVER

721.

Le Foie Gras de Canard aux Raisins. Season a fine fat duck's liver with salt, pepper and spices and wrap it in a thin slice of larding bacon. Next line a casserole with sliced onions, carrots, a pinch of thyme and a broken bay leaf and on this place the liver. Add a glass of Madeira or failing that of Port, place on the lid and put the casserole in a moderately hot oven for about forty minutes, basting occasionally. At the end of that time remove the liver to an earthenware cocotte (for service), skim off the fat from the braising liquor and strain this over, then add a good handful of de-pipped fresh grapes, replace the lid on the cocotte and return this to an oven cooler than before for about half an hour. Rectify the seasoning and send to table with croûtons or toast.

722.

Le **Ragoût de Foie Gras de Toulouse.** Clean and trim a prime quality fat goose liver. Put this into an earthenware terrine with an onion, cut into four, a clove of garlic, a few parsley stalks and a seasoning of pepper and salt. Add sufficient water to reach one-third the way up the liver, place on the lid and cook in a moderate oven until the liver is 'à point'—a state best determined by means of a skewer. Make a roux of goose fat and flour, adding a spoonful of chopped shallots, cook together for a few minutes then add enough white wine to make into a sauce. Dish the cooked goose liver and cover with the sauce, sending to table as hot as possible.

723.

Le **Pâté de Foies de Volailles Cévenol.** Take one and a quarter pounds of chicken livers and one pound of lean pork and chop these together very finely. Add five ounces of double cream, three eggs, the necessary seasoning of salt and pepper and if possible a few pieces of chopped truffle, the last for the exquisite flavour imparted, and mix together. Line a pâté mould with short paste and fill with the above preparation, cover with a lid of the same paste, bake in a slow oven—or the filling will 'souffler'—and serve hot.

724.

Le **Pâté de Foies de Volailles Truffés.** The recipe for this is similar to the last, but the preparation is cooked in gratin dishes in a layer about one and a half inches in thickness, instead of in a pastry-lined mould. Take one and a quarter pounds of chicken livers and one pound of pig's caul. Chop these together finely or put them through the fine plate of the mincer. Season the mixture with pepper, salt and, by way of a change this time, a tiny pinch of 'quatre épices' and add the three eggs but two ounces of cream only. Mix as much chopped truffle as can be spared with the foregoing ingredients. Cook in a slack oven and when the preparation leaves the sides of the gratin dish and the rendered fat becomes clear, the dish is ready to send to table. Care should be taken that a crust does not form on the top surface during the baking; a few thicknesses of kitchen paper will be of help here.

MAZAGRANS

725.

Mazagrans. For these you make a duchesse, mixing well, bound with yolks, allow it to cool and then roll it out and cut it into whatever shapes you fancy. Put half of these shapes on a slightly greased baking sheet and arrange neatly on them small heaps of a selected salpicon. Give the border a slight touch of beaten egg and place on this another piece of paste of exactly the same shape and size. You must be careful about this for nothing looks so unsightly as a mazagran that is carelessly made. Egg-wash the top and bake in a fairly hot oven. An alternative way of making mazagrans is to line patty pans with circles of paste cut out with a crimped cutter and to use similar circles for the top; in fact, patty pans, owing to the ease in handling and moving, make for simplicity.

Nouilles or Noodles

Nouilles or noodles may be served as hors-d'œuvre. **The recipe is** very simple, and varies slightly in different countries. Take one egg (more if required) or a mixture of yolks and whole eggs, with or without the addition of cold water, add a pinch of salt and work into this as much flour as possible. The size of the eggs and the absorbing power of the flour determine the amount of it required, the only safe guide to readiness being when the paste no longer sticks to hands or table. A very tight, stiff dough must be made which is then covered with a damp cloth and allowed to rest for half an hour.

726.

To make nouilles take a lump of this paste the size of a cricket ball and roll it out with a rolling-pin to the thickness of a sixpenny piece. Not an easy job unless you have a marble slab to work on (or a good pastry board) and a rolling-pin which is a true cylinder; the local joiner will soon put to rights a pin which shows signs of wear in the middle. Give the thin sheet of paste a slight dusting of flour and roll it up like a Swiss roll. Then with a sharp knife, and on the board this time please, for the slab will ruin the edge of any knife, cut slices of about three-sixteenths of an inch in thickness. This gives thin ribbons of paste. Strew these about on a slightly floured board to dry a little, then cook them in plenty of boiling salted water until they are done, but avoid over-cooking—about six or eight minutes should suffice. If you are using dried nouilles as bought ready-made, they will take longer. Toss them in a sauteuse with a pat of butter and serve.

727.

Nouilles aux cèpes or **Nouilles aux champignons.** You must first prepare a little ragoût of ceps or of mushrooms by cooking a spoonful of finely chopped onion in a little oil without browning. Add to this some tomato purée, the fungi and a spoonful or two of sauce demi-glace or of meat glaze. Toss these ingredients together and allow them to cook for a few minutes. Likewise toss the required amount of nouilles in butter and mix with grated cheese. Put a layer of the prepared nouilles in an oven dish, and on them place the mushrooms or ceps, then a similar layer of nouilles. Finish by sprinkling on the top some grated cheese and a little melted butter. Re-heat the dish thoroughly in the oven and send it to table.

728.

Nouilles à la polonaise. Dry some breadcrumbs and sieve them. Cook them carefully in butter until they are light brown and the butter has reached the noisette stage. This is known as polonaise and in the old days was part of the 'mise en place' of both saucier and entremettier; ready for any dish à la polonaise or for gratinating one quickly. Add the well-drained nouilles and toss all together. Grated cheese should be served apart.

OEUFS WASHINGTON
729.

To prepare Œufs Washington. Select fairly large tomatoes and cut off the top third, i.e. cut a slice one-third of the way down from the end opposite the stalk. By means of a vegetable scoop empty them of seeds, etc., leaving a shell that will hold a raw egg. Season the egg and place on top of it a spoonful of well-reduced Duxelles purée. If liked, the slice of tomato may be restored as a cap or the tomato may be put into the oven without it. In either case bake the dish until the egg is set but not too much so and, in serving, use extra care as the tomatoes, when cooked, are very fragile. This is a satisfying dish and should be served when the rest of the meal is light in character.

PÂTES À LA POCHE

This hot hors-d'œuvre is delicious, and has some resemblance to gnocchi au gratin.

730.

Method. Take the number of eggs required, break them into a basin and, having seasoned them with salt, mix in as much flour as they will take. Then stir in enough milk to make a paste of dropping consistency. Put this paste in a savoy bag furnished with a three-eighths-of-an-inch plain tube, and pipe it out into a pan of nearly boiling salted water in about four-inch lengths. They will come to the top of the liquid when they are cooked, so skim them off and drain them well. Next place them in an oven dish in layers alternately with grated cheese. Pour over a good, well-flavoured, well-reduced veal stock. Sprinkle a little more grated cheese on the top surface and gratinate.

Petits Pâtés

731. (I.)

Several methods. These are similar in many respects to bouchées, the difference between them being that whereas bouchées are filled or 'garnished' after baking, petits pâtés and their fillings are baked together. This means that they must be made with two pieces of paste, one for the bottom and one for the covering or lid. The first circle of paste may be placed direct on a wetted baking-sheet, the filling in a neat heap placed in position, the border dampened, the top put on and the back of a round cutter less in diameter than the one used for cutting out the paste used to seal it on. The top surface may now be egg-washed and the top of the pâté pierced with the point of a knife. Use good puff paste with plenty of spring and bake in a hot oven.

732. (II.)

Another method of making them is to use shallow patty pans (the English equivalent of pâté?) and line them with puff pastry trimmings —a very thin lining this, for you do not wish your pâtés to be so light that they topple over! Fill them as before with a salpicon or mince, place the lid in position and seal it on firmly. Bake as before.

733. (III.)

Petits pâtés may also be made in brioche dough, made without sugar and kept on the firm side. If you have the chance to chill the dough so much the better, it will be so much easier to handle when firm. Roll out the dough, cut the pieces out with a round cutter or as a change cut them with a knife into squares or rectangles. Garnish half of them with the filling, wet the edges and place the cover in position. Press the border, then egg-wash and put the pâtés on a warmed baking-sheet and then into a warm draught-free place to 'prove'. Bake in a fairly hot oven.

A few suggestions for the fillings:

734.

Reduce a spoonful or two of good fish sauce with some concentrated tomato purée, then add a salpicon of anchovy fillets and a seasoning of chopped tarragon.

735.

Dice of foie gras and truffles bound with reduced sauce Madère.

736.

Sweet pimento, skinned and chopped, allowed to 'fall' in oil, mixed with twice the quantity of diced cold braised mutton and bound with a spoonful or two of well-reduced tomato purée.

737.

Petits pâtés de veau et jambon. Small veal and ham patties. Put some lean veal through a coarse plate of the mincer and mix with it one-quarter of its weight in ham similarly treated. Season with half an ounce of general seasoning (page 86) to every pound. Line the patty pans with circles cut from rolled-out puff pastry trimmings, put a neat ball of the meat in place, splash with water and place on the lids, which have been cut from good paste and are slightly thicker than the bottoms. Thumb the edges to seal the two pieces of pastry together, egg-wash the tops, stab with the point of a knife and bake in a hot oven.

738.

Small chicken patties may be made in a like manner by using dice of left-over chicken bound with sauce velouté and with the addition of a little chopped truffle parings.

739.

Small game patties. As above, using minced cooked game bound with sauce demi-glace or sauce salmis.

PIEDS DE MOUTON OU DE PORC

Sheep's trotters or pigs' feet. These should be cooked as already indicated and allowed to cool in the cooking liquor. Subsequent treatment is very simple and either grilling or frying will cover this.

740.

Fritot de Pieds de Mouton (Porc). Dry well, remove most of the bones and divide the feet into convenient-sized pieces (this is done for hors-d'œuvre only) and marinate them in a mixture of oil, lemon juice, chopped parsley, salt and pepper for thirty minutes or so. When required for service, dip the pieces into a light frying batter and fry in hot deep fat. Dress them on a folded serviette, decorate with a few sprigs of curly parsley and send to table with a sauce boat of tomato sauce or sauce Périgueux.

741.

Pieds de Mouton (Porc) en Crépinettes à la Périgourdine. Proceed as above and place each piece of cooked pied between two layers of farce fine truffée. Wrap each in a piece of crépine and when the moment for service arrives, brush each with melted butter, toss in fine breadcrumbs and grill slowly.

742.

Variant of the above. Replace the bones by well-seasoned sausage meat to which has been added a little chopped, partly cooked onion. Egg-and-breadcrumb the pieces and fry them when required in hot deep fat. Serve as before accompanied by a suitable sauce.

743.

Croquettes de Pieds de Mouton (Porc) may also be made and the procedure does not differ from that already described under Croquettes, q.v., i.e. a salpicon of cooked sheep's trotters or pigs' feet is mixed with mushrooms and truffles and bound with sauce Parisienne. When the mixture is thoroughly cold, form it into any desired shape (preferably flat rectangular). Egg-and-breadcrumb these and fry them in deep fat. Send to the table with sauce tomate.

Pissaladière

744.

Method. Though ordinary short paste can be used for this, I advise your making a paste with olive oil. One pound of flour will take six ounces of olive oil and about one-third of a pint of water to make it into a dough of the right consistency. Add a good pinch of salt when mixing. Spread this paste out on a baking-sheet in a rectangle about twelve inches by eighteen, and on it put a layer of sliced onions which have been slowly cooked in oil. On this arrange a lattice work of fillets of anchovy with a few black olives dotted here and there. Bake this in a medium oven and cut it into pieces about four inches by two on withdrawal.

Pommes de Terre Fourées

Certain stuffed potatoes are served as hot hors-d'œuvre. The flat oval type is chosen, baked in the oven and an incision made in one of the flat sides so that a piece may be removed. This piece may be required as a cover later and the pulp of the interior is more or less completely emptied through the opening thus made.

745.

The first is a **simple stuffed potato**. Cook the potatoes as indicated above, cut them in half lengthwise, empty all the interior pulp into a basin and for every pound add three yolks of egg, four ounces of butter, half a pound of lean ham cut into small dice, three ounces of chopped mushrooms, pepper, salt, a grating of nutmeg, a spoonful of chopped parsley and a good handful of grated cheese. Mix these ingredients well together and fill the emptied potatoes, smooth the surface, sprinkle with cheese and gratinate.

746.

Pommes Georgette. Peel the potatoes and bake them in the oven. Cut off about one-third (of the thickness) as a lid and empty the shells, leaving the walls as thin as safely possible. Prepare a salpicon of mushrooms, prawns and a few small dice of truffle. Bind this with a good sauce vin blanc and use to fill the potato cases. Replace the lids and serve.

747.

Pommes Léontine. Prepare the potatoes as before, but this time fill them with a salpicon of lambs' or calves' sweetbreads, white chicken meat, ox tongue and a few dice of truffle bound with a sauce supreme. As a variant they may be brushed on the top surface with melted butter, sprinkled with grated cheese and gratinated under the salamander.

QUICHE

There are a number of preparations known as quiches which are in reality flans, i.e. shallow pans lined with pastry or metal rings placed on baking-sheets and lined with pastry. These large-sized tarts are sometimes partly baked before being filled and the baking of filling and pastry shell completed. Occasionally they are filled in an uncooked state and the baking of both case and filling is done together.

748.

Quiche à la Lorraine is the most renowned and for this you require some blanched lardons of 'petit salé' (belly pork). These you sprinkle over the bottom of a half-cooked flan shell. Now fill the case to within a quarter-inch of the top with a savoury custard made from sour-milk cheese and eggs at the rate of four eggs to the pint of liquid or a richer one at six yolks and seasoned with salt and pepper. Failing sour milk cheese you may use ordinary cheese which you should cut into small blocks about half-inch square, and in this case you use ordinary sweet milk for the custard. You can of course use grated cheese, but guard against using too much or your quiche will not set properly. Give a dusting of grated nutmeg on top and bake in a moderate oven. Always make sure that your baking-sheets do not twist when in the oven or your flan case may be cracked and that means a leak when the custard filling is put in later. More serious still is a leak that develops in an unbaked flan complete with filling, that is, if ever you feel tempted to cook the two together.

749.

Quiche Remiremont. For this you cover the bottom of the flan case with finely cut chives and fill with a custard made from sour cream with yolks, seasoned with salt and pepper. Cook off a small sample of the custard in a greased dariole mould (about a dessertspoonful will be enough) in order to verify the setting powers. More eggs or yolks may be added if necessary.

750.

Quiche Savoyarde. Blanch, slice thinly, and sauté in butter two small potatoes. Add these at the last minute to the filling mixture which should consist of cheese cut into thin slices, and a custard as before in which has been incorporated some sweet cream with a little chopped tarragon and chervil and of course the usual seasoning of salt and pepper.

751.

Quiche Forestière. Morilles are required for this flan, but as they are not obtainable here, use plenty of thinly sliced mushrooms. Allow them to 'fall' in butter, then bind with a spoonful or two of well-reduced Béchamel sauce, fill your prepared flan case, sprinkle with grated cheese and finish baking in an oven hot enough to gratinate the cheese slightly.

RAMEQUINS

These are a survival of ancient cookery; a type of cheese on toast, with or without chopped or pounded onions, probably the forerunner of the Welsh rarebit.

751, 752

Two kinds. Today they take the form of short paste tartlets filled with a cheese cream, or secondly a pâte à choux mixture containing grated Gruyère and Gruyère in small dice. This is piped out on to a baking-sheet in small choux, the tops of which are egg-washed and sprinkled with more cheese dice. The amount of cheese to be added to a pâte à choux mixing must not exceed that of the flour.

753.

Ramequins de Camembert. Camembert cheese, paper removed, and the exterior well scraped, is passed through the sieve. Mix the purée thus obtained with yolks of egg and double cream. Season with cayenne pepper. Test the setting powers by poaching a little in boiling water, correct if necessary by adding more cream or more yolks, fill into buttered dariole moulds and poach them en bain marie in the oven. When they are cold cut them into even round slices, pass them through cream and grated Parmesan cheese, then egg-and-bread-crumb them and fry in deep fat.

RAVIOLI

Ravioli can be an excellent hot hors-d'œuvre. I recommend you to use the correct mixture for these. It differs from the noodle paste generally used for this purpose in that it does not contain eggs or egg-yolks.

754.

Recipe. Make a paste from one pound fourteen ounces of flour, a pinch of salt and half a pint of olive oil, using sufficient cold water to make into a very tight dough. This paste will give you a very much better eating ravioli than if you use a paste bound with yolks. To proceed: Roll out your paste into a very thin sheet and on half of this put small heaps of the stuffing which may be one of several varieties. Then egg-wash the other half of the paste and place it carefully over the one with the little heaps of stuffing. Press the paste together in the spaces between the heaps of filling and then cut out the ravioli, either with a round crimped cutter or by running a pastry wheel between the rows.

Have a pan of salted water at near boiling point, throw in the ravioli and poach them for ten to fifteen minutes, but do not let them boil or some will open, lose the stuffing and become useless. When they are sufficiently cooked, lift them out with a skimmer and place them in a soufflé dish or timbale and put a few spoonsful of good gravy or a rich brown or tomato sauce over them, sprinkling liberally with grated cheese. Then place the timbales in a moderate oven for a few minutes in order to blend the different elements of the dish together thoroughly.

755.

Suggested fillings. The classic farce for ravioli has as its principal ingredients brains and spinach; but there seems to be an almost endless variety of fillings that can be made from veal, chicken, sweetbread, sour-milk cheese, various vegetables, with of course a binding of eggs and Parmesan cheese. My preference is for three ounces of chicken livers sauté with a little finely chopped shallot and a touch of garlic. Season with nutmeg, basil and add an equal volume of blanched spinach, finally one and a half ounces of butter and an egg. Mix well in the mortar then pass through the sieve.

RIZOTTO

Rizotto is a dish which may well in these days appear as a hot hors-d'œuvre. There are many varieties of rizotto, every district seems to have its own particular recipe, but we will confine ourselves to a few of the more common ones.

756.

Rizotto à l'Italienne. For this you should allow a finely chopped onion to fall in a spoonful or two of olive oil. Add two and a half times as much Italian rice, violona or Avorio, stirring all the time, and allow it to fry slightly. Next add twice as much chicken or good stock (by volume), bring to the boil and, having covered the pan with paper and a close-fitting lid, place it in the oven for twenty minutes by the clock. At the end of that time, mix in as much grated Parmesan cheese as you had chopped onion in the first place. Dress the rizotto in service dishes and sprinkle grated cheese over.

757.

Rizotto alla Milanese. Foundation as above adding saffron before cooking and a garniture Milanaise after, i.e. a julienne of tongue, ham, truffles and mushrooms. Terminate with a spoonful of tomato purée and a handful of grated cheese.

758.

Rizotto con funghi. For this add a few sliced mushrooms to the onions when frying for the Rizotto à l'Italienne and finish as before.

759.

Rizotto alla fiorentina. To some Rizotto à l'Italienne add a few pieces of cooked chicken giblets. Finish as before with grated Parmesan.

760.

Rizotto alla parmigiana. As above, substituting small pieces of sauté chicken livers in place of the giblets and adding more grated Parmesan cheese.

RISSOLES

Oh, rissoles, what abominations are perpetrated in thy name! Yet a properly made rissole, one with a certain amount of respect for tradition in its make-up, is a very good dish. Many cooks, those of the half-trained type, think that all they have to do is to slap some sort of a mixture that will hold together with egg and crumbs or batter and fry it—et voilà! Contrary to this debased practice the filling, which should be a salpicon made exactly as for croquettes, is enclosed in either a sheet of brioche dough made without sugar, puff pastry trimmings or short paste. The rissole is then fried in deep fat, dressed on a papered dish and garnished with a bunch of curly parsley.

761.

Rissoles à la Bergère. Make a salpicon of cooked lambs' breads and mushrooms bound with a sauce Béchamel flavoured with an onion purée. Cut out rounds of puff pastry trimmings with a crimped cutter and on half of them put a small heap of the above. Wash the border with egg-wash and seal on the lid. Egg-wash the top and fry at the last moment.

762.

Rissoles à la Bressane. The filling is made of a salpicon of cooked chicken livers and sliced cooked mushrooms bound with a reduced sauce duxelles. Use short paste cut out with a large crimped cutter to make the rissoles like turn-overs. Finish as before.

763.

Rissoles Cendrillon. A salpicon of white chicken meat and truffles is bound with a purée of foie gras and this mixture used to garnish circles cut from brioche dough. Allow them about twenty minutes, covered and in a warm place, for the fermentation of the dough to continue before frying them in deep fat.

Soufflés (Petits)

764.

Other rissoles may be made from chicken either as a salpicon or as a mince bound with a creamy Béchamel, white fish (such as sole), lobster or shrimps with sauce Normande, game, grouse and pheasant left-overs are particularly good cut into a salpicon and bound with a demi-glace sauce.

SAUCISSON DE LYONS

765.

Saucisson de Lyon chaud en croûte. Use a saucisson de Lyon with skin removed and naturally you will pick one as straight as possible. Roll this in a sheet of pie paste, q.v., and place it in a small long mould or make a suitable one by using a piece of bent tin plate inside a straight-sided plaque or roasting-tin (plaque d'office). Bake this sausage in pie paste and serve it on a long dish, cutting slices about half an inch in thickness and serving at the same time a salade de pommes de terre chaude.

SALADE DE POMMES DE TERRE CHAUDE

766.

To prepare salade de pommes de terre chaude. Boil sufficient potatoes in their jackets, peel them while they are still hot and either slice or cut them into pieces. Sprinkle with chopped chives or finely chopped onion. Cut some fat bacon into dice and cook in its own fat until crisp and brown. Season the potatoes with pepper and salt, add a few spoonsful of vinegar to the hot bacon fat (carefully, for it will immediately froth up) and pour over the potatoes.

SOUFFLÉS (PETITS)

These may be served as hors-d'œuvre.

767.

The preparation. The principle governing their preparation is that a purée of the ingredient giving its name to the soufflé is bound with a small quantity of well-reduced Béchamel sauce to which is added the yolks of three eggs for every half-pound of purée. This is done off the fire and the mixture seasoned highly, then the whites of the three eggs whipped into a firm froth are very lightly mixed in. Have ready the number of small, individual cassolettes in either metal, fireproof china or oven glass well greased with butter and fill them to within half an inch of the top with the mixture. Bake the soufflés in a moderate oven for twelve to fifteen minutes. Serve at once.

The following purées are used for soufflés.

768.

Brains, calves' or sheep's. Soak them in running water for several hours to get rid of as much blood as possible, then run your forefinger between the folds to remove the membrane which covers the whole. This must be carefully done for this membrane, if cooked, is like fine wire. Poach the brains in salted vinegar and water. Reserve the best escalopes for other uses and make use of the débris for your purée.

769.

Cooked **chicken** to which may be added a salpicon of mushroom and truffle or a spoonful of well-reduced tomato purée to give it a rosy tint. In this case it is known as Petit Soufflé de Volaille à l'Aurore.

770.

Cheese. Make a roux with two ounces of butter, two ounces of flour and a quarter of a pint of milk. Add two ounces of grated cheese, bind with three yolks and lastly stir in gently three whipped whites. Fill to within half an inch of the top the little soufflé moulds which have been greased with butter and dusted with dry grated cheese. Bake in a moderate oven for a quarter of an hour.

771.

Various fish soufflés: **Shrimp, Lobster** and **White Fish.** Part of the garnish may be as a salpicon.

772.

Game. Eight ounces of a purée of left-over game bound with a quarter of a pint of reduced sauce salmis to which the usual three yolks and three whipped whites are added.

773.

Ham. Proceed as above, substituting sauce Béchamel for the sauce salmis and a purée of lean ham for the game purée.

774.

Liver. Pound eight ounces of cooked calves' or chicken liver with an ounce and a half of butter and a sixth of a pint of reduced Béchamel sauce stirred in with the pestle at the end. Pass this preparation through the sieve, then add the usual three yolks and three whipped whites and finish as before.

Subrics

775.

Spinach. Pass eight ounces of cooked spinach through the sieve, bind with three yolks and add three whipped whites carefully—this last operation off the fire, of course. Complete the dish as before.

776.

Variant of above. By adding two ounces of grated Parmesan cheese you make the mixture into Soufflé d'Épinards à la Florentine.

777.

To turn it into **Soufflé d'Épinards à la Romaine** merely add the diced, de-salted fillets of two anchovies to the last mixture.

778.

Tomato. Bind half a pint of well-reduced tomato purée with a sixth of a pint of Béchamel sauce then add the three yolks and three whipped whites and finish as above.

SUBRICS

779.

Method of making subrics. Make a batter by beating two eggs until well mixed and adding a spoonful of flour. Season with pepper and salt. The batter should be of a creamy consistency, and after standing for a little time is ready to receive dice or small escalopes of the principal ingredient of the dish, which may be left-over beef from the stock pot, cooked chicken, foie gras or chicken livers, sweetbreads, left-over fish, cold meats and potato. Mix the dice of the selected ingredient with the batter and fry spoonsful in shallow oil. When the subrics are brown on one side turn them over and cook them on the other. With a little care in putting out the batter the subrics may be formed of even shape.

780.

Subrics à l'Italienne. Cut two calves' brains, which have been poached in salted, acidulated water and allowed to become quite cold, into dice. Mix them carefully with the batter and drop by spoonsful into a frying-pan containing hot olive oil as indicated above.

781.

Subrics Piémontais. These are slightly different and can be made from any left-over rizotto by adding a handful of chopped cooked ham and more grated cheese if required. Bind with one or two eggs, verify the seasoning and shape into little cakes, which may then be fried until brown on both sides as already explained. Serve hot. In some places a sauce-boat of tomato sauce is handed at the same time.

782.

Talmouses. Line some fluted bun tins with short paste and pipe in each a ball of choux paste with which has been mixed some grated Gruyère cheese. Sprinkle a few small dice of Gruyère cheese on top and bake in a moderate oven. The talmouses may now be filled with a cheese cream or not as desired.

783.

Talmouses à l'Ancienne. Use a large round cutter, three-inch diameter, to cut out circles of thin short pastry. On each of these pipe a ball of the cheese choux pastry and sprinkle the dice of cheese on the top surface as before. Now make your talmouses by folding the edges of the pastry to make tricornes, i.e. three-cornered hats. Pinch the edges together slightly where they meet and give a touch of the egg-wash brush to the exterior. When baked the talmouses should be stuffed with a cheese cream, a fromage blanc mixed with a little fresh cream and highly seasoned, or a crème pâtissière made without sugar and mixed with a little grated Parmesan cheese. The stuffing can be done from a savoy bag furnished with a quarter-inch plain tube—merely push the tube in any convenient spot and squeeze the bag until sufficient cream has been deposited in the interior.

784.

An alternative method of making these is to cut the short paste into squares of three-inch sides and finish as above, this time bringing the corners of the paste to the centre.

785.

To prepare the tartelettes. For these use sharp-edged patty pans placed close together on the 'tour'. Roll out a thin sheet of pâte à foncer, pick it up on the rolling-pin and extend it over the assembled patty pans, then, having depressed it into each with a pad of paste, pass the pin over to cut off the surplus. Thumb each one to ensure that the paste fills the moulds, and having allowed sufficient time for the recovery of the paste, place the usual piece of paper and beans inside and bake. When cool remove from the tins and empty out the paper and beans, then reserve for use as directed.

786.

Tartelettes aux Gnocchi. Prepare some tartelettes as above. Garnish these with gnocchi made smaller than usual, bound with a minimum of sauce Béchamel. Sprinkle with grated cheese and gratinate.

787.

Tartelettes à la Reine. Bake the pastry shells as above and when they are cold, spread the interior with a layer of chicken farce. Poach this at the mouth of a moderately hot oven, then garnish with a little ragout made of escalopes of cooked breast of chicken, slices of mushroom and a few thin slices of truffle all bound in a sauce Suprême. Cover with a thin layer of the chicken farce and again poach this in a gentle heat.

788.

Variations of this may be made by using a game farce and escalopes of cooked game bound with a brown game sauce.

789.

Tartelettes à l'Indienne. Bake the tartelettes 'blind' as before and, when cool, garnish them with a curry of prawns. Place a teaspoonful of boiled rice in the centre and surmount this with a neat piece of mango chutney.

790.

Tartelettes à la Polonaise. Line some patty pans with short paste and fill them with a mixture of half a pound of sauerkraut, one chopped hard-boiled egg and a heaped tablespoonful of cooked kasha. Cover with a thin lid of paste, properly fastened in place and egg-wash them before baking in a moderate oven. Pour a few drops of sauce demi-glace through the hole in lid into the interior before serving.

791.

Tartelettes—Scotch style. Fill the pastry tartlets with a purée of cooked salmon bound in cream, cover this with a sauce Mornay, sprinkle with cheese and gratinate.

792.

Tartelettes with soufflé mixture. The tartelettes, baked blind as before, may be filled with a soufflé mixture and put into the oven until the filling is cooked. The centre of this may be garnished with a salpicon of the principal element of the soufflé, with or without the addition of dice of mushrooms and truffle.

TIMBALES

793.

Various methods of preparation. These are usually made in dariole moulds, but several methods of lining and filling these are used. Sometimes they are spread internally with a 'farce fine', sometimes with a pancake made, of course, without sugar. Again a timbale made in pâte à savarin is hollowed out after baking and filled with the selected stuffing. Another variety is made by lining semi-spherical moulds with spaghetti blanched long enough to make it pliable.

794.

Timbales Agnès Sorel. Butter some dariole moulds and spread them internally with a 'farce fine' of chicken, having placed a round slice of tongue or truffle at the bottom. Make the lining of farce no thicker than a quarter of an inch, fill the centre with a salpicon of chicken, tongue and truffle bound with a sauce velouté. Smear the top with a layer of the farce, poach the moulds for about fifteen minutes, unmould on to a service dish and serve with sauce demi-glace.

795.

With fish farce. Butter the dariole moulds as before, sprinkle them with chopped truffle and line them with a fish farce. Garnish the centre with a salpicon of lobster bound with sauce Normande, cover with farce and poach as before. Unmould on to the service dish and serve with a sauce Normande.

796.

Make some **small babas**—without sugar, of course—and allow them to become stale, one day old is sufficient. Hollow them out, leaving a wall of about one-third of an inch in thickness. Fill them at the moment of service, with a salpicon of tongue, foie gras and truffle bound with a sauce Allemande tinted with a small quantity of tomato purée. As a lid place a slice of truffle cut with a crimped cutter on top.

797.

Timbales lined with pancakes. Place a round of thin pancake at the bottom of a buttered dariole mould and line the sides with overlapping strips of the same. Smear the interior carefully with a chicken farce and fill with a purée of chicken with a brunoise of langue à l'écarlate added. Poach as before and serve accompanied by a sauce Suprême to which has been added a little melted meat glaze and a few finely crushed sweet peppers.

798.

Timbales à la Milanaise. Blanch sufficient spaghetti in salted water, leaving the paste in its full length. Use this to line well-buttered semispherical moulds in a spiral, having placed a round of thinly sliced ox tongue at the bottom. Mask this spiral with a carefully applied layer of farce and fill the interior with a 'macaroni à la Milanaise'—having cut the paste into short lengths.

799.

Timbales de Macaroni à l'Américaine. Line a timbale mould with a good quality short crust, fill it with beans or sea shells and bake it 'blind'. When it is cold, empty it of beans and fill it with alternate layers of the following preparations: (*a*) a salpicon of homard à l'Américaine and (*b*) macaroni, cooked in salted water in the ordinary way, bound with a pat of butter and a small handful of grated Parmesan cheese. Make the last layer one of escalopes of lobster and coat with sauce Américaine.

YORKSHIRE PUDDING

This dish, when served as is correct before the meat and not as an accompaniment to it, can be an excellent hors-d'œuvre. My recipe and method is at variance with accepted practice and will horrify any Yorkshire housewife.

800.

My recipe. I make the batter with more eggs than she does, prepare it just prior to use and do not add the traditional spoonful of cold water before pouring it into the pudding-tin. In fact I discard even this last and use instead individual Pyrex pie-dishes. Take one pound of plain flour, add a good pinch of salt, six to eight eggs and sufficient milk to make a batter of required consistency—best found by practice, a little thicker than that of evaporated milk is the nearest I can tell you. Put the small pie-dishes in the oven with a nut of dripping in each and allow them to become thoroughly hot. Then pour a spoonful of the prepared batter in each and return to the oven. You will find that owing to the presence of so many eggs in the batter the puddings will swell up and become very light, the nearest substitute for the real thing that I know and very much different from the usual disgraceful soggy mass that masquerades under the name of York-shire pudding. Serve one of these small puddings with a spoonful of good gravy in the hollow to each guest before the roast meat and rejoice that you are able to serve at least one dish in the traditional style.

ZEWELWAÏ

801.

Zewelwaï, an Alsatian dish, may be described as an onion tart. Cut into fine rings sufficient spring onions or syboes (or failing these use small onions) and allow them to 'fall' in butter. Season with salt, pepper, and a suspicion of nutmeg. Add several spoonsful of fresh cream and boil up well. Then add three or four eggs and continue to cook slowly on the side of the stove stirring until the mass shows signs of thickening. Now remove from the fire and pour into a ready prepared flan which you then return to the oven to gratinate. Some cooks strew small cubes of blanched smoked bacon over the surface before the final gratination, but this is not essential.

HOT HORS-D'ŒUVRE—RUSSIAN SPECIALITIES

PIROSCHKI

Piroschki, Pierajki or Pierogi. I have lumped together these different ways of spelling the same article and other hot hors-d'œuvre into a small section. Although I have referred to them as Russian, I am conscious that not all of them are and that Eastern European would be a better description.

Piroschki, the indispensable accompaniment to Bortsch or Barszcz (pronounced Barchtch), those slightly sour soups of the Slav cuisine, may be made in three ways.

802.

To make Piroschki. You may use fermented dough similar to, but less rich than, the pâte à brioche already given. For this, take the following quantities: one pound plain flour, one ounce yeast, three eggs and one-third of a pint of milk and make into a smooth dough, adding a pinch each of salt and sugar. Allow to rise, then beat in four ounces of soft butter. Chill the dough thoroughly in the refrigerator, then roll it out quickly to a thickness of about an eighth of an inch. Now cut strips two and a half inches across and the full length of the paste. On half the width place tiny heaps of the selected filling,

238

egg-wash the other half then fold it over the filling, press lightly between the heaps and cut out the piroschki by means of a plain or fluted round cutter. Use a knife to make square, rectangular, diamond or triangular shapes. Each variety should be distinct in form from its companions. Next place them on a warmed baking-sheet which has been slightly greased and allow them to rise. Then egg-wash them twice, stab them with the point of a knife and bake in a hot oven.

803.

(II.) The second way of preparing piroschki is to use good quality puff paste in place of the brioche dough referred to above and is to be preferred for it is so much easier to work and the resultant goods are, to my mind, superior.

804.

(III.) The third way is to bake a sheet of pâte à choux and when it is cold cut it in half. Spread one piece with grated cheese and sliced cooked mushrooms bound with Béchamel sauce and seasoned highly with cayenne pepper. Cut this into rectangles, daub each with Béchamel sauce bound with grated cheese and dip into breadcrumbs. Egg-and-breadcrumb and fry in deep fat. These are known as

805.

Kavkaskie Piroschki (Caucasian). Other fillings may be treated in like manner. Remember that piroschki must be small in size—not any larger than a two-shilling piece.

The following are recognized fillings:

806.

Cabbage filling. Take a large white head of fresh cabbage and slice it thinly. Blanch it well in slightly salted water, that is to say allow it to boil for a few minutes before cooling it under running cold water and then draining it thoroughly. Complete the draining by placing the shreds of cabbage in an old towel and with the help of an assistant, twisting it to extract as much moisture as possible. Next fry a few thinly sliced onions in butter until slightly brown and add the cabbage. Moisten with a spoonful or two of stock and cook over a slow fire, stirring constantly until the cabbage is tender. Season to taste with salt and pepper, add a few chopped hard-boiled eggs and the mixture is ready.

807.

Carrot filling. Prepare carrots as for carottes Vichy (though as an alternative you may cut them into small dice) that is, cook them with sliced onions, and a seasoning of sugar, salt, pepper with a pat of butter adding sufficient water to cover. Bring to the boil and continue cooking until the water has evaporated. If the carrots have been cooked in slices they may now be chopped until fine enough, or if in small dice left as such.

808.

Egg filling. Boil an egg four minutes only, cool it under the running water from the cold tap, remove the shell, chop the egg, season it, adding chopped parsley and melted butter. Mix well and use as required.

809.

Fish filling. In Russia sigue and sturgeon are used, but as these are unobtainable here any white fish such as fillets of haddock, sole, brill or halibut may be used. It is not necessary to use the prime cuts, the belly or jowl is equally suitable. Salmon may also be used. Poach in the ordinary way, that is in slightly salted water, and use when cold. Mix with kacha or rice.

810.

Minces of various meats may be used, such as beef, chicken, game débris or veal. For the beef, boiled shin from the stock pot may be minced. Fry finely chopped onions in butter but do not brown them. Add the minced meat and a spoonful of stock. Season with salt and pepper and add a few chopped hard-boiled eggs, with or without kacha or riz au gras. Other meats may be treated in the same way. As a variant, chicken, ham and tongue may be made into a salpicon with truffle and mushrooms—chopped hard-boiled egg may also be added—and the whole bound with well-reduced Béchamel to which chopped parsley and chives have been added as a seasoning.

811.

Mushroom filling. Slice sufficient mushrooms and allow them to 'fall' in butter. Then bind them with a sauce Béchamel, cool and use as required.

812.

Rice filling. Add a few sauté mushrooms (sliced) to the desired amount of pilaff rice.

813.

Sauerkraut and ham filling. Take sufficient cooked sauerkraut and chop it slightly, then add to it a short julienne of cooked ham. Mix the two together and use as required.

814.

Sour milk filling. Take some sour-milk cheese (twarogue) made as already described, season it with salt, pepper and a pinch of sugar. Then stir in a little flour and an egg yolk or two, mixing well. Use as required.

815.

Vegetables, cooked and of divers kinds, may be sauté in butter and mixed with either kache or riz au gras.

816.

Vesiga filling. Vesiga is the spinal 'marrow' of the sturgeon and is little used except in Russian cooking. It comes to you in the form of a hard gelatinous band and requires five hours' soaking in cold water before being cooked (preferably by steaming) until soft. Chop the vesiga and mix it with a few chopped hard-boiled eggs, some finely chopped onions which have been allowed to 'fall' in butter, and a little chopped parsley. Finally add sufficient well-reduced fish stock to bind the mixture and allow this to cool before use.

817.

An alternative method of preparing vesiga filling is to mix cooked white fish, five ounces, cooked vesiga, three ounces, with two hard-boiled eggs, the whole chopped together.

818.

Moskowskie Piroschki. Chill some pâte à brioche commune (recipe above) in the refrigerator, roll it out and cut from it sufficient ovals of the size required. Garnish the centre of these with a spoonful of either of the mixtures given for vesiga filling. Wash the borders, fold over, press the edges together with the back of a cutter, place on a warm baking-sheet, egg-wash the top surface, stab with the point of a knife, prove and bake in a hot oven. On serving pour a few drops of maître d'hôtel butter melted and mixed with glace de viande, through the hole where stabbed.

819.

A simpler variety may be made by using puff pastry and chopped cooked white fish as a filling.

820.

Moulds—small dariole ones—may be lined with the pâte à brioche above mentioned and filled with seasoned twarogue. Cover with a round of the same pâte as a lid. Allow to rise, then bake in a hot oven.

Hot Hors-d'œuvre

821.

Ciernikis belong to the Polish cuisine. They are made by adding flour, eggs and butter with seasoning to twarogue and forming the resultant paste into little cakes about two inches in diameter by half an inch thick. The amount of flour required depends upon the moistness of the twarogue, but in general, it is safe to begin by adding slightly more than half the weight of the cheese in flour. Take ten ounces of twarogue and mix with it five ounces of flour, two ounces of melted butter, three beaten eggs, a grate of nutmeg and the necessary seasoning of salt and pepper. You may need as much as three ounces more of flour before the paste is of the right consistency. Drop a little of it into a pan of boiling water; add more flour if the paste is not firm enough or a little cream if it is too much so. Next form it into little cakes of the dimensions indicated and poach them in salted water. When they are cooked lift them out with a skimmer, place them in a serving dish and sprinkle them with melted butter. Re-heat and serve hot.

822.

Koulibiatschki are diminutive koulibiaka. The ingredients required are: a sheet of puff paste, a supply of kasha (semolina cooked in stock is a substitute), slices of hard-boiled egg, cooked mushroom in slices and thin slices of salmon cooked in butter. If possible, a little cooked vesiga will be required. On a round of puff paste assemble the filling thus: kasha, slice of egg, tiny escalope of salmon, a few pieces of cooked vesiga, some slices of mushroom and terminate with a little more kasha. Bring the edges of the paste up to form a purse-like shape and seal well. Egg-wash, bake, and on removing from the oven pour a little melted butter into the aperture left on top.

823.

Nalesnikis (Russian cuisine) are a type of kromesquis. Mix equal weights of twarogue and softened butter, eight ounces of each, and bind with a beaten egg, adding a seasoning of salt and pepper. Make some thin pancakes without sugar and put a spoonful of the mixture in the centre. Fold the pancake to enclose the filling and seal the edges with beaten egg. When required, dip the nalesnikis in frying batter and fry in deep fat.

824.

Ogorki Zapiekane is a Polish dish of baked pickled cucumbers.

Take the required number of cucumbers (agoursis) and slice them thickly. Arrange these sliced cucumbers in an earthenware oven dish. Then make a sauce in the usual way, using half milk and half pickle in which the cucumbers were preserved. Cover the sliced cucumbers with this sauce, sprinkle with grated cheese and browned breadcrumbs, dot with tiny pats of butter and heat thoroughly whilst browning in a hot oven.

825.

Sibierskie Pelmeni. A dish from Siberia, which is a variety of ravioli. Roll out thinly some ravioli or noodle paste and cut from it a sufficient number of discs about two inches in diameter. On half the number place a small heap of the stuffing. Wet the others with beaten egg and turn them over on to the garnish. Press the edges well together and poach the pelmeni in salted water at about simmering point for fifteen minutes. Drain them, dish them in a hot dish and sprinkle with melted meat glaze to which has been added the juice of a lemon, some chopped parsley and a pat of butter. For the stuffing make a salpicon of cooked ham, lean and fat, with an equal amount of the flesh of roast hazel hen. Season with salt, pepper and a grating of nutmeg and bind with a little sauce Espagnole.

826.

Rastigaï. As in the case of koulibiaka this is normally a large-sized dish, but a diminutive one is made for hors-d'œuvre. They are prepared similar to the Moskow Piroschki detailed above, substituting dice of raw salmon for the white fish in the second of the two recipes given for vesiga filling. Note carefully the distinction between rastigaï and koulibiaka.

827.

Litovskie Vareniki. Chop separately equal weights of fillet of beef and kidney fat, eight or ten ounces of each and add to two chopped onions which have been allowed to 'fall' in butter. Cook the mixture well, stirring constantly. Season with salt, pepper and a grating of nutmeg, finally bind with a spoonful or two of well-reduced Béchamel sauce. Roll out thinly some nouille paste, for here again these Lithuanian Vareniki like the Siberian Pelmeni are a variety of ravioli. Place small heaps of the above filling at regular intervals, egg-wash the other half of the paste and place it carefully over the filling. Press the paste between the heaps to make it adhere and cut out the vareniki with a pastry wheel in squares of about two and a half inch sides.

Poach these as before in near-boiling salted water, then dress them in a hot dish and pour over them a little melted butter.

828.

Varenikis Polski—the Polish variety—are similar in preparation, the filling is twarogue, they are cut out with a crimped round cutter, and a sauce-boat of sour cream (Smitane) is handed with them.

829.

Vatrouschka. There are two ways of preparing this interesting little hors-d'œuvre. First, you can roll out some puff paste about a quarter of an inch in thickness and cut out rounds two inches in diameter with a crimped cutter. Next with a plain cutter a size smaller, dipped occasionally in hot water, mark the centre, cutting slightly into the paste. From a bag and half-inch plain tube pipe a blob of twarogue which has been bound with a few egg yolks and seasoned with salt and pepper on to the circle you have just made. Give a dab with the egg-wash brush to the cheese and bake in a hot oven. You will probably be amazed at the result on withdrawing them from the oven, that is if your puff pastry is well made. You will find that this has risen to the top of the twarogue, which itself has flattened out, giving the appearance of a bouchée filled with cream.

830.

A second way of making these hors-d'œuvre is to take some of the pâte à brioche commune already noted and after chilling it, roll it out to a quarter of an inch in thickness. From this cut out rounds four inches in diameter and garnish these with the above-mentioned sour-milk cheese. Wet the borders and fold over, press the edges slightly and egg-wash the top surface. Allow to prove for about fifteen minutes, then bake them in a hot oven.

831.

Visnisckis. Chill and roll out some pâte à brioche commune and from it cut out the required number of rounds about two and a half inches in diameter. Garnish half the number of these with a mixture of chopped cooked fish (any kind) flavoured strongly with either chopped fennel or dill, seasoned with pepper and salt and bound with a stiff fish sauce. Cover these with the remaining rounds, pressing to ensure adhesion, and, after allowing time for the fermentation of the paste, drop the visnisckis into deep fat and fry them for about eight minutes. Drain them well and serve in a pile on a papered dish.

Glossary

In a work such as this, terms in current use in the French kitchen are bound to creep in. The definition of these cannot be found in any dictionary. It is essential, therefore, that the exact meaning be clearly established; the more common expressions are given below.

ASPIC WORK. This is not easy and demands a certain amount of experience which can only be obtained by trial and error. Remember these points: when you have brought your aspic jelly to that oily consistency which indicates the 'near' setting point, have ready two pans of water, one hot the other cold with lumps of ice in it. By judicious immersion of your pan of stock jelly in these you will be able to keep your aspic in a serviceable state over a long period. If you are making moulded aspics, chill the moulds, pour in sufficient jelly to mask them to the height required, then pour out the surplus and return the moulds to the chill, whether refrigerator or pan of ice water. Then proceed to build up your aspic slowly, a layer of garnish and a little aspic, allow to set, then continue. Put any decoration immediately under the masking layer of jelly as it obscures the sometimes untidy-looking interior. Avoid putting salt into your ice mixture, for if you freeze the aspic, however slightly, it will become cloudy. I have advised your using a brush to glaze canapés and the like with aspic in order to brighten and take away that dull look from them. For this purpose use aspic as indicated above. See page 120.

ASPIC CROÛTONS. Cut from your solidified stock of aspic a slice of the required thickness, using a sharp knife with cold water as a lubricant. Place this slice on a scrupulously clean marble slab or hardwood table and proceed to make triangles, diamond shapes, rectangles, circles with which to decorate the border or well of the service dish or the top of the glazed tongue, galantine, pie, pâté, etc. If you use chopped jelly to fill up the odd corners and holes, see that it is evenly chopped. Then mix this chopped jelly with a little melted jelly and you will be able to pipe it where wanted from a paper cornet.

BAIN-MARIE. This is a term loosely applied to a method of cooking in a water-bath, a means of keeping a sauce, purée or garniture hot for service or even the pot or pan used for this purpose. This last may easily be distinguished from the others in a 'batterie de cuisine' by the fact that it is made of thinner metal than a pan made for cooking, is taller in relation to its breadth in order to save space in the water bath and is tinned both on the outside and inside.

BAIN-MARIE, Cooking in a, see pages 121–122.

BEURRE MANIÉ. Softened butter mixed with an equal weight of flour and used for the quick thickening of sauces or binding of purées, etc.

BLANC. See page 94.

BLANCHIR. To blanch or to scald. An operation which consists in bringing certain foodstuffs to the boil from cold and thereafter cooling them under running cold water (see RAFRAÎCHISSEMENT). This procedure is used to rid (*a*) artichokes, cabbages, onions of bitterness; (*b*) salt belly pork cubes of saltiness; (*c*) to facilitate the removal of skins from tomatoes, peaches and other fruits; (*d*) to cook in salted water for a more or less prolonged time young vegetables such as peas, haricots verts, brussels sprouts, broad beans, spinach, etc.; (*e*) calves' heads and feet, pigs' feet, sheep's trotters, calves' sweetbreads, lambs' breads after a soaking in running water for twelve hours to purge them and in the case of the last two items, to firm the outer skin; (*f*) potatoes and other root vegetables, to pre-cook them partially before finishing them in butter.

BOUQUETS. Used here in the sense of 'dresser par bouquets'. This means to place the elements composing a dish in small neat heaps, using art and symmetry in their arrangement. I have tried to impress on you the great advantage to be gained in dressing mixed salads in this way as the service of the first portion does not spoil the appearance of the whole.

BOUQUET GARNI. A bay leaf, a branch of thyme and a few parsley stalks or a green leaf of leek made into a bundle and tied with string. Leave a length of string attached to the bundle and fasten this to the handle of the pan, the bouquet may then be easily withdrawn.

BRIOCHE A TÊTE. See page 170.

Glossary

BRUNOISE. Very small dice of vegetables used principally as a garnish in clear soup. It is easily made by cutting a julienne into tiny cubes.

CASSEROLE. This refers to a pan used in cooking, generally made of copper, straight-sided with a circular base. In a large 'batterie de cuisine', three depths appear for each diameter; depth approximately equal to diameter; depth about three-quarters of diameter and depth about half diameter. The first and last of these are known as 'russe' and 'grec' respectively. The word casserole is also used for a glazed oval earthenware receptacle, usually brown or green on the outside and white or cream on the inside and provided with a close-fitting lid. These are unsurpassed for the slow cooking of various viands and for the holding of pâtés or terrines.

CHAMPIGNON. This name describes the article perfectly. It is a piece of wood shaped like a large mushroom cap with a handle where the stalk would be. It is used for pressing pulps and the like through a sieve. In every case where you are instructed to pass some article through the sieve after pounding, a champignon would be used.

CHAUD-FROID. This seeming contradiction in terms signifies a fricassée of chicken or a salmis of game cooled, covered with its own sauce, decorated and brightened with aspic jelly. The piece may be whole or jointed prior to cooking, but for our purposes it is the sauce chaud-froid, i.e. set with aspic jelly, which is of interest. Note that the term is neither applied to fish nor to meat, the one exception being lamb cutlets.

CHINOIS. This is the name given to a pointed strainer used for the straining of sauces, soups, stocks, etc. This implement is made either with pierced holes of sizes from fine to coarse or with a fine wire mesh.

CLARIFYING STOCK. To clear stock, see page 120.

CONCASSER. To chop or cut into pieces of gross size. To chop roughly.

COURT BOUILLON. A specially flavoured liquid for cooking fish, see pages 41, 45.

CRÉPINE. The name given to a large fold of connective tissue lying loosely round the stomach of a pig, and known here as pig's caul. When soaked in warm water and stretched out carefully it is used as an envelope for certain preparations of farce or stuffing known as crépinettes.

CUISSON. Although this word means 'cooking', by extension it includes the actual liquor in which a piece of meat, fish or vegetable is cooked, or the liquor resulting from a method of cooking. This last is often made into the accompanying sauce or reduced by quick boiling and added to such sauce. Cuisson or pickle for hard herring roes, see page 31.

ÉMINCER. Means to cut into thin slices and is generally used when referring to carrots, turnips and the like. It does **not** mean to mince.

FALL (LAISSER OU FAIRE TOMBER). This refers to a short preliminary cooking usually given to vegetables in company with a fat of some kind, which renders them limp, and may be allowed to colour them slightly. The appropriate term in the case of meat is 'revenir' though la cuisine ancienne used the term for the cooking of meat without any liquid other than that furnished by the piece itself. TOMBER À GLACE is used to indicate the cooking of a vegetable where the cuisson is allowed to evaporate completely thus leaving a rich GLACE or GLAZE.

FARCE FINE DE PORC. See page 84.

GENERAL SEASONING. See page 86.

JARDINIÈRE is the name given to a cut of vegetables used in clear soup as a garnish and also cooked and cooled as an element in vegetable salads. Carrots and turnips are cut into little sticks about one inch in length and three-sixteenths-inch square section; the other vegetables into pieces approximating as nearly as possible to this, peas and cauliflower buds excepted.

JULIENNE. Another cut of vegetables. Make these as long as a match-stick but much thinner. Ox tongue, ham, cooked fish, mushrooms, artichokes and fillets of chicken or game may also be cut into thin slices and then into julienne.

MANDOLINE. This is the name given to a knife set in a piece of wood after the manner of a plane. It is used for the rapid slicing of vegetables, and probably gets its name from the motion of the hand holding the carrot, etc., being sliced. An adjustment is provided for the varying thicknesses.

MARINADE À LA GRECQUE. See page 109.

MAYONNAISE COLLÉE. This is the name given to a mayonnaise sauce which has aspic jelly added to it to give a coating consistency or to make a coating less liable to 'run' or 'slip'. A dish which has been prepared with mayonnaise collée should not be allowed to stand too long before use as beads of oil are apt to appear on the surface.

MIJOTER means to simmer.

Glossary

ŒUFS FILÉS (for Huevos hilados), see page 69.

OYSTER KNIFE. See page 34.

PAYSANNE is another cut of vegetables which are given a semi-circular shape, sometimes with the centre removed and the outside notched before being sliced or at others being made into slices about the size and thickness of a halfpenny.

PLUCHE is the term employed for the little groups of leaves which form a branch of chervil. They are plucked off and dropped into a basin of cold water awaiting further use either as a garnish in soup or as a decoration on an aspic or other cold dish.

POLONAISE. A definition of this is given under NOUILLES À LA POLONAISE. Do not confuse this with the dressing of, say, Chouxfleurs or Choux de Bruxelles à la Polonaise. These dishes have sieved hard-boiled eggs and chopped parsley in addition, with a squeeze of lemon juice over all before being sauced with a beurre noisette.

RAFRAÎCHIR, RAFRAÎCHISSEMENT is the act of cooling under running cold water of a meat, fish or vegetable that has just been blanched or brought to the boil from cold in order to rid it of an unwanted taint or bitterness, to pre-cook it slightly or cook it completely.

RAVIER is the name given to the small oval or diamond-shaped dishes used for the dressing of salads or hors-d'œuvre.

RIZ PILAFF. See page 131.

SALPICON signifies a single element or a mixture of several cut into regular-shaped dice of about a quarter of an inch sides. Some cooks cut the material for a salpicon into little batons. An appropriate sauce is used to bind the single or multiple elements.

SAUTEUSE. This is a shallow pan specially made for the cooking of vegetables. It is wider at the top than at the bottom and has, therefore, sloping sides. This enables one to toss the contents easily, a facility necessary when making glazed carrots, turnips or onions for garnishing. Owing to its shape and shallowness, this pan is also useful for the poaching of eggs or fish and for the cooling of aspic jelly to the degree necessary for masking various items.

SIMPLE SYRUP. See pages 154 and 157.

SPICE IN SAUCISSON. See page 76.

Bibliography

L'Art de la Cuisine: Ch. Chemin.   1891
Dictionnaire de Cuisine: J. Favre.   1902
La Grande Cuisine Illustrée: P. Montagne et P. Salles.   1902
Le Guide Culinaire: A. Escoffier.   1907
Les Œufs: A. Bautte.   1906
Larousse Gastronomique.   1938

DO NOT FORGET THAT IT WAS THE
GREAT CARÊME HIMSELF WHO SAID
THAT TO ACQUIRE THE SKILL OF THE
'OFFICE'—THE PANTRY WHERE SALADS
AND HORS-D'ŒUVRE WERE PREPARED—
THE WHOLE LIFE OF MAN WAS
HARDLY ENOUGH

Index of Recipes

Index of Recipes

252

Index of Recipes

Fish filling for Piroschki, **809** (240)
Fish for smoking, to prepare, **52** (51)
Fish salads, **23** (40)
  twenty-three suggestions for, **94-116** (61-5)
Flutes, filled (crusty rolls), **536** (183)
Foie Gras, to serve, **143** (79-80)
Foie gras, ham, tongue, in Attereaux, **557** (188)
Foie Gras en Terrine, **144** (80)
Foie Gras en Hérisson, **145** (81)
Foie Gras de Canard aux Raisins, **721** (219)
Foie gras, ham and tongue (Attereaux), **557** (188)
Fondants, **708** (216)
  of purée of foie gras, **709** (216)
  of purée of foie gras and chicken purée, **710** (216)
  of purée of cooked chicken livers, **711** (217)
  of purée of game, etc., **712** (217)
Foundation Royale, **257** (122)
French Mustard Dressing, **204** (109)
Fritelli di Spinachi, **713** (217)
Fritots, **714** (217)
Fritot de Pieds de Mouton (ou Porc), **740** (224)
Frittons, **195** (97)
Fromage de Tête de Porc, **169** (91)
Frozen tails (crustacea), **49** (50)
Fruit cocktails, **392, 393** (153-4)
Fruit compotes, **415-21** (157-9)
Fruit compote presentation, **421** (158-9)
Fruits, dried (canned), **414** (157)
Fruit in mixed salads, **424-49** (160-4)
Fruit juices, **404-11** (155-6)
Fruit salads, **422-3** (159-60)
Fruits, stewed (for serving cold), **413** (157)

Gaffelbitar, **67, 480** (55, 173)
Galantine of Chicken, **161, 162** (87-8)
Galantine of Veal, **163** (88)
Game patties, **601** (197)
Game patties, small, **739** (224)
Game Pie, **155** (84)
Game, poultry or meat toasts, **495, 496** (176)
Game Royale, **262** (123)
General Seasoning, **159** (86)
Gherkins, large, **246** (117)
Gherkins, pickled, **245** (117)
Gherkins, small, **247** (117)
Gnocchi au Gratin, **715** (217-18)
  all genovese, **719** (218-19)
  alla Toscana, **716** (218)
  di semolino alla romana, **717** (218)
  verdi alla Bolognese, **718** (218)

Grapefruit, **391** (153)
Grapefruit and orange skin baskets (with melon balls), **390** (153)
Grapefruit and orange cocktails, **393** (153)
Grapefruit juice, **404** (155)
Gratterons, **195** (97)
Grattons, **195** (97)
Green butter, **211** (111)
Green Gooseberry compote, **419** (158)
Green olives, **402** (155)
Green Pea and Carrot (Mixed) Royale, **263** (123)
Green peppers, **318** (135)
Green tomato chutney, **250** (118-19)
Grouse in Attereaux, **555** (188)
Grouse cheese paste, **226** (113)

Ham mousse cornets, **525** (181)
Hams, **120, 121-5** (69-71)
Hard-boiled eggs, **335** (138)
Hard-boiled egg variants, **340-7** (139-41)
Harengs à l'Esthonienne, **720** (219)
Harengs Marinés au Vin Blanc, **63** (54)
Hare Pie, **154** (84)
Herring butter, **217** (111)
Herring roes, hard, **4** (31)
Herring roes, soft, **5** (31); in Carolines, **532** (183)
Herring roes, mayonnaise of soft, **6** (31)
Herrings, canned, **78** (58-9)
Herrings, kippered, **79** (58-9)
Horseradish butter, **225** (112)
Hot Water Paste, **158** (85)
Hungarian Salami, **135** (74)
Hure de Sanglier, **165, 166** (90)

Imam Bayeldi, **575** (191)

Jamon Dulce Huevos Hilados, **120** (69)

Kavaskie Piroschki, **805** (239)
Kipper cheese paste, **227** (113)
Kippered herrings, **79** (58)
Kipper Snacks, **77** (58)
Koulibiatschki, **822** (242)

Langue de Boeuf à l'Écarlate, **174** (93)
Leeks, **288-90** (129)
Lentilles en Salade, **291** (129)
Lettuce, banana, beetroot and horseradish salad, **435** (161)
Liver Dishes, Hot, **721-4** (219-20)
Liver Paste, **147** (81)
Liver paste, Béchamel, Truffle (in Allumettes), **546** (186)
Litovskie Vareniki, **827** (243)
Lobster, cooking of, **34** (45)
Lobster, to cut up alive, **33** (44)

255

Index of Recipes

Index of Recipes

R 257

General Index

((a) *refers to* Index of Recipes)